AF477910

POLITICAL PARTIES IN POST-COMMUNIST SOCIETIES

Political Parties in Post-Communist Societies

Formation, Persistence, and Change

Maria Spirova

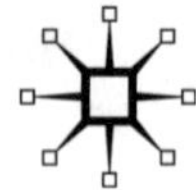

POLITICAL PARTIES IN POST-COMMUNIST SOCIETIES
© Maria Spirova, 2007.

First published in 2007 by
PALGRAVE MACMILLAN™
175 Fifth Avenue, New York, N.Y. 10010 and
Houndmills, Basingstoke, Hampshire, England RG21 6XS.
Companies and representatives throughout the world.

PALGRAVE MACMILLAN is the global academic imprint of the Palgrave Macmillan division of St. Martin's Press, LLC and of Palgrave Macmillan Ltd. Macmillan® is a registered trademark in the United States, United Kingdom and other countries. Palgrave is a registered trademark in the European Union and other countries.

ISBN-13: 978-1-4039-7815-8
ISBN-10: 1-4039-7815-8

Library of Congress Cataloging-in-Publication Data

Spirova, Maria.
    Political parties in post-communist societies : formation, persistence, and change/ by Maria Spirova.
        p. cm.
    Based on author's thesis.
    Includes bibliographical references and index.
    ISBN 1–4039–7815–8 (alk. paper)
  1. Political parties—Bulgaria. 2. Political parties—Hungary.
  3. Political culture—Bulgaria 4. Political culture—Hungary.
  5. Bulgaria—Politics and government—1990- 6. Hungary—Politics and government—1985- I. Title.

JN9609.A795S65 2008
324.2439—dc22   2006053260

A catalogue record for this book is available from the British Library.

Design by Macmillan India Ltd.

First edition: August 2007

10 9 8 7 6 5 4 3 2 1

Printed in the United States of America.

Contents

Acknowledgments

This book would not have materialized without the advice, support, and encouragement of a large number of people; I am deeply grateful to all of them. Eric Browne and Georg Vanberg read numerous versions of this work and pushed me to explore further; Shale Horowitz, Howard Handelman, and Donald Pienkos read and commented on the later versions. James Derleth, Antony Todorov, Ronald Weber, Andras Bozoki, and Laszlo Vass helped with contacts in Bulgaria and Hungary; without them my work would have been impossible. To Robert Sata, who interpreted at many of the interviews in Hungary: *köszönöm szépen*. Petr Kopecký and my other colleagues at the Leiden University, the Netherlands, provided a wonderful work environment at the stage of final revisions and gave me help and advice whenever needed. The editorial staff at Palgrave Macmillan and their anonymous reviewer have made the review and submission process a pleasure.

I owe a lot to the party leaders and strategists in Bulgaria and Hungary who agreed to talk to me and share their experience and knowledge. They are too many to name, but here are the ones I am most obliged to: Dr. Penka Krusteva, Mr. Roumen Zankov, Mr. Kiril Avramov, Mr. Georgi Pinchev, Mr. Azer Melekov, Mr. Zahary Petrov, Mr. Vladimir Murdzov, Mr. Ivaylo Kutov, Mr. Kasim Dal, Mr. Nikolay Mladenov, Ms. Julia Stoianova, Mr. Petar Dzudzev, Mr. Georgi Vanev, Mr. Zahari Petrov, and Dr. Milan Milanov in Bulgaria; and Mr. Peter Hack, Mr. Janos Vajda, Mr. Tibor Navracsics, Mr. Gabor Fodor, Mr. Laszlo Szoke, and Dr. Mihaly Kopa in Hungary.

Financial support from the University of Wisconsin–Milwaukee Graduate School allowed me to carry out the fieldwork for my doctoral dissertation on which this book is based; the New Bulgarian University, the Central European University and the European University Institute hosted me and provided invaluable resources during the winter and spring of 2002–2003.

Finally, none of this would have been possible without the encouragement and support of my loved ones: Jim, my family, and my friends, to all of whom this book is dedicated.

LIST OF TABLES

List of Figures

List of Abbreviations

Bulgarian Parties

ASO – Alternative Socialist Union
ASP – Alternative Socialist Party
BBB – Bulgarian Business Block
BDS – Bulgarian Democratic Union-Radicals
BEL – Bulgarian Euro Left
BESDP – Bulgarian Social Democratic Party (United)
BKP – Bulgarian Communist Party
BLP – Bulgarian Liberal Party
BNRP – Bulgarian National Radical Party
BNS – Bulgarian National Union
BSD – Bulgarian Social Democracy
BSDP – Bulgarian Social Democratic Party
BSDP-2 – Bulgarian Social Democratic Party–2
BSP – Bulgarian Socialist Party
BZNS – Bulgarian Agrarian National Union
BZNS-AS – Bulgarian Agrarian National Union–Alexander
        Stamboliiski
BZNS-M – Bulgarian Agrarian National Union–Mozer
BZNS-NP – Bulgarian Agrarian National Union–Nikola Petkov
CPoB – Communist Party of Bulgaria
CSII – Coalition for Simeon the Second
DAR – Democratic Alternative for the Republic
DP – Democratic Party
DPS – Movement for Rights and Freedoms
DSB – Democrats for a Strong Bulgaria
GOR – Citizens' Union for the Republic
K(F)TsB – Confederation/Federation "Tsardom Bulgaria"
KhRP – Christian Republican Party
NDSV – National Movement Simeon the Second
NI, SNI – New Choice Alliance
NLP "St. Stambolov" – People's Liberal Party Stefan Stambolov
NOSII – National Union for Simeon the Second

NDPS – National Movement for Rights and Freedoms
NL – New Left
NS – People's Union
NV – New Time
ODS – United Democratic Forces
ONS – Union for National Salvation
OPT – United Party of Labor
OT – Alliance for the King
OTP – Fatherland Party of Labor
PDC – Party of the Democratic Center
PDS – Political Movement Social Democracy
PS – Patriotic Union
RDP – Radical Democratic Party
SDS – Union of Democratic Forces
SDS-L – Union of Democratic Forces–Liberals
SDS-C – Union of Democratic Forces–Center
SNI – New Choice Union
SSD – Union of Free Democrats
VMRO – Internal Macedonian Revolutionary Organisation
ZP – Green Party

HUNGARIAN PARTIES

CP – Center Party
FIDESZ – Federation of Young Democrats
FIDESZ-MPP – FIDESZ Hungarian Civic Party
FKGP – United Smallholders Party
HVK – Patriotic Election Coalition
KDNP – Christian Democratic People's Party
MDF – Hungarian Democratic Forum
MIEP – Hungarian Justice and Life Party
MSZMP – Hungarian Socialist Workers Party
MSZP – Hungarian Socialist Party
NS – People's Union
SZDSZ – Alliance of Free Democrats

EUROPEAN PARTIES

EPP – European People's Party
PES – Party of the European Socialists

CHAPTER 1

POLITICAL PARTIES IN OLD AND NEW DEMOCRACIES

The evolution of democracy in the post-communist world has been a fascinating and challenging process. Over seventeen years after the fall of the Berlin Wall, some formerly communist countries have established strong and functioning democracies, while others are still struggling with basic principles of representative government. But one of the most challenging tasks that all post-communist systems have faced has been the transformation of one-party systems into functioning multiparty polities. This process is a demanding one for any new democracy, but the pervasive nature of communist parties' monopoly over political life during the years of one-party government has left a legacy that makes the process even more difficult.

In most Eastern European states, political life after the changes of the early 1990s continued to be dominated or strongly influenced by the successor parties of the defunct communist parties.[1] For the most part, these successor parties inherited strong organizations and human and material resources that put them in a class of their own. They also had seasoned political elites and an ideology that made them popular in the context of increasing social and economic dislocation. The presence of the successor parties in multiparty systems created specific dynamics among the contenders for power in the post-communist world, which in some cases made it difficult for new left-leaning parties to enter the competition.

In addition, the years of forced political mobilization by communist parties left many people unwilling to join political formations and, in some cases, even uncertain about the benefits of political parties operating in the new multiparty systems. These attitudes contributed to the difficulty faced by new parties in attracting members, establishing strong organizations, and finding a persistent core of supporters, although the extent to which this has been the case has varied from system to system. However, political parties remain essential components of modern democratic government, and this has made it necessary for the young post-communist democracies to establish stable parties and functioning party systems for them to be accepted in the family of democratic states.[2]

POLITICAL PARTIES AND DEMOCRATIC GOVERNMENT

Despite their relatively late arrival in political life, multiple and free political parties[3] have come to be seen as major prerequisites for a functioning democratic system.[4] Parties are indispensable to any democratic system of government because they serve as channels for the expression of people's demands, as instruments of popular representation, and as routes of communications between state and society (Sartori 1976, 27 and 56). Parties are essential to a democracy both because they provide its institutional channels and because they maintain the stability of the system.

Political parties shape citizen participation and determine the stability of political leadership, and can inhibit or exacerbate turmoil and violence. So "a strong system of political parties is essential for a strong democracy" (Powell 1982). As parties manage both elections and the legislatures—the two main possible sources of instability—they remain crucial for the maintenance of both the stability and the legitimacy of the system (Yanai 1999).

Despite the recent "decline" in the centrality of political parties in the democratic process, they have not been replaced by any new institutions of similar importance (Bartolini and Mair 2001).[5] Parties have encountered numerous challenges and have adapted their structures to deal with them: a recent taxonomy of political parties identified fifteen different "species" of political party, each of them belonging to a "broader *genus* of party types" (Gunther and Diamond 2001, 9). However, despite these challenges, parties continue to be "one of the most prominent institutions of liberal democracies" (Lewis 2001b, 1).

POLITICAL PARTIES IN NEWLY ESTABLISHED DEMOCRACIES

Although they might not play a very large role in the actual transition to democracy, parties play a crucial role in the consolidation of democracy in newly democratized states.[6] The most difficult challenge that a new system faces is its freshly mobilized electorate. As parties are the key institutions for organizing mass involvement, the ability of parties and party systems to expand participation through the system; preempt or divert any revolutionary activity; and moderate and channel the participation of newly mobilized groups without disrupting the system is a strong determinant of the stability of the democratic polity (Huntington 1968, 412). Recent studies of democratic consolidation have expanded the analysis regarding the roles parties play in this process (Pridham 1995; Heywood 1996; Diamond and Linz 1988; Pridham and Lewis 1996; Schmitter 2001; Lewis 2001b).

Political Parties and Post-Communist Systems

There seems to be general agreement that "analyzing the role of parties and the emerging shape and quality of a party system . . . provides important and potentially long-standing evidence about how new democracies are functioning and beginning to root themselves" (Pridham and Lewis 1996, 8). The study of party development in the post-communist states has been extensive and diverse. However, in many ways it has reflected the difficulties faced by the party formation process itself. Authors have argued that political parties in the post-communist systems are, and should be, different from parties in the West, not only because of the novelty of the democratic process, but also because they are developing in a period during which the nature of parties is changing (Mair 1996; Pridham and Lewis 1996; Bielasiak 1997). Some authors have even argued that the disarray brought about by the transition prevents the formation and consolidation of a structured party system. Known as the *tabula rasa* hypothesis, this view stresses the major differences between the process of party development in Eastern and Western Europe and argues against the use of any classic theories to explain party development in the post-communist world (Bielasiak 1997).

Alternatively, other works have focused on the legacy of the one-party communist state; the continued presence of the "successor" parties; the challenges presented by the simultaneity of political, economic, and, in some cases, national reforms; the absence of strong social cleavages; and the weak party identification among the electorate. Studies carried out at the party level have focused on the evolution of "successor" parties in the democratic polities (Agh 1996, 1997, 2000; Ishiyama 1995, 1997, 1999a, 1999b; Racz 2000; Ishiyama and Bozoki

2001; Bozoki and Ishiyama 2002; Grzymala-Buse 2002) and the legacy of the communist regimes for the development of party identification (Wyman et al. 1995; Rose 1995; Bacon 1998; Bielasiak 1997). Studies at the system level have followed Lipset and Rokkan (1967) in their analysis of the impact of social cleavages on party system development (Kitschelt 1995a, 1995b; Kitschelt et al. 1999; Markovski 1995; Toka 1995a; Karasimeonov 1996; Lawson et al. 1999; Whitefield 2002)[7] or have used Sartori's framework to compare and analyze the level of fragmentation and polarization of party systems (Clark 1995; Bielasiak 1997, 2003).

The nature of the evolving party organizations in the post-communist world has been a favorite topic of party research as well. These studies have concentrated on parties in several party systems (Hungary, Poland, the Czech Republic, and, more rarely, the Baltic States) and have either used the institutionalization theories of Panebianco (1988), Huntington (1968), or Mainwaring (1999) or have kept the discussion at a descriptive and procedural level. Their main argument is that parties in the region are parliament-centered, have few or no local branches, and are not supported by any voluntary organizations; instead, they are elite-dominated and highly professional (Lewis 1996; Olson 1998; Klima 1998; Krapavicius 1998; Golosov 1998; Toole 2000, 2003; Szczerbiak 1999, 2001; van Biezen 2003).

Yet another major group of studies has concentrated on analyzing the impact of the turbulent nature of the political process on the development of political parties. This work has focused on the interplay of electoral and parliamentary cycles and the effects that the "game" of politics has on political parties. The studies have investigated the various "strategies" adopted by the parties in terms of their alliance partners, their ideological positions, and their policies while in government. Of particular note is the volume edited by Gordon Wightman (1995), *Party Formation in East-Central Europe,* which includes studies of the party formation process from the party strategy perspective in Czechoslovakia, Hungary, Poland, and Bulgaria. Individual studies (Agh 1996, 1997, 2000; Lewis 1994a, 1994b; Bacon 1998; Olson 1998; Kreuzer and Pettai 2001) have looked at the development of parties in Eastern Europe from this perceptive as well. Starting from either the assumptions of rationality or those of learning theory, these studies maintain the centrality of party elites in party formation and political competition.

THE RATIONALE FOR THIS WORK

This book follows partly in the tradition of this latter body of research by assuming a rational approach to the understanding of political parties. It believes that electoral strategies and fortunes are key to a party's evolution and views party evolution in some ways as a by-product of electoral competition. However, rather than simply describe this evolution (as many of the existing studies have done), this study borrows from the existing literature on political parties in the West to develop a general understanding of why parties form and how they choose their electoral strategies. To understand this process better, this work addresses two key questions: why parties form in the post-communist context, and how and why they choose their electoral strategies. This study thus rejects the idea that post-communist party development is unique; instead, it maintains that party evolution can be explained with some of the existing theories about political parties as long as the specifics of the post-communist context are incorporated. Thus, it contributes to the development of party theory by testing a model of parties as endogenous institutions in the context of post-communist political development.

Unlike most of the existing works on post-communist party development, this work assumes that because developments at the party-system level are a result of the dynamics between individual parties in the system, we need to understand how individual parties behave in order to understand developments at the system level. To achieve this understanding, the study examines how features of individual parties impact their own electoral strategies and those of their competitors. In doing so, it incorporates arguments from the literature devoted to the ideological and organization development of post-communist parties. The study avoids a major pitfall in the existing literature, namely, its failure to link individual party behavior to the behavior of other parties and to the development of the party system.

This book also ventures into uncharted territory—it investigates the impact of public financing on party evolution and the role played by transnational parties in the party politics of the post-communist countries. While the study of public financing has recently become a popular topic, political scientists and policy analysts rarely examine the role of public financing in the evolution of the political parties. Instead, they tend to concentrate on issues of transparency and political corruption (Roper 2002; Protsyk 2002; Nassmacher 2004; Pinto-Duschinsky 2002). Similarly, due to the sporadic and selective nature of transnational party involvement in national party politics, no detailed examination of its nature and consequences exists. This study attempts to address both of these gaps by incorporating public financing and external influence as two of the constraints on party behavior.

Finally, this work uses the experience of Bulgarian political parties as a major object of study, something that has not been done on a large scale in the literature on the subject in the English language. While Hungarian, Polish, and Czech parties have received a considerable amount of scholarly attention (the Hungarian Socialist Party being probably the most studied party in the region), and the parties in the Baltic States and Romania have been studied to some degree, works on Bulgarian parties are rare and they do not as a rule study Bulgarian parties from a comparative perspective.[8] Much of the information on Bulgarian parties presented here is thus original and not available elsewhere, including complete election results for all post-1989 elections and data on the organization of the Bulgarian political parties.

CHAPTER-BY-CHAPTER OVERVIEW

Chapter 2 outlines the study's theoretical framework. It begins by discussing the conception of parties as endogenous institutions and proceeds to develop a model of party formation and electoral competition. Its main argument is that political parties exist to help politicians realize their political ambition, and defines political ambition, in the tradition of the work of John Aldrich (1995) and Joseph A. Schlesinger (1994), as access to political office. The chapter maintains that politicians, including those in this study, define their political goals in electoral terms and form parties only because doing so promises to help them achieve their electoral targets. Once formed, parties will select the electoral strategy that has the potential to deliver their electoral targets from among a range of choices—from running alone to seeking alliances, merging, disbanding, or hibernating. During every inter-electoral period, politicians and parties will reevaluate goals, redefine electoral targets, and, based on these analyses, choose the most promising electoral strategies at the next election.

The choice of strategy will depend on how much electoral support a party believes that it enjoys, whether this support is enough to allow politicians to achieve their respective electoral targets, and how stable that support is expected to be until the elections. Previous electoral support, an expectation of electoral volatility, the electoral system threshold, the presence of ideological competitors, the availability of resources, and the party's organizational strength are suggested as factors that influence this choice. As a result of this process, parties will form and then persist or change as political entities. If the propositions developed in chapter 2 are correct, then parties that do not achieve their electoral targets should become discouraged from running alone and should seek allies, thereby contributing to the eventual stabilization of the party system.

Based on these theoretical assumptions, chapter 2 develops nine hypotheses and defines their observable implications at the party and party-system levels. The chapter then discusses the methodology used to study these hypotheses. To test the model at the party level, this study employs a comparative analysis of the electoral strategies of parties in Bulgaria and Hungary. Data from interviews and primary and secondary sources are used in the analysis. To test the model at the system level, the study employs a larger, statistical analysis, using the number of parties in 12 post-communist systems over several consecutive rounds of elections as its dependent variable. The methodological issues involved in the use of these approaches are also discussed in the chapter.

Chapter 3, the beginning of the empirical part of the study, opens with a brief overview of the development of party politics in Bulgaria and Hungary. In order to test the understanding of party formation and electoral competition presented earlier, the chapter then proceeds to describe the process of the formation and of the electoral competition of six parties. The chapter examines the evolution of three Bulgarian and three Hungarian parties over the 1990–2005 period—respectively, the Bulgarian Socialist Party (BSP), the Movement for Rights and Freedoms (DPS), the Bulgarian EuroLeft (BEL), the Federation of Young Democrats–Hungarian Civic Party (FIDESZ-MPP), the Alliance of Free Democrats (SZDSZ), and the Hungarian Workers' Party (Munkaspart). The discussion defines the parties' electoral targets, describes the processes that have led to their formation, and follows their choice of electoral strategies over several rounds of elections. It also touches briefly upon the different factors that have impacted the decision of these parties to form, run alone, forge alliances, or merge.

A more detailed analysis of the factors that have impacted the decisions of these six parties in regard to their formation and electoral competition is presented in chapter 4. The chapter preserves the party level of analysis and tests several of the hypotheses suggested in chapter 2. It focuses on the influence that electoral performance and expected electoral volatility (hypotheses H1, H2, and H3), ideological crowdedness (H5), and party organizational strength (H9) have had on the decisions of political parties in Bulgaria and Hungary. In addition to examining in detail the experience of the six parties described in chapter 3, the analysis also incorporates examples from other parties in the Hungarian and Bulgarian party systems. Drawing on data from interviews and other sources, and placing these in the context of the evolution of the parties over the years under study, the analysis finds evidence in support of hypotheses 1 and 3, and mixed evidence in support of hypotheses 5 and 9. Both individual party data and the development of these two party systems indicate that, overall, these parties reacted to anticipated and actual success and failure at elections as proposed. Although there are exceptions that complicate the overall pattern, in general, both party systems have seen increasing stability with the passage of time, both in terms of the number of new entries and the exit of unsuccessful contestants.

The evidence is not as conclusive with regard to the roles that ideological crowdedness and organizational strength play in the decision of parties to form and their choice of electoral strategies. Political party leaders point to the importance of ideological considerations in choosing electoral strategies, and these leaders emphasize a commonly held belief that "ideological space" needs to be consolidated if parties are to be successful electorally. However, at least in Bulgaria, the actual behavior of political parties partially contradicts this claim. The number of competitors within ideological families continues to be relatively high, and new entries within already crowded ideological space continue to appear. More limited examples of this trend exist in Hungary as well.

The data are equally mixed on the relationship between organizational strength and electoral strategies. Parties in both systems indicate that organizational considerations play a role in their choice of electoral strategies, and that the presence of already established parties is often a deterrent for new entrants and an incentive for allying or merging. However, while parties seem to be more interested in strengthening their organizations in Bulgaria than in Hungary, an examination of the evolution of the party systems in these two countries reveals a tendency for the number of parties in Hungary to decrease, but does not find a consistent trend in Bulgaria. After a short examination of some external factors that seem to have influenced parties' decisions, but which have not been fully accounted for by the theoretical understanding of party behavior, the chapter concludes with the observation that a consideration of system-level factors is clearly needed for a better explanation of party behavior.

Chapter 5 shifts the level of analysis to the system level in order to test the empirical implications of the theoretical model. The chapter begins with a brief examination of the electoral systems and of party financing regulations in Bulgaria and Hungary, and examines their apparent influence on the outcomes described in chapters 3 and 4. Chapter 5 then proceeds to formulate a model that can be used to test the system-level implications of the theoretical model. Using the number of electoral contestants at every election in twelve post-communist party systems, the model estimates the impact of expected electoral volatility (H3), stability of support (H6), electoral threshold (H4), the regulations of party financing (H7 and H8), and electoral experience (H1) on party behavior. The analysis finds support for all but one hypothesis and discusses the implications that the results have on the conclusions reached in chapter 4. These results indicate that overall, politicians and parties in the post-communist world appear to behave rationally and in accordance with the understanding of party behavior suggested in chapter 2. They seem to define their ambitions in electoral terms and to contest elections with a strategy that best promises to deliver their target. While the party-level analysis presents plenty of exceptions to this pattern from the two systems in this study, the general relationships between the components of the model seem to be well established.

The major conclusion of this study, presented in chapter 6, is that an understanding of the general processes that shape a certain party system might not help us to learn about the behavior of any given individual party within the system. The party-level analysis points to the importance of several factors that are not incorporated by a rational and electorally centered view of political party behavior. Some politicians, at least in Hungary and Bulgaria, seem to value the autonomy of their parties more than the theoretical assumptions regarding party behavior suggest. Personality factors and party histories also can stymie otherwise beneficial cooperation among parties.

This book also suggests the importance of system-level factors for a party's choice of electoral strategies, particularly regarding the relatively uninvestigated role that party-financing regulations play in the evolution of parties and party systems in the post-communist world. The study also sheds some light on the trends in organizational development of Bulgarian parties and the role external actors have played in the evolution of party interactions in the post-communist region.

NOTES

1. The term "successor" party/parties will be used throughout this study to mean the party or parties that succeeded the communist party in each system. The term was introduced by John Ishiyama in his extensive studies of the revamped communist parties in the post-communist region (Ishiyama, various works; Bozoki and Ishiyama 2002).

2. In fact, the European Union required that any candidate state achieve "stability of institutions guaranteeing democracy, the rule of law, human rights and respect for and protection of minorities," thus making the establishment of stable parties even more important in the post-communist context (European Commission 2004).

3. A political party is defined as "any group, however loosely organized, seeking to elect governmental officeholders under a given label" (Epstein 1967, 9).

4. Historically, political parties only came to be accepted with the realization that "diversity and dissent are not necessarily incompatible with, or disruptive of, political order" (Sartori 1976, 13). Political parties evolved from the clubs, committees, philosophical societies and parliamentary groups of the premodern period (Duverger 1951, xxiii). All of these bodies strived to acquire and exercise power, but the differentiating element of political parties was their connection with the people. Parties emerged when a permanent connection between parliamentary groups and electoral committees was established. Alternatively, externally generated parties emerged when groups outside the parliamentary setting organized themselves and started competing in elections (Duverger 1951, xxiv).

5. This decline, arguably, has been brought about by declining party membership and widespread party identification, and the advent of new technology as a means of political communication (Katz and Mair 1995; Gunther and Diamond 2001).

6. While transition implies the actual replacement of an authoritarian regime with a democratic one, the consolidation of democracy involves the process that leads to the establishment of democracy as the "only game in town" (Linz and Stepan 1996, 5–6). According to Mainwaring, the consolidation of democratic regimes necessarily involves the institutionalization, or wide acceptance, of its rules and procedures (Mainwaring 1992, 296). Parties might not play the most important role in the breakup of the previous regime because during this stage other actors, such as the military or the country's elite, might be of more significance (Pridham 1995; Heywood 1996, 158). The more established a democracy becomes, the more central the role played by the parties tends to be. The consolidation of democracy thus requires the presence of stable parties and party systems. It is important to note, however, that stable political parties might be

a necessary condition for the consolidation of democracy, but they are by no means a sufficient condition. Most of the democratization literature studies the role of parties as only one of the factors contributing to the stabilization of democracy. Other important determinants of the stabilization of democracy include historical conditions, political culture, political leadership, state structures, the military, civil society, socioeconomic development, economic performance, and international factors (Diamond and Linz 1988, 2–47; Pridham and Lewis 1996, 1–2).

7. These studies, however, disagree on how applicable the theory is to the post-communist world. The Lawson et al. volume (1999) is quite skeptical about the strength of social cleavages, especially in regard to their reflection in the platforms of political parties. In contrast, Kitschelt's work assumes a stronger impact of social divisions and uses extensive survey data to investigate the linkages between public and political parties in terms of various social cleavages.

8. The major exceptions are Georgi Karasimeonov (1996), Waller and Karasimenov (1996), and a study of the Bulgarian Socialist Party by Murer (2002) published in several edited volumes.

C H A P T E R   2

PARTY FORMATION, PERSISTENCE, AND CHANGE: THEORETICAL FRAMEWORK, METHODOLOGY, AND DATA

During the last two decades, political parties in post-communist political systems have formed, disbanded, merged, and split. In the process, one-party systems have evolved into multiparty systems. However, the experiences of individual East European states have been quite diverse in this respect. Some of them have witnessed the appearance and maintenance of relatively stable political parties while others have seen a substantial degree of fluctuation in the number of parties. The diversity of these countries' experiences raises three basic questions. First, why, given the post-communist political and institutional context, do parties form? Second, why, once formed, do they persist more or less intact or undergo significant change? And third, how do the institutional, legal, and political characteristics of the post-communist political systems influence this evolutionary process?

Although abundant, the existing literature on parties and party system change rarely addresses these questions, mainly because it has focused on Western European parties. It therefore tends to assume a set of existent parties and concerns itself with answering the question of whether change has occurred and measuring change when it does occur (Pennings and Lane 1998; Daalder and Mair 1983; Mair 1997). Further, studies of change have usually been conducted on a country-by-country basis with little consideration of general evolutionary patterns (Wellhoffer 2001; Niedermeyer 1998; Hazan 1998). Studies of new party emergence—one of the elements of system change—have been relatively rare (Hug 2001; Golder 2003).

The literature devoted to Eastern European developments has also failed to address these questions. It tends to contain descriptive accounts of either party system developments or individual parties. There have been few attempts to analyze how an individual party's development is influenced by the development of other parties or by the legal and institutional arrangements of the political system.[1]

However, the decisions of parties to form, merge, ally, or dissolve is a crucial question for the analysis of parties and party systems. This chapter will develop a model to describe and explain the decision-making process that results in these outcomes, which we shall consider to be a choice made by politicians. It borrows from insights into this process developed in several fields of the literature: studies on party system change in Western Europe, including the literature on new party emergence in established systems; the literature on party development in new democracies, specifically those in Eastern Europe; and more general discussions of the role of political parties in democratic systems.

PARTY FORMATION, PERSISTENCE, AND CHANGE: AN OVERVIEW

Political Parties as Endogenous Institutions

The current understanding of party formation and change is consistent with the understanding of party behavior as the result of the actions of rational, goal-oriented individuals, constrained by structural and institutional factors. This approach to the study of party development has been taken by Aldrich (1995), Perkins (1996), Hug (2001), and Hauss and Rayside (1978). If we consider politics to be a "game," then institutions can be treated as equilibrium outcomes of this game, or put in other words, humanly devised constraints on human behavior (Calvert 1995). Although institutions are outcomes of people's behavior, they also represent "stability that can arise from mutually understood actor preferences and optimizing behavior" (Crawford and Ostrom 1995, 582). Institutions thus become necessary only as long as they perform a function that serves to increase the benefits for individuals.

While parties are seldom studied by "institutions as equilibria" scholars, who usually focus on electoral arrangements and constitutional frameworks, Aldrich views parties as "the most endogenous of all institutions." That is, they are seldom part of the legal framework defining the institutional arrangement of a polity (Aldrich 1995, 19).

Aldrich argues that parties can, and should, be treated as political outcomes—they "result from actors seeking to realize their goals, choosing within and possibly shaping a given set of institutional arrangements, and so choosing within a given historical context" (Aldrich 1995, 6). Parties are thus seen as "tools" that allow people with political ambition to realize their goals. Instead of viewing political parties and, by extension, party systems as the results of sweeping societal and historical forces, Aldrich sees them as a consequence of the actions of goal-oriented individuals, who are subject to institutional, political, and legal constraints.

Some people have political ambitions—for example, they might want to influence the political outcomes, to express political ideas, or to simply enjoy the spoils of political office. Conceived this way, "ambition" becomes associated with conventional understanding of the concept of "political participation," where political action (behavior) includes activities intended to "influence" the process or outcomes of political decision making (Nie, Verba, and Kim 1978). For our purposes, however, we consider the concept of "ambition" to denote activity beyond an attempt to exert a single influence on political decision making. Rather, we conceive of ambition as a motivation to acquire leadership positions or status related to the achievement of personal and public goals associated with or resulting from political action. Thus, all people who are characterized as having political ambition are participants in the political process, but not all political participants have political ambition. Our concern in this research is with those who pursue political ambition. In particular we are interested in the activities of such individuals as these relate to the formation of political groups and parties as instruments for the furtherance or achievement of their goals.

For some, political ambition is associated with winning political office. They might want to win office because of benefits associated with the "politically discretionary governmental or subgovernmental appointments" or because they are interested in policy and desire to dominate the executive in order to influence policy (Muller and Strom 1999, 5). Regardless of whether office is valued instrumentally or intrinsically, it is only achievable by running candidates in elections. The two processes—party development and electoral competition—are thus very closely intertwined. For politicians, however, winning office, is not a *goal* in itself, but only the instrument for achieving their underlying goals.

Other people with political ambition might not need to win office to realize this ambition. For them expressing their ideas may be enough. Even so, some of these people might form parties and even run in elections because elections provide them with an opportunity to present and express their ideas. Political science commonly considers behavior motivated in this way to be inconsequential. Schlesinger, for example, argues that "for parties which use elections for some purpose other than gaining office, the goals and means are unspecified by the democratic institutions," and excludes these parties from his discussion (1994, 7). In contrast, others have argued that motivations can include goals that are not dependent on winning office (Browne and Patterson 1999). Making a political statement, establishing a political presence, enjoying the financial benefits of being a party, and participating in elections are also possible motivations that can encourage parties to form and run in elections even when chances of winning office are slim, if not nonexistent. More recently, in his study of right-wing parties in Western Europe, Golder similarly distinguishes between political parties that are motivated by instrumental ends and those motivated by expressive ends (2003, 442). The members of the latter group are satisfied with simply expressing their political (in this case right-wing) ideas. The belief that parties and voters can be driven by expressive motivations has probably been best developed by Schuessler (2000). For the present purposes, however, parties that form and run in elections but are not interested in office per se are not considered. Thus, the conception of ambition is narrowed to its conventional definition: a desire to win office (Schlesinger 1994, 33–46).

Overview of the Model

The proposed understanding of how parties form, choose their electoral strategies, and evolve over time is based on the belief that politicians will define the realization of their goals in electoral terms and form a party only when doing so promises to achieve the electoral target that they have set for themselves. Once parties are formed, they will similarly define the realization of their members' ambitions in electoral terms and choose electoral strategies that promise to achieve that electoral target best. After an election, and as a result of their electoral performance, politicians will reevaluate and adjust their ambitions, set new electoral targets that reflect these reevaluated goals, and so on. The process will thus repeat itself at every election and during every interelection period. As a result of the process, political parties will form, continue to exist, merge, or disband. This process is represented in figure 2.1.

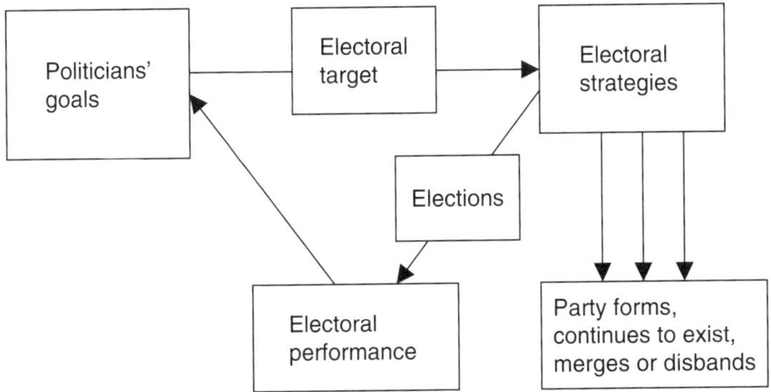

Figure 2.1   Overview of the process of party formation and electoral competition.

The following sections will discuss these processes in turn. First, the section on setting an electoral target examines the possible targets that politicians can set for themselves. The section on party formation elaborates on the choices that politicians have in terms of forming or joining a political party. The next one discusses the electoral strategies available to parties at their first, and at each succeeding, election. Finally, the section on evaluating the likelihood of success discusses how various institutional constraints impact the choice of electoral strategies.

SETTING AN ELECTORAL TARGET

Forming a party only serves the goals of politicians when it can achieve enough electoral support to allow the winning of office. Similarly, a party only needs to continue to exist as an entity if it provides its leaders with the chance of getting into office (Schlesinger 1994, 33). However, what exactly "winning office" means will differ substantially from one case to the next. As Schlesinger has argued, "ambition for office" can be either "static" or "progressive"—politicians might be interested in winning the same office over and over again, or might move from one office to another (1994, 39–41).

Political parties then will respond to the varying office ambitions of their leaders. These ambitions can range from participating in the legislative process to holding a ministerial position or being prime minister.[2] However, at the party level, these ambitions will be reflected in the target that each party sets for itself at each election—getting representation in the national legislature, being in a position to participate in the government, or dominating the formation and functions of the national government.[3] Which one of these targets a party sets for itself will depend on the ambitions of its leaders *and* the capability of the party, defined as the level of electoral support that the party can gather at each election. As access to the executive is only possible through legislative seats, each of these targets will lead to a respective *electoral target* defined in terms of a sufficient number of legislative seats.

All parties that try to get representation in the legislature are expected to set their immediate objectives as *at least* surpassing the electoral threshold. Parties that have already won seats in previous elections might try not only to get seats, but also to *increase* their share of seats. As a result, parties will differ in their definition of what constitutes a satisfactory number of seats, depending on their popularity and their experience of legislative representation.[4]

Parties that seek legislative representation are what we usually call short-term seat-maximizers (Gunther 1989). They want representation in the legislature and consider anything less to be a failure. However, in most cases, parties try to win seats *and* secure their participation in the government.[5] Gaining executive office might dictate different electoral targets than gaining parliamentary seats. A place in the governing coalition might be achieved through presence in parliament *and* appropriate ideological positioning rather than simply by securing a large number of seats. This might allow smaller parties to define their electoral target as surpassing the threshold, but not necessarily as getting as many seats as possible.[6]

Parties that want to participate in the government and are popular enough might want to dominate the governmental process. Thus they will try to achieve more than just representation in parliament—in most cases they will need to gain at least a near plurality of seats. Parties that have a chance of dominating the governing process usually consider gaining a plurality or near plurality of seats in parliament to be the decisive element in their being able to achieve the dominant position. Although policy positioning can influence their ability to form a government, achieving a near plurality of the seats is usually the dominant strategy. Politicians who want to control the government formation process will define the electoral target of their party to be that of achieving enough seats to be one of the top parties in parliament.

The exact electoral targets of each party will thus depend on the ambition of its leaders, the party's capability, and its electoral and legislative experience. Thus, it becomes impossible to define exactly how many seats each party will be trying to get at each election. What we can do is define the minimum targets for each type of party. There are thus two distinct *electoral* targets that politicians can set for

Table 2.1 Party electoral targets

Party target	(Minimum) Electoral target at each election
Participate in legislative politics (legislative parties)	Surpass threshold
Participate in government (executive parties)	Surpass threshold
Dominate government (Prime Ministerial parties)	Achieve near plurality of seats

parties—surpassing the threshold and achieving enough seats to be one of the top parties in the legislature. These options are represented in table 2.1.

PARTY EVOLUTION: FORMATION (PHASE 1)

When a few people decide that they want to *cooperate* for the purpose of winning office (defined in any of the ways presented in the earlier section), they are transformed into what may be called a "proto party." Belonging to a party provides benefits to people who seek office: the party coordinates local and national vote-getting, regularizes candidate recruitment and protects against new entrants, and provides patronage appointments. The party also regularizes legislative and ministerial advancements and minimizes campaign costs by providing economies of scale, using its organizational structures (Aldrich 1995, 45–55; Kruezer and Pettai 2002). Party formation is thus only part of an electoral strategy that helps people who seek office to maximize their goals through running for office.

Once members of the group have decided that they can best realize their goals by participating in the electoral process, they evaluate their options. If the members of a proto party believe that by forming a political party they can best realize their ambitions and the electoral target that they have set, we should expect that the group will not seek electoral support of other groups but would constitute itself, officially, as a new political party.[7] Alternatively, if members of a proto party decide they cannot realize their goals alone, they will seek the support of other such groups or that of existing political parties. If their attempt to find partners is unsuccessful, they might either join an existing party,[8] in which case we would not see the emergence of a new party, or they might form a new party together with other groups in a similar situation. If these attempts at cooperation fail, no party can form.[9] This process is represented in figure 2.2.

Once the decision to form a party is made, the members adopt a label, register the party appropriately, and begin to develop an

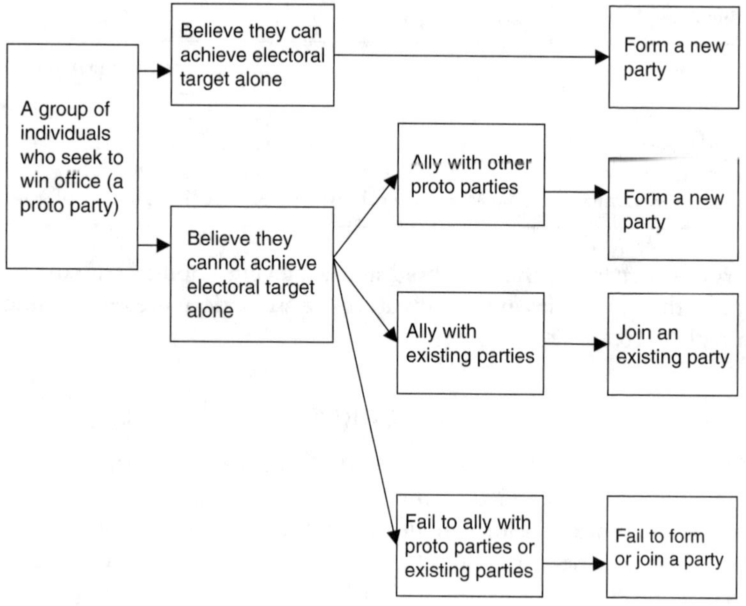

Figure 2.2   Process of party formation and electoral competition, phase 1: Formation.

electoral strategy.[10] For the current purposes, this is the decision of primary interest.

PARTY EVOLUTION: ELECTORAL STRATEGIES

Choosing an Electoral Strategy at the First Election (Phase 2)

Figure 2.3 presents the elements of electoral strategy for a newly formed political party. Starting at any point after formation, but before an election is held, a new party will reevaluate how much electoral support[11] it needs in order to achieve its electoral target. Next, it will evaluate the likelihood that this electoral target can be achieved. Based on this evaluation, the party then may be expected to choose from among three possible strategies: run candidates in the elections on the party's own label; seek to join or form an electoral alliance with another party or parties; or not contest a current election. In this third case, the party may decide to dissolve itself, to merge with another party or parties, or to "hibernate" electorally.

If the party believes that it can achieve its electoral target, it is expected to contest elections alone and thus "persist" as a party through the election period. However, if the party is uncertain about

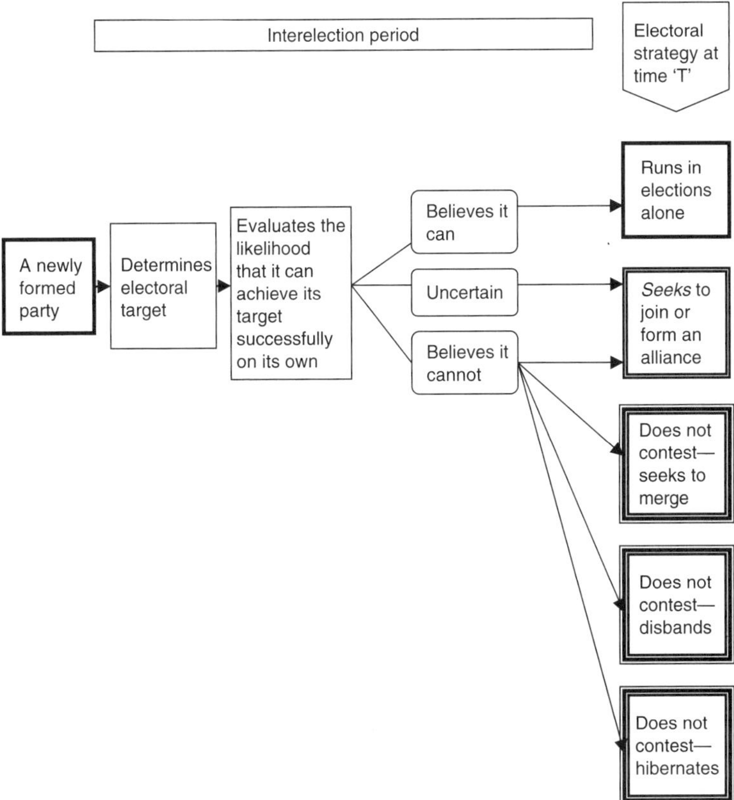

Figure 2.3   Process of party formation and electoral competition, phase 2: Possible electoral strategies at first election.

the likelihood of achieving its electoral target, it is expected to negotiate with others in an attempt to join or form an electoral alliance.[12]

An electoral alliance is an explicit agreement between two or more parties to coordinate their electoral strategies for their mutual benefit. Such alliances are typically concluded for the purposes of fighting elections and do not imply further cooperation. This definition thus includes both alliances that use a label different from the labels of each of their constituent parts *and* alliances that use a combination of the parties' labels. Similarly, the definition also incorporates both alliances in which parties run joint lists and alliances in which the parties run separate lists but their votes are counted as if cast for one party (*apparentements*).[13]

Forming an alliance increases the likelihood of achieving the electoral target as the alliance pools the support of two or more political parties (Pettai and Kreuzer 2001, 113). Alliances do not typically compromise the autonomy of their members beyond the specific terms of the electoral agreement. However, joining an alliance, and especially a non-*apparentement* one, also restricts the independence of the party in terms of its ability to place candidates on lists or control its policy positions, thus limiting the benefits it brings in terms of helping politicians win office. In fact, the fear that allying will result in the party's loss of integrity as an institution has been shown to serve as a deterrent to the formation of electoral alliances in some cases (Gunther 1989, 845).[14] Thus, for a party to seek an alliance, it needs to be highly uncertain that it will win office on its own, and certain that the party that it is allying with will contribute enough electoral support so as to improve the chances of both winning office. The formation of an alliance is graphically represented in figure 2.3 by a double line.

Alternatively, after an evaluation, the party might realize that it cannot achieve the electoral target. In this case, it may try to negotiate to join an alliance, decide not to contest elections and to merge with another party, sit out the current elections (hibernate), or dissolve. A merger refers to the decision of two or more existing political parties to end their independence as a party, combine their structures and leaderships, and register as a new political party. Thus, an alliance allows for the party to remain in existence, but a merger implies the end of the party (graphically represented in figure 2.3 by a triple black line).

Mergers are relatively rare, especially where a new party has just formed and has not fought an election. They bring electoral benefits because they promise to combine the electoral support of all its members into one, but they also carry the danger of alienating the supporters of all or some of the new entity's members. A merger can give members and supporters the idea that their leaders have betrayed them ideologically; as Mair has argued, voters might decide that the merger is "strategically irrelevant or ideologically distasteful" (1990, 131). Mergers are thus usually the last resort of parties faced with prospective electoral defeat.

Because of this, parties that have just formed and believe that they cannot achieve the electoral support needed for the realization of their immediate goals are more likely to try to join or form an alliance than to try to merge. As the party has just formed, it might be unwilling to forego its independence, but it might be willing to withdraw from the election in an attempt to build up support and do better next time. Similarly, the party is also relatively unlikely to disband and thus end its existence before running in elections. If it decides not to run in elections and hibernate, the party becomes of no consequence to the present discussion until it appears at elections again.

Choosing an Electoral Strategy at Each Succeeding Election (Phase 3)

Parties Contesting Elections Alone at the Previous Election
Since parties exist to make it easier for politicians to win elections, the parties' continuing existence is closely linked to their electoral performance. Once a party has fought an election under its own label, regardless of whether it has won office or not, it will again confront three options when deciding on an electoral strategy for the next election: running alone, trying to ally, or not contesting elections (because of an attempt for a merger, a dissolution, or hibernation). In order to choose an electoral strategy, the party undergoes a process that is similar to the one followed by a new party. It determines the electoral target it needs to achieve, and if it believes that the likelihood of achieving the target is high, the party continues to run alone. If achieving the electoral target is uncertain, the party is expected to try to ally with others in an attempt to increase its electoral support without losing its identity. If it believes that the likelihood of achieving the target is low, the party can then decide to seek to form or join an alliance, to seek a merger with another party, to disband, or to "hibernate." The process is represented in figure 2.4.

It can be seen from the figure that parties emerging intact from their first elections continue to confront the full range of election strategy options. Of these options, the two most probable choices for a party are to run alone in the next election under its own label (if the party believes it can achieve its electoral target) or to seek alliances (if it is uncertain about achieving its target and if it believes it will not achieve it). In other words, the party is unlikely to go from running alone at its first election to merging at the next (thus ending its independent existence), without going through the alliance stage. For the political leaders the party serves, a merger means that they have to renegotiate their control over candidate lists, office allocation, and any other party feature. As they are driven by a desire to win office, and as allying can make achieving office more likely without eliminating all control, a party in this situation is not likely to merge.

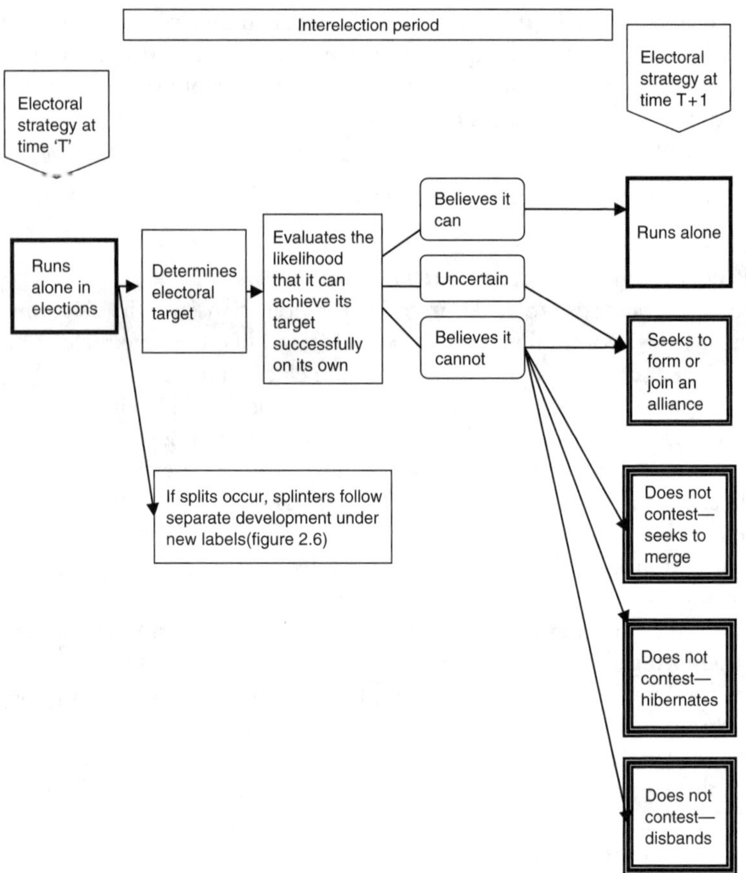

Figure 2.4   Process of party formation and electoral competition, phase 3: Possible electoral strategies at time T + 1 for parties that run alone at time 'T'.

Parties Contesting Previous Elections in an Alliance

Some parties that seek alliances will succeed in forming or joining them and will then contest elections as part of the alliance. However, they will also have to choose a new electoral strategy before the next election. All possible electoral strategies are presented in figure 2.5. An attempt to merge is a more likely choice in cases where the party does not believe that it can achieve its electoral target. This is because the party has already tried the alliance strategy. At this point, if office is unlikely to be won by running alone and more likely to be won through a merger, the party may be willing to transform itself into

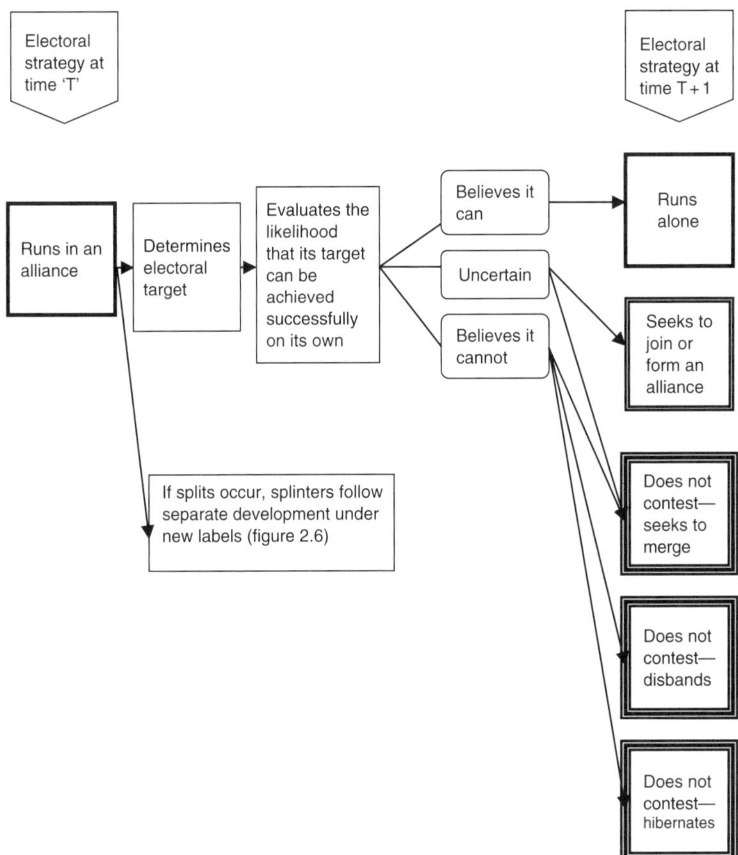

Figure 2.5 Process of party formation and electoral competition, phase 3: Possible electoral strategies at time T + 1 for parties that run in an alliance at time 'T'.

a new political entity. Once a merger is accomplished, the new entity behaves as a new party and goes through phases 2 and 3 again.

Splits in Existing Parties

The uncertainty of electoral politics also makes it possible that parties will experience divisions during an interelection period, some of which might lead to formal splits.[15] If none of the resulting constituent parts ("splinters") preserves the original label, the original party ends its existence and the splinters follow a separate developmental process.

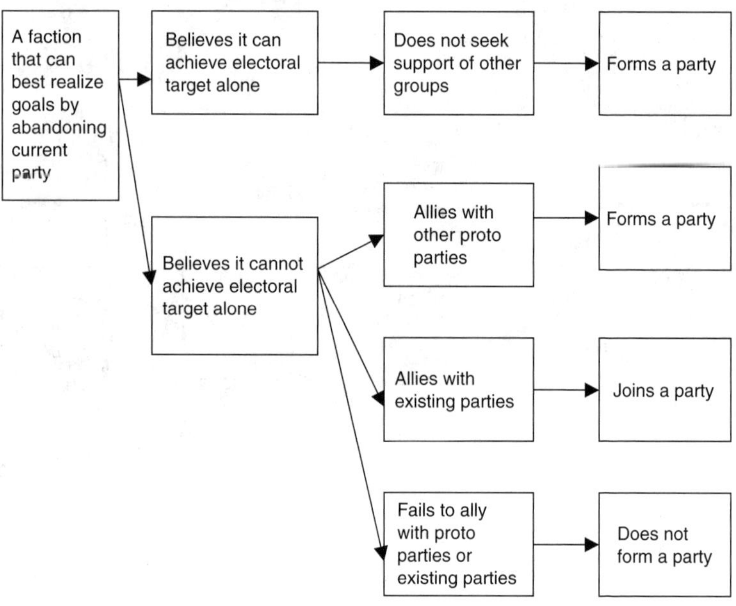

Figure 2.6 Process of party formation and electoral competition, phase 1: Splinters.

Alternatively, the party can survive despite splinters breaking off. In this case, the remaining members, now diminished in number, retain the original label, and the party behaves in the way described in the section on choosing an electoral strategy at succeeding elections. In both cases, the splinters follow different developmental paths.

The process that leads to the possible formation of a new party as a result of a split from an established one is similar to the process of new party formation. In fact, both are usually conceptualized and studied as part of the same process (Hug 2001, 13). Individuals depart from established parties regularly. The cases that are of interest here, however, are the ones that involve a *group or groups* of party members, and not just individuals. The existence of such groups in parties is commonly conceived as "factionalism." When a party is "factionalized," it becomes an arena for coalitional politics and leadership struggles, and sometimes this situation leads to the desertion of the losers of factional disputes to pursue alternative strategies. Such disputes are most commonly defined as ideological disagreements, conflicts over party strategy, or personality conflicts.

If a faction decides that abandoning the current party is the best road to achieving office, it returns to the status of a proto party and follows the usual developmental path of any proto party. There is one difference, however. The members of a proto party that takes shape as the result of a split have to decide that they can best realize goals not only by cooperating with one another (since they already are within the larger group), but by abandoning their current party and limiting their cooperation to the members of the faction only. This process is presented in figure 2.6.

Once a new party is formed from a splinter, it follows the process of development a new party goes through, and repeats stages 2 and 3 as presented and discussed in the further sections.

Evaluating the Likelihood of Success

The preceding sections presented the possible developmental paths of any group of people with ambitions to office. The sections discussed the group considering party formation (Phase 1), proceeding to contest elections for the first time (Phase 2), and contesting elections subsequently (Phase 3). While the electoral strategy options have been presented and some propositions about parties' choice of strategies have been made, there has been no discussion of the process that leads to this choice, a topic the discussion will turn to presently.

It has been suggested that a party's choice of an electoral strategy is based on an evaluation of how likely it is for the party to achieve its electoral target. At the point when a specific electoral strategy needs to be chosen, the party (or proto party) is expected to estimate its current support and to assess whether the support is sufficient to enable it to achieve its electoral target.[16] The party will also be concerned with the likelihood of its current level of electoral support remaining stable (or increasing) until election day. This process is represented in figure 2.7.

The choice of electoral strategies is expected to reflect not only the ambitions and target of the politicians and parties, but also the structure of electoral competition. As Schlesinger has argued, this structure, defined by its competitiveness and rules, "helps inspire and temper political ambitions" (Schlesinger 1994, 99). Here, several factors are proposed to define the electoral competition structure and thus influence the likelihood that a party will achieve its electoral target successfully. These are the nature of the electoral system, the presence of ethnically based support, the availability of public financing for parties, ideological crowdedness, and the extent of the organizational development of the parties in the party system. These factors will be discussed in turn.

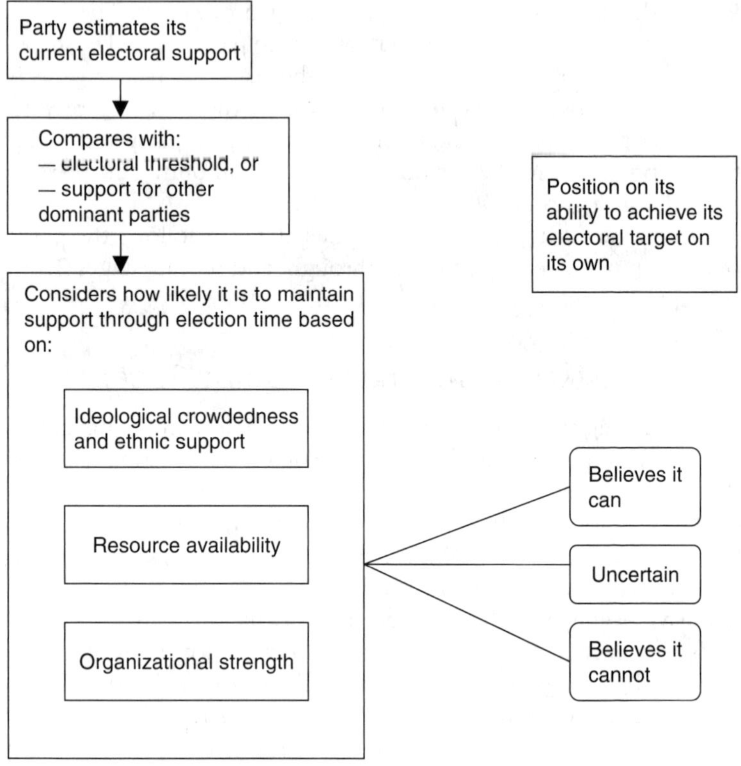

Figure 2.7　Evaluation of the likelihood of achieving electoral target.

Estimating Current Electoral Support

The choice of an electoral strategy is made well before an election. As parties cannot know how much support they will receive at election time, they need to update any information they have acquired. As noted earlier, we assume that established parties have a relatively precise idea of how much electoral support they have at any given time, on the basis of past performance. Past electoral experience is therefore of great importance. Success at achieving the electoral target at previous elections may be expected to encourage the choice of the same strategy, while failure would most certainly lead to a change in the strategy. Of course, to assume that developments between elections do not influence the choice of electoral strategies is illogical. Party popularity can suffer for a multitude of reasons, and the party itself might undergo changes during the interelection period. If there are clear indications that the previous strategy would not be conducive to success at the current election, *and* a strategy that promises to achieve the electoral target successfully exists, this new strategy will be chosen. Opinion polls will provide key information in this case, and parties will have to judge the desirability of strategies on the basis of their potential electoral support at the time the decision needs to be taken.

However, proto parties will be disadvantaged in this respect owing to their having no prior history. Their leaders must use other means to infer the party's prospective level of support. The decision to convert a proto party into a full-fledged party will likely involve the use of indications of electoral volatility as a proxy for potential electoral support. This is particularly important when a proto party's likely supporters must transfer their votes from an established party to a new one. An *expectation* of high electoral volatility will thus lead to an expectation of higher electoral support. The presence of "new issues" in society or the persistence of old issues that are not being resolved by the established parties are often seen as conducive to high electoral volatility. In particular, disruptions of political and economic life, such as high unemployment, inflation, corruption, environmental problems, and foreign policy crises, are among the factors likely to make the electorate more volatile and thus more likely to support new parties (Muller-Rommel 1989; Hug 2001; Sjoblom 1983; Wellhofer 1998; Jackman and Volpert 1996).

Assessing the Adequacy of Support: Electoral Thresholds

Once a party has an idea of how much electoral support it has, it needs to assess whether this support will allow it to achieve its electoral target. The party thus needs to take into consideration the actual electoral threshold it needs to surpass.[17] The higher the threshold, the higher the level of electoral support a party needs in order to get into parliament. As thresholds are highest in single-member-district plurality (SMD) electoral systems, and lowest in proportional representation (PR) systems, the rules of these electoral systems impose an important constraint on a party's behavior. That this is so is probably the best-established proposition in the study of democratic institutions and one of the most developed theoretical arguments in political science.

SMD plurality systems have a high threshold, which makes it difficult for each party to achieve its electoral targets on its own. This creates such a strong disincentive to form and run alone that the SMD electoral system is seen as "favoring" a two-party system

(Duverger 1969, 217). Reduction in the party system is expected from both a mechanical and a psychological effect. The former works in the following way: as only one candidate (party) can win in each district, two of three parties are encouraged to reach agreements whereby one party's candidate is withdrawn in order that the other can present a stronger challenge to the third front-running candidate (Duverger 1969, 225). Over time, this cooperation should lead to the fusion of the two parties. When fusion does not occur, elimination through the electoral process will work to limit the number of parties in the system. As parties that come third have no chance of winning, they suffer from underrepresentation, which in turn affects its participation in government, funding, and other benefits associated with winning in elections.

In addition, when confronted with three (or more) parties in an SMD plurality system, voters may realize that their votes will be "wasted" on the third party and, accordingly, may abandon this party and transfer their votes to the "lesser of two evils" (Duverger 1969, 226). Because of this psychological effect, in the longer run the third parties may become discouraged from running its own candidates and be encouraged either to join one of the two dominant parties or disband.

In contrast, PR systems have much lower thresholds and allow for more parties to make it on their own. PR systems were thus seen as providing little or no reward for fusing (merging) and no punishment for splitting (Duverger 1969, 248–254). Neither the psychological nor the mechanical effects are expected to play any significant role here, as proportionality between seats and votes at the national level is generally preserved. Although the specifics of the PR system result in different levels of proportionality, and "full proportional representation exists nowhere," PR systems tend to have a "multiplicative effect" on the number of parties (Duverger 1969, 253).

An enormous amount of work has been done to test, qualify, and revise Duverger's formulae (Rae 1971; Riker 1986; Sartori 1986; Cox 1997; Lijphart 1990, 1994). However, the basic underlying logic of main interest remains more or less intact. Parties do seem to react to the constraints of the electoral system in their decision-making process—"Elites rationally calculate the effects of the institutional context in making decisions" (Willey 1998, 651–678; also Jackman and Volpert 1996; Rohrschneider 1993). The picture, however, is not as clear-cut as Duverger described it: strategic voting does happen in PR systems, and third parties do persist in SMD plurality systems (Cox 1997). Even in PR systems, parties are thus not completely free to split and have to take into account the level of the electoral threshold. In addition, variations of the PR type of electoral systems can impact the behavior of parties (Lijphart and Gibberd 1977; Powell and Vanberg 2000, 380). Different levels of thresholds, applying higher thresholds for electoral alliances, or requiring parties to field a specific number of candidates in order to qualify for seat distributions are just a few examples of the way in which electoral rules might substantially influence the behavior of parties.

In the current understanding of party decision making, when the electoral threshold is lower, proto parties and established parties will be more likely to be able to gather enough voter support to cross it. Thus, they will be more likely to decide to form parties and run alone at election time.

The electoral threshold does not impose a strong constraint on parties that set their electoral targets as achieving a near plurality of seats. By definition, these parties are capable of achieving levels of electoral support that exceed the level required for entry into parliament. For them, the yardstick for comparison will be obtaining a near plurality of seats.

Evaluating the Stability of Support: Ideological Crowdedness, Ethnic Support, Resource Availability, and Organizational Strength

After support is determined and its adequacy is assessed, parties need to evaluate the probable trend of support level (whether support will increase, decrease, or remain the same) until election time. As already mentioned, parties determine this trend in light of the competition they are facing within the party system, the availability of resources, and their ability to carry out electoral campaigns.

Ideological Crowdedness

To evaluate the probable trend of support, parties need to account for the presence of competitors in the system. To be able to attract voters, a proto party needs to be seen as being distinct from the currently available alternatives, but yet not so different as to fail to attract potential voters. Focusing more on individual parties, Rochon (1985) and others have stressed the importance of a prospective party's ideology in relation to the existing ideological "space" for its decision to enter the political competition (Lacardie 2000; Muller-Rommel 1989; Andrews and Money 2002). According to their studies, parties that are "too extreme" tend to be unable to attract enough votes to "make it," but this is also true of parties that present an ideological position that is too close to the positions of already established parties. As the number of votes is limited, the more competitors there are within one ideological family, the more difficult it becomes for a new party to enter it successfully. Spatial models of elections have also considered the implications of ideological positioning of existing parties for the chances of entry of new ones (Palfrey 1984, Shepsle and Cohen 1990).

Parties in the post-communist world are no exception to this trend. Although there is a large body of literature that suggests that ideology does not play an important role in the behavior of individual politicians, this claim cannot be sustained in the case of parties (Shabad and Slomczynski 2004; Zielinski et al. 2003; Mair 1997; Grofman et al. 2000; Kreuzer and Pettai 2002).[18] Parties must position themselves electorally in an ideological space, and they commonly base their appeal to voters on ideological positions. Thus, the presence of ideologically close competitors is expected to make it more probable that the support of any party will be contested and possibly eroded.[19]

Ethnic Parties and Ideological Crowdedness

Electoral support for ethnic parties is often considered to be more stable than that of nonethnic parties. Ethnic parties are parties that draw their electoral support from an exclusive electorate (the ethnic group) (Horowitz 2000, 291). According to Birnir's study of ethnicity and parties in new democracies, the support of ethnic parties in such democracies is particularly stable (Birnir 2001, 219–221). This is so because ethnic identity is among the very few group identities that could not be eliminated by authoritarian regimes, and in some cases, was even mobilized by them. As a result, when the multiparty system becomes an option, voters more readily associate themselves with ethnic divisions than with any ideological divisions. Ethnicity remains a very powerful and in many ways a more salient category even after the development of other identities. Ambitious politicians are tempted to exploit this stable allegiance and form parties based on ethnicity (28–61).[20] An ethnic party thus often enjoys a stable level of support no matter what the other social and political circumstances are.

Ethnic parties tend to have platforms and programs that reflect the demands of the ethnic minority. These are usually seen as opposed to the will of the dominant majority in the political system. As successful opposition to the majority requires unity of the relatively smaller group, ethnic parties tend to stress the need for unity.[21] This unity is usually achieved through socialization of the minority members and tends to translate into an absence of political opponents within the group (Birnir 2001; Alionescu 2003). Original mobilization of support tends to be easier and more lasting, and voters' allegiances tend to be stronger.[22]

Thus, the support of an established ethnic party is less susceptible to challenges from both nonethnic and new ethnic parties. As a consequence, the presence of high levels of ethnic heterogeneity in a given political system is often credited with the maintenance of a higher number of parties in systems with otherwise similar characteristics. The link between ethnic heterogeneity and the number of parties has been established in various systems and in various electoral settings (Cox 1997, 220–221; Ordeshook and Shvetsova 1994; Norris 2004, 209–230).

Our current understanding suggests that established ethnic parties should be more likely to maintain their support through elections, but ethnic proto parties should be less likely to maintain their support in cases when there already is an established party, because the "ethnic space" is already crowded.

Resource Availability
For prospective electoral support to be transformed into actual votes, the party needs to carry out electoral campaigns and maintain an active presence in society. Both of these require financial resources. Thus, the availability of resources becomes of consequence for the ability of a party to maintain or increase its support by election time.[23]

In most of the post-communist world, parties have relied heavily on direct state funding in running their campaigns and operations.[24] Public funding can provide financial resources for one or more of the following: day-to-day operations of parties, election campaigns, and salaries and other support for parliamentary groups and their membership (Lewis 1998, 141). Most commonly, however, party financing refers to subsidies disbursed directly to parties on a regular, usually annual, basis and those disbursed to fund electoral campaigns.

There are both theoretical arguments and empirical evidence to suggest that the type and very existence of public funding influence the development and behavior of political parties in the post-communist world (Lewis 1998, 141; Roper 2003; van Biezen 2004). Public funding has been a major source of income for a large number of parties in these systems and thus a factor that has allowed parties to compete in elections and maintain operations between elections.

Within the present framework, availability of funding directly influences the probability that a party's electoral support will remain stable during the campaign. Direct public funding varies in terms of the basis on which it is disbursed and the amount of money given to parties. A large variation in both the basis and amount of funding is observed in Western as well as Eastern Europe (Duschinksy 2002, 80; Ikstens et al. 2002, 33–34).

The more "restrictive" type of public financing limits state subsidies to parties that have parliamentary groups or those that have some parliamentary presence.[25] This type of financing decreases the likelihood that electoral support of proto parties and parties that are outside parliament will remain stable until election time, as it will not provide them with resources to organize campaigns and compete in elections. To compensate, they would have to rely on other funding sources, which tend to be scarce in the post-communist world.[26]

Less restrictive are public financing regulations that are based on the party's performance at the previous election but are not limited to the parties currently holding seats in the legislature.[27] Thus, in a system with a 4 percent threshold, a extraparliamentary party with 3.8 percent of the vote may expect to get only marginally less funding than another such party that won seats with 4.2 percent of the vote.

While this less-restrictive system of public funding still makes it more difficult for new parties to maintain their electoral support, it is more supportive of parties that are established but have not yet made it into parliament. Because they have resources to carry out campaigns they should be more likely to be able to maintain or increase their support. A similar argument has been put forth by Koole regarding the development of parties in Germany and Italy (Koole 1996).

Finally, the least-restrictive form of public funding uses the number of candidates put forward in the current election as a basis of funding the electoral campaigns of parties.[28] These two types of funding legislation are most inclusive in that access to public funds benefits all electoral contenders rather than being limited only to established parties.

In the current understanding of party behavior, the availability of funding relates directly to the likelihood of any party maintaining its electoral support. If finances for campaigns are available, parties will see their chances of winning as higher. Proto parties will thus be more likely to transform into parties, and established parties will be more likely to run alone.[29]

Party Organization

In addition to money, running an electoral campaign necessitates an organization. Parties can use their branches and members to advertise, create supporters, and get them to turn out and vote.[30] Having members, for example, ensures that the party has a certain number of loyal voters, who are not only going to turn out and vote, but will also provide free advertisement (Scarrow 1994, 47). Members and local offices serve as a means of communication and even if not the only such means, they still play a substantial role in election campaigns (Scarrow 1996, 86–112; Kreuzer and Pattai 2002).

Within the current framework, the stronger and more complex[31] the organizational structure of a party, the greater the likelihood that it will maintain or increase its electoral support through election time. At the same time, however, the party needs to compete with the other parties in the system and prevent them from eroding its own support. Thus, if competitors have strong organizations, parties need to be able to match these with their own organizational development.

As proto parties tend not to have strong organizations, the stronger the organizational level of the rest of the parties in the system, the more likely it is for the support for proto parties to erode by election time, even if the proto party is popular initially. A similar argument has been made by critics of the popular studies of party and party system institutionalization (Randall and Svasand 2002).[32]

Whether organizational factors play any role in the process of party development in the post-communist world has been subject to much debate. Numerous studies have examined the level of organizational development of individual parties in the post-communist world (Krupavicius 1998; Golosov 1998; Bacon 1998; Bielasiak 1997, 2001; Lewis 1996; Clark 1995; Kopecky 1995; Miller et al., 2000; McFaul 2001; Szczerbiak 2001; Toole 2003; van Biezen 2003). This research indicates that, overall, post-communist parties lack strong organizational structures and have weak electoral and partisan linkages with society, but are for the most part professional, personalized, and closely linked with the state (Lewis 1996, 1–13; van Biezen 2003; Szczerbiak 2001; Toole 2003).

This general pattern is relatively uniform across parties in post-communist systems: these parties have lower memberships and less-extensive organizations, and give less importance to building organization than do parties in the Western and Southern European systems. However, variations within and across party systems do exist and seem to matter. First, at least one party in each system—the party that succeeded the old communist party—has membership and an organization that is superior to most Western European parties. Second, most of the research on party organization has been carried out in Central Europe, but its conclusions have been generalized to the whole region. Because of both arguments, we cannot ignore the importance of organization as a factor that influences the behavior of parties in any post-communist system until we have a better understanding what the level of organization development of parties there is.

Evaluating the Likelihood of Success: Summary

This section has presented an understating of how parties and proto parties will estimate the likelihood that they can achieve their electoral target by contesting elections alone. After estimating their current electoral support and evaluating it in light of the electoral threshold and the stability of support, each party will conclude that it can either achieve its electoral target alone, or that it cannot, or the party will be uncertain in this regard. Low electoral support, high electoral thresholds, crowded ideological space, inadequate resources, and the absence of a strong organization make a party unlikely to achieve its electoral target on its own. In contrast, high and stable support, unique ideological appeal, abundant resources, and a strong organization will make a party more likely to achieve its electoral target on its own. These factors will combine in a different way in the case of every party.

PARTY EVOLUTION: RANDOM EVENTS AND EXTERNAL SHOCKS

To gain a theoretical understanding of the process of formation and evolution of political parties in the post-communist democracies in Central and Eastern Europe, we have posited as determinants the goals of politicians, the electoral targets that they set for themselves, and the constraints of the structure of electoral competition. As a result of the processes presented in figures 2.1–2.7 and discussed in the earlier sections, parties choose electoral strategies that best promise to deliver the benefits that politicians are after. However, sometimes events of political significance occur unexpectedly in the decision environment of politicians, upsetting expectations relative to the development of parties through time. As a consequence, parties might choose electoral strategies that do not follow the logic presented in this model because they are driven by different forces.

The effect of stochastic events on political outcomes has been studied in the context of cabinet coalition dissolution. The basic argument in this tradition maintains that governmental coalitions are often destabilized by the appearance of certain random exogenous shocks

such as political scandals, international crises, or economic down-
turns. This aspect of cabinet durability has been explored in detail in
works by Browne, Freindreis and Gelebier (1984, 1986), Warwick
(1992, 1994), Strom (1985), King et al. (1990), and Diermeier and
Stevenson (2000).

Analogously, disruptive events may on occasion also impact party
development in the post-communist systems. For example, it has been
common in these party systems for the leadership of a certain alliance
or party to expel one or more of its members. As a result, individuals
or factions may find themselves searching for new homes in other
existing parties or be encouraged to form a new one. Examples of this
abound in the recent history of Eastern European party development.
Although it might be the case that the expulsion is correlated with
other factors accounted for by my model, it is an important part of
the decision-making process and needs to be considered.

In addition, events outside the national political system often
have an impact on domestic politics as, for example, the impact of
international events on the opening up of the authoritarian systems
during the late 1980s, or, later, the influence of the European Union
(EU) integration process on the development of various policies and
institutions in the post-communist systems. In some cases, however,
the influence is less visible, and can only be discerned by a careful
examination of particular cases.

An example of the influence of international events is the way in
which the EU integration process has weighed on the behavior of
individual parties in the post-communist candidate states. A focus on
party-specific consequences for particular cases is seldom associated
with the burgeoning, if relatively recent, literature examining EU
impact on candidate states (see, among others, Goetz 2000, 2001;
Grabbe 2000, 2001; Schimmelfennig 2001; Kopecky and Mudde
2000, 2002; Vermeersch 2002, 2003). And when this literature
does focus on the party consequences, it tends to concern itself
with the consequences of EU-level processes as they relate back to EU
issues: the rise of Euroskeptic parties, for example. However, detailed
examination of party evolution reveals the direct role of several
European-level actors even in areas of party behavior that have little to
do with the EU directly. For example, pan-European political parties
(Europarties[33]) and other international organizations of various ideologies (the Socialist International and the Liberal International) have
influenced the status of Eastern European political parties in their
domestic party systems in several ways. They have given membership
status to some parties but refused it to others; provided financial and

personnel assistance to certain parties; and in some cases, intervened to encourage certain electoral behavior on behalf of their kin parties.

The Europarties' interest in the East dates back to the mid-1990s. It is at least partially explained by the future electoral benefits that the European parties were hoping to get after accession (Deldosato 2002, 274; Dakowska 2002, 284). After the Treaty of Nice redistributed the seats in the European Parliament, 198 seats (out of a maximum of 732) are to be filled by the electorates in Bulgaria, Cyprus, the Czech Republic, Estonia, Hungary, Latvia, Lithuania, Malta, Poland, Romania, Slovakia, and Slovenia. Engagement in the East was thus well worth it, especially since the volatility of politics in the post-communist countries allowed for things to change in favor of one or the other party when the time for European parliamentary elections came.

In addition to seats, engagement with parties in the East allowed Europarties to influence policy making in these countries, which they could hope would have consequences for the policy making in the EU after integration (Deldosato 2002, 274). Finally, engagement in the East helped heal the legitimacy crisis that some of the Europarties were suffering at the time (Dakowska 2002, 285). Media attention and the generally higher attention the Europarties received in the East helped them gain more visibility and claim a more important position in EU politics. Thus, probably because Europarties have only a limited and indirect impact on national party systems in member countries (Poguntke et al., forthcoming), their involvement in the East has been more pronounced.

Resources and legitimacy are also the main reasons behind the willingness of political parties in candidate countries to accept the interest of the Europarties and abide by their rules. Membership in the European federations bestows legitimacy on member states even when the parties in the party system are new and in need of legitimacy—Poguntke et al. give the examples of Forza Italia and the Democratic Party of the Left in Italy, which sought legitimacy by associating with the European People's Party (EPP) and the Party of the European Socialists (PES), respectively (Poguntke et al., 5).

Similarly, parties in the newly established and volatile system in the post-communist world have sought legitimacy in the Europarties (Dakowksa 2002, 285; Deldosato 2002, 275; Dorget 2000). Given that EU integration was a primary and undisputed national priority in most of the post-communist states in Central and Eastern Europe, an association with the Europarties made them appear modern and distant from the communist past. Especially as the 1990s progressed, this association seems to have been of crucial importance for any political party that sought national prominence.

An understanding of the electoral behavior of parties in the post-communist world thus cannot be complete without allowing for the external shocks that pan-European parties sometimes provide to the system. In certain situations, the decision of a party to run alone, seek to ally, merge, or hibernate might be the result of the direct influence of an outside actor. Thus, a model based on traditional explanations of party behavior might either fail to explain or blur the choice of political parties. What would, statistically speaking, be considered an error term, could be explained by the intervention of Europarties.

Theoretical Framework: Summary

The present framework presents an understanding of party formation and evolution closely intertwined with its electoral performance. It is argued that office-seeking parties will preempt an anticipated failure to achieve their electoral targets by allying, merging, and disbanding, and will react to electoral success by persisting in a relatively unchanged form.

On the basis of their goals, politicians will define certain immediate targets for themselves, which will have an electoral dimension. Once targets are determined, politicians will estimate the likelihood of achieving these targets by forming a party. If party formation follows, the new party will approach elections with similar considerations in mind: it will reevaluate its target and the likelihood of achieving it, and when elections approach, it will decide to either run alone, seek alliances, or not contest elections. The process will repeat itself at each succeeding election with the politicians' goals and the party's electoral targets updated to reflect the electoral performance of the party at the previous election and its current standing in the political system.

As a result of this process, the party system is expected to achieve a certain level of stability and continuity, with successful parties persisting in the system and unsuccessful parties being discouraged from further participation. This process, however, is based on the assumption that politicians are rational, that they want to win office(s), and that they understand the institutional constraints imposed on them. These assumptions are fundamental and are usually unchallenged in political science literature. The rest of this work will therefore attempt to analyze the process of party development in the post-communist world within this framework and test its usefulness to understanding party politics in this part of the world.

HYPOTHESES AND THEIR EMPIRICAL IMPLICATIONS

On the basis of the discussion so far, I suggest the following hypotheses regarding the behavior of parties in post-communist systems. The empirical implications of the hypotheses are discussed after each proposed hypothesis.

Political Parties as Means to Winning Office

As parties exist to make it possible for politicians to win office, their existence will be closely intertwined with their electoral performance. Parties are expected to form when politicians believe that new parties will allow them to achieve their electoral target; the parties are expected to continue to exist as long as they promise to achieve the electoral target. However, when the target proves to be unachievable, parties are expected to have no reason to maintain their existence, and should merge or disband.

> H1: Over time, parties that repeatedly fail to win office should disappear as political entities because of a dissolution or a merger.

At the party level, we should observe that parties react to expected and real electoral success and failure: success should lead to a preservation of the party's electoral strategy and thus to the preservation of the party as a political entity; failure should encourage parties to change their electoral strategies in a direction that should bring electoral benefits (from running alone to allying, merging, or dissolving). At party level, over time, we should observe a decrease in the number of parties in the system as unsuccessful parties disappear.

However, a party will not be willing to forfeit its autonomy by merging before trying out an alternative electoral strategy first. This is so because the people behind a new party or one formed through a splithave decided at a relatively recent point that forming a party does promise to bring office rewards. It is thus unlikely that the party will right away decide to give up its autonomy and merge.

> H2: Newly formed parties and parties that have run alone in previous elections will not consider merging to be a possible electoral strategy at the current election.

At the party level we should observe that parties only consider merging when they have no other options to expand their electoral support. If allying allows for the achievement of electoral targets, mergers will not be necessary.

Expected Electoral Volatility

As proto parties rarely have reliable information about their electoral support, they will use an expectation of electoral volatility as a proxy for an estimation of their support. Thus, we can expect phenomena leading to an expectation of high electoral volatility to be conducive to the formation of new parties and their entry into the electoral competition alone.

> H3: Disruption of the polity's political, economic, and social life will lead to an expectation of high electoral volatility, which will encourage the formation of new parties and their entry into electoral competition under their own label.

At the system level, we should observe that elections following a major disruption of political life are contested by a larger number of parties than elections that are held in "normal" circumstances.

Electoral Thresholds

Before any (proto) party can take a decision to form, run alone, ally, or merge, it needs to evaluate the adequacy of its electoral support by comparing the support to its minimum electoral target. The minimum electoral target for most parties is assumed to be the percentage of votes needed at the national level to gain representation in parliament.

> H4: Higher thresholds will increase the level of electoral support needed by a party to achieve its electoral target.

At the system level, we should observe that electoral systems with higher thresholds discourage the formation of new parties and encourage a faster reduction in the number of parties over time by providing higher incentives for allying and merging.

Ideological Crowdedness and Ethnic Support

Whether a party's popularity will be transformed into votes at the election is partly determined by the number of competitors in the system. However, as parties attract votes based on their ideology, the relevant competitors are those within each party's ideological family. We can thus expect that the more competitors for the same vote there are, the less likely it is for a party to achieve its electoral target on its own.

> H5: Ideological crowdedness will decrease the stability of electoral support for any party.

The presence of ideologically close competitors will discourage proto parties from transforming into parties and encourage established parties to seek alliances or mergers. Within ideological families, we should observe the gradual decrease in the number of new entries, and thus of competitors, over all.

However, ethnic support is arguably less susceptible to challenges than nonethnic political support, making it easier for ethnic parties to maintain themselves in the party system.

> H6: Established ethnic parties will enjoy more stable support and experience fewer challenges from new competitors than nonethnic parties.

Within systems, we should observe that ethnic parties enjoy consistent levels of support over time. At the system level, we should observe that higher levels of ethnic heterogeneity lead to a higher number of parties in the system.

Public Financing

Parties also need finances to carry out their electoral campaigns and everyday activities. The availability of resources works at two levels to influence the development of political parties.

> H7: Availability of regular public financing for extraparliamentary parties will encourage parties and proto parties to seek to win office in the long term; and
> H8: The availability of resources for electoral campaigns will make it more likely for the electoral support of parties to remain stable or increase until election time.

Thus, at the party system level, less restrictive regulations of party financing are expected to lead to a larger number of parties in the system compared with systems that provide more restrictive funding. This will be the case because proto parties will be encouraged to transform into parties (H7), while established parties will be encouraged to run alone in elections (H8).

Party Organization

Besides funding, parties also need members and facilities to establish their social presence, carry out campaigns, and solidify their support.

> H9: The organizational strength of a party will contribute to the stability of its electoral support.

The stronger the organizations of existing parties, the less likely it should be for proto parties to see themselves as able to achieve their electoral target on their own, thus discouraging them from transforming into legal parties and running alone at their first elections. Thus, over time, assuming that parties do strengthen their organizations, we should observe fewer new parties entering the party system.

Testing the Model at Party Level: Methodology and Data

Methodology: Research Design

To study these hypotheses at party level the book employs a qualitative examination of the behavior of a small number of political parties in two party systems—those of Bulgaria and Hungary. It describes the process that has led to the formation of these parties and their choice of electoral strategies at several elections cycles (chapter 3) and examines the role various factors have played in this process (chapter 4).

The advantage of a "small N" qualitative study is that it provides the opportunity to discuss the different cases and to investigate the proposed relationships in detail, and to incorporate contextual variables. The difficulties in using such an analysis arise from the limited number of cases and the large number of independent variables that could possibly affect the dependent variable. This effectively prevents observation of the relationship in enough settings so as to allow the establishment of a general causal relationship (Smelser 1975, 77). Thus, the analysis presented in chapters 3 and 4 is limited mainly to the validation of the theoretical propositions and to conducting a very preliminary test of the proposed theory.

There are several strategies for dealing with this problem. Lijphart, for example, has suggested increasing the number of cases and limiting the number of variables examined (Lijphart 1975, 163). However, Lijphart's concrete suggestions are likely to be incompatible; as we increase the number of cases it becomes more difficult to keep them strictly comparable. Alternatively, Lijphart focuses on the selection of comparable cases ("the most similar system design") as a solution to the "small N, many variables" problem. To avoid the problem of insufficient variation in the independent variables, Lijphart advocates the selection of cases that exhibit most variation on the independent variables but differ least on the control variables (Lijphart 1975, 163). A problem remains, however, in finding comparable cases that are similar enough in the dependent variable and yet have enough variation on the operative variables.

This study employs a similar research strategy to support its conclusions. Six parties from the Bulgarian and Hungarian party systems were selected for analysis. They will be presented and analyzed in pairs that reflect the typology of parties presented earlier in this chapter. Two of them have dominated and tried to dominate governments, two have participated in the executive, and two have not been in a position to participate in the executive at the national level. Each pair of parties have a similar experience in the party and political system but provide enough variance on both the dependent and the independent variables. The six parties represent different ideologies, have different organizational trends, and exist in different electoral systems and party financing regulatory frameworks. This variation should allow us to isolate specifics of the theoretical relationships proposed.

The three Bulgarian parties are the BEL, the BSP, and the DPS. Munkaspart, FIDESZ, and the SZDSZ are the three Hungarian parties chosen for analysis.

The six parties have had differing success in elections. The BSP, the DPS, FIDESZ, and the SZDSZ have gained representation in parliament on a regular basis since 1990. BEL has been represented in parliament for only one term since 1990, and has failed to pass the electoral threshold on two occasions. Munkaspart has not been able to pass the electoral thresholds although it has contested elections repeatedly.

The six parties also have quite diverse experiences of participating in government in Bulgaria and Hungary. BEL and Munkaspart have never held executive office, the BSP and FIDESZ have led coalition governments, and the DPS and the SZDSZ have played important roles as coalition partners in several governments during the 1990s and early 2000s.

The six parties represent all major ideological trends in the post-communist party systems: reformed Marxism (Munkaspart), socialism (BSP), social democracy (BEL), conservatism (FIDESZ), and liberalism (SZDSZ). The DPS is included as an example of an ethnic political party, although it can also be considered a liberal party in some ways.

The six parties examined in detail vary substantially on the dependent variable as well. The BSP is the only one that has existed from the pre-1989 period; BEL, formed in 1997, is the youngest party, and the other four parties formed during the initial demo-cratization process. In terms of electoral strategies too, the parties vary significantly—Munkaspart always runs alone in elections, the SZDSZ, the BSP, and the DPS have both run alone and sought electoral alliances, and BEL and FIDESZ have each run alone and sought alliances *and* mergers over the last five election cycles. This variance on both the dependent and independent variables allows me to examine in detail how parties have behaved in the post-communist systems, taking into account their own nature and their position in the system and the impact of other parties and the institutional con-text on their evolution.

A second way that scholars have proposed to deal with the degrees-of-freedom problem is to conduct replications at different analytical levels. For example, in the case of cross-sectional, national-level studies, shifting the analysis from the unit (state) to the intraunit (regions within the state) increases the sample size and preserves the comparability of cases (Smelser 1975, 79). Doing so should also alleviate the problem of overdetermination. This problem, particularly dangerous in the view of Przeworski and Teune, arises from the fact that even though the number of variables on which the cases differ is limited, there are still too many differences that could explain the variation in the dependent variable. This leads to overdetermination of the problem and inability to establish the true causal links (Przeworski and Teune 1982, 34). Selecting additional cases from the same system would increase the sample size without increasing the number of differences (Lijphart 1975, 172).

This solution, of course, presents a problem, because it increases the number of cases studied but decreases their independence of one another. The process of establishing a certain relationship relies on the assumption that the cases under investigation (and thus the processes that go on within them) are independent of one another.

However, when we increase the sample size by choosing additional cases from the same system, we increase the likelihood that development in one case will influence the processes in another. Thus, finding two cases in which a certain relationship holds true might actually be a result of a link between them.

Although problematic, this solution will be used here. The analysis of the impact of the independent variables on the decision of parties to form and choose certain electoral strategies (chapter 4) examines the pattern of behavior of individual parties in the two systems, drawing on the experience of the six parties that were selected while also incorporating insights about the behavior of other parties in these two systems.

Choosing Bulgaria and Hungary as the two systems for detailed analysis might come as a surprise to some. Although both countries belonged to the communist bloc, their paths to democracy have been quite divergent. The transition to democracy in Bulgaria was regime controlled while the one in Hungary was negotiated between regime and opposition; 17 years later Hungary is probably the most successful of the post-communist states in terms of democratic and market reforms, while Bulgaria is still struggling to achieve stability in both. In addition, the patterns of party-system dynamics in the two states have also been quite dissimilar; Hungary again displays much higher levels of stability and continuity than does Bulgaria.

However, for the purposes of this research, we are interested in the behavior of political parties in any post-communist systems. As touched upon in the introduction, what makes post-communist party development different is the fact that most parties are "new" and that most of them emerged and developed in the presence of a strong "successor" party in the system. In both Bulgaria and Hungary, this has been the case. The variations that the two countries provide in terms of system-level factors, such as electoral system and party financing arrangements, only allow for a better analysis of the behavior of similar entities under partly different constraints.

Data: Personal Interviews

The data used in chapters 3 and 4 come from three main sources: interviews with party leaders, archival sources of a primary nature, and other published works that deal with the questions under study. Interviews were conducted during fieldwork done in the winter and spring of 2002–2003. Representatives of a total of 16 parties were interviewed, ten in Bulgaria and six in Hungary. Respondents included party chairmen, deputy party chairmen, party strategy analysts, members of party executive councils, and party international secretaries. Interviews were conducted in Bulgarian, Hungarian, and English. The interviews conducted in Hungarian were assisted by an interpreter. Eight follow-up interviews were conducted with the six parties studied in most detail in an effort to verify the information received and to clarify details.

Most interviews were not recorded (unless the interviewees requested otherwise). Using the method advocated by Feno (1978), notes were taken during the interview, and, upon its completion, detailed notes were recorded. When interpreters were used, the detailed notes were validated by them as well. This method was chosen because it allows for more spontaneity and sincerity during the conversation (Feno 1978). In addition, it also prevents any confusion about the purpose of the interview and helps preserve the guarantee of confidentiality (Peabody et al. 1990).

Elite interviews can provide an invaluable wealth of details and insider information about actual events and occurrences. However, their use as a source of data has several potential problems. Primary among these problems is the objectivity of the respondent in reporting data (Dexter 1970, 125; Putnam, 1973, 18; Peabody et al. 1990, 454; Lieber 1975, 323–325). There is no doubt that respondents inject their own experience, ideas, and value judgments into their responses. In addition, some of them may have limited knowledge or selective memory of what has happened in the past, making their opinions about distanced events unreliable (Dexter 1970, 119–138).

There are several ways in which a researcher can attempt to verify and validate the information received. It can be compared for consistency with data reported by other respondents or with information available through primary and secondary sources. In addition, a good understanding of the position of the respondent in the party hierarchy and the respondent's political experience allows the researcher to estimate better the level of reliability and plausibility of the information (Dexter 1970, 15–127). In the present case, information obtained through interviews was validated by other sources (primary and secondary). In addition, every effort was made to ensure the interviewer's familiarity with the interviewees by collecting background information and conducting discussions with political experts.

Problems can also arise from the way an interview is conducted. Closed-ended questions and questions that suggest an answer often lead to biased answers (Peabody et al. 1990, 453). To prevent this problem, questions were kept as open-ended as possible; interviews started with easy, objective questions and moved on to more judgmental ones once familiarity with the interviewee was established. Questions for all interviews followed a general protocol, although the specifics were changed to accommodate each party's experience. In general terms, the questions were about the goals and electoral targets of the party, the reasons for its formation at a certain time, the factors that have made it choose a certain electoral strategy at each election (including the role electoral rules, organization, and ideology play in this decision), the general trends in party cooperation with other parties, and the personal political goals of the interviewees. A sample list of questions that were asked is provided in appendix A. When clarification was needed, more specific questions were asked in the course of each interview.

Data: Primary and Secondary Sources

The second type of data used was derived from primary and secondary sources discussing the actions, events, and other developments of interest related to the parties under consideration in this research. Primary sources include documents produced by political parties (programs, statutes, and conference and congress materials); newspaper and other archival articles; and published interviews with party leaders. Secondary sources include other research on party development published in books and political science journals by both native (Bulgarian and Hungarian) and nonnative authors.

TESTING THE MODEL AT PARTY SYSTEM LEVEL: METHODOLOGY AND DATA

Methodology: Research Design

Several of the hypotheses developed here can and should be tested at the party-system level, especially as some of them (H5, H7, and H8, particularly) are only observable at this level. To test these hypotheses directly, I use a statistical model that incorporates a larger number of party systems. To capture the theoretical propositions and their empirical implications, I conceptualize the *number of parties* contesting each election as a function of several factors: the level of electoral volatility, the level of ethnic heterogeneity in the country, the presence of public financing for extraparliamentary parties, and the level of electoral threshold needed for entry into parliament as specified by the electoral system. In addition, I add a factor that attempts to capture the temporal dimension of the model as well as indirectly reflect the implications of H9: the number of the election counted since the initial democratization point. In equation form, this conceptualization can be represented in the following way:

$$\text{Number of parties} = \alpha + \beta_1 \text{ electoral volatility} \\ + \beta_2 \text{ heterogeneity} + \beta_3 \text{ funding} + \beta_4 \text{ threshold} \\ + \beta_5 \text{ number of election} + e$$

The model is estimated using a pooled cross-sectional times series design and Ordinary Least Squares regression with panel-corrected standard errors. The use of statistical cross-sectional studies to confirm a causal mechanism is often criticized on the premise that it only establishes a correlation between outcomes and does not provide a detailed examination of the process that leads to this correlation.[34] However, in this case, the statistical analysis is only meant as a final test of the proposed relationships; discussion of the processes that go on within parties to lead to come up with the aggregate observation is provided in the party-level, qualitative analysis of the model.

Data: Twelve Post-Communist Systems

Data from democratic elections in the following countries is used for the estimation of the pooled model: Bulgaria, the Czech Republic, Estonia, Hungary, Latvia, Lithuania, Poland, Romania, Russia, the Slovak Republic, Slovenia, and the Ukraine. Countries were selected on the basis of the relative similarity in their experiences with democracy, although enough variation on the independent and dependent variables was provided to allow for the testing of the hypotheses proposed by the model.

Main sources of data include the *Political Transformation and the Electoral Process in Post-Communist Europe Project at the University of Essex*, the *IFES Central and Eastern European Electoral Law Compendium*, the *IDEA Handbook on Political Parties Financing*, *Lijphart Electoral Archive*, and Rose and Munro (2003). Precise specification of the model and operationalization of variables will be presented in chapter 5.

NOTES

1. While institutional and legal arrangements can and do change over time, and this analysis takes account of these changes, it is beyond the focus of this book to investigate how the political parties might try to

change the legal and institutional frameworks of the political systems for their own benefit.

2. In addition, politicians might be interested in running and winning office for reasons that do not involve participation in any policy-making structures: parties might be interested in winning a minimum amount of votes in order to get party financing, or to maintain their status according to party law requirements. However, these parties are of no interest to this study; presently we are concerned with parties that seek office for the benefits associated with it.

3. Getting into local and regional government offices is also a legitimate realization of political ambition. However, here we are concerned exclusively with politicians who want to realize their political ambition at the national level.

4. We assume that the electoral support for any given party is a set figure at any point in time, and that the party has a relatively precise idea of what it is. In other words, why a party wins/loses popular support is beyond the scope of this study.

5. Others might prefer to just enjoy the benefits of legislative office. Parties have avoided participation in the executive on various occasions and for various reasons. Strom, for example, has discussed various reasons why parties might avoid participating in *certain* governmental coalitions (Strom 1990; Strom and Liepart 1993). In the post-communist world, we have even seen a principled commitment to nonparticipation in the governing process. Some have been unwilling to participate in the government because of the unpopularity of reforms that had to be implemented and the electoral risks associated with being in government. Although this certainly changed with time, there is enough evidence to argue that some parties were only interested in holding legislative office. An example of such a party was the Radical Democratic Party (RDP) of Bulgaria. It was not until 1993, for example, that its leader, addressing a convention of the party, advocated a change of party goals from mere parliamentary presence to participation in government, and urged the RDP members to embrace such a goal. Michail Nedelchev, then RDP Chairman, argued in 1993: "We need new criteria [for party building]. Criteria of political professionalism. Which also calls for a re-orientation of our goals. We are proud of our tradition of parliamentary presence, but we can no longer stress only the parliamentary presence. The new professionalism which we are striving for is participation in all branches of government" (Nedelchev 2000, 44). In addition, and this is not limited to post-communist systems only, some parties are too radical, or too marginal, to participate in the government. Parliamentary representation thus is the only political goal they *can* achieve.

6. In addition, some parties seek to win office (legislative or executive) in the short *and* long run (Gunther 1989, 854). For the latter group,

surviving as an independent entity is part of the strategy to win office in the long run. Thus, in situations when achieving the support needed for surpassing the threshold is uncertain, parties with long-term office goals will be more likely to risk staying out of parliament *if* getting in would mean losing their independent identity. While making it into parliament increases the chances of winning office next time, parties can find other means to compensate for not being in parliament (winning office at the local level, getting resources through other means, etc.). Thus, although all parties try to surpass the electoral threshold, in some cases not doing so is not necessarily seen as a failure.

7. The evaluation of electoral realities that leads to this belief is probably the most important stage of this process. However, it is currently sidestepped, but will be discussed at length in section, "Evaluating the Likelihood of Success."

8. Whether they join as a "faction" (a group that is recognized as having positions that are distinct from those of the party) or as individuals is of consequence, but for purposes of conciseness cannot be accounted for in this study.

9. A party could form in this case, even without expecting to win any seats, if it wants instead to prepare for a future attempt to win seats.

10. To be a political party, in the most general terms, an organization or a team of people does not need to run in elections. However, political parties only become of consequence if they compete in elections, which is why most political science definitions of political parties use running in an election as the one key element of being a political party. Epstein, for example, considers any "group, however loosely organized, seeking to elect governmental office-holders under a given label" to be a political party (Epstein 1967, 9). Richard Rose similarly defines a party as "an organization concerned with the expression of popular preferences and contesting control of the chief policy-making offices of government" (Rose 1974, 3).

11. Defined as the percentage of the popular vote that a party receives or expects to receive at election.

12. The outcome of an electoral strategy that involves the cooperation of another party or parties (forming or joining alliances and merging) will depend on the success of this attempted cooperation. Thus, one party seeking an alliance will not necessarily lead to the party contesting elections in an alliance. However, for the purposes of this research, the important elements are the decision of the party *to seek alliances* and how the outcome of this electoral strategy influences the choice of electoral strategy at the next elections.

13. This definition of an "alliance" is narrower than some others. Duverger (1969) for example, sees "electoral alliances" as one of several things—"putting up joint candidates or joint lists at the first

or at the only ballot, reciprocal standing down on the second ballot, agreements for the distribution of remainders or friendly arrangement in certain proportional systems, and so on" (Duverger 1969, 331). In addition, Duverger argues, alliances might be either tacit or explicit.

14. Because of the complicated nature of electoral alliances (they are not "new" parties but they are different from two independent parties) they are very rarely studied (Hug 2001, 13–14).

15. Party splits have been common in Western European party development and even more so in the post-communist world (Mair 1990, 1997).

16. In most cases, the factors influencing proto parties and established parties in their evaluation of support and choice of electoral strategy are the same and impact both in a similar way. Because of this, and for purposes of conciseness, from this point on, the term "party(s)" will be used to denote both a proto party and an established party. Distinctions will be made only in the cases where the processes differ.

17. This is true for parties of the "legislative" and "executive" kind only. The constraint of electoral laws on the dominant parties will be discussed later.

18. The assumption that politicians in the post-communist world are policy neutral has been relatively common among students of Eastern European party development. This assumption has its origins in the observation that politicians tend to switch parties and parliamentary factions quite frequently (Shabad and Slomczynski 2004; Zielinski et al. 2003; Mair 1997; Grofman et al. 2000). However, although this might be a warranted assumption in the case of some individual politicians, it is untenable in the case of parties as such.

19. The presence of many parties that are close ideologically also obviously decreases the level of support that each of them enjoys.

20. Birnir's study builds on a large body of literature that deals with social cleavages, group identities, electoral shortcuts, and other related subjects. The most prominent examples of studies dealing with ethnicity as a determinant of electoral preferences are Lipset and Rokkan 1967; Crawford 1996; Powell 1982; Rhabushka and Shepsle 1972; and Horowitz 2000.

21. This is particularly so in cases where the ethnic group's size approaches the electoral threshold needed to gain representation.

22. Of course, exceptions do exist. For a more detailed examination of these issues in practice, see Barany 2001; Friedman 2002; Alionescu 2003; Reilly 2003; Shafir 2000; and Stroschein 2001.

23. Party funding here is assumed to be the means to achieve the party goals of legislative or executive office, and not an end in itself.

24. The regulation of party and campaign financing is a particularly important constraint on party behavior in the post-communist world, because parties in these systems rely more heavily on public funding than parties in the Western European systems. This is partly because other sources of financing are more limited, and also because public

financing has always been available in the post-communist world. Unlike other party systems, the establishment and initial development of the post-communist party systems happened at a time when public funding of parties had become the norm worldwide (Roper 2002; van Biezen 2003, 178–179). Research on party financing has centered mostly on the effects party financing has had on issues of corruption, accountability, and transparency, and for the most part has focused on the regulation of private financing (Roper 2002, 2003; Protsyk 2002; Nassmacher 2004; Pinto-Duschinsky 2002). Similarly, studies have investigated the effects high dependence on public financing has had on the development of organizational structures and the internal shifts of power within individual parties (van Biezen 2003, 177–200). Relatively little research has been done on the ways in which the regulation of public financing can influence the party system through the dynamics of interparty behavior.

25. Based on data from the *IDEA Handbook on Political Finance*, 10 of the 65 (about 15 percent) countries in the world where public financing of require that public money go only to parties currently represented in parliament (IDEA 2004).

26. Some scholars have concluded that the legislation specifying this kind of financing results from a conscious effort of existing parliamentary parties to discourage the formation of new parties and challenges from parties outside (Katz and Mair 1995). Although a discussion of the endogeneity of party financing legislation is important, it is beyond the scope of this work. Just as with other institutions, that is the electoral system, party financing legislation is assumed to be exogenous in this case.

27. About 22 percent of all systems where there is public funding of parties use performance at the previous elections as the guiding principle of monetary allocation (IDEA 2004).

28. About 19 percent of all party financing arrangements in the world use this as the basis for funding, while about 10 percent use an "equal funding" criterion as a basis for public funding (IDEA 2004).

29. The type of funding available also influences the likelihood that parties will be able to seek office in the long term (see section "Setting an Electoral Target"). In the context of the most restrictive system of funding, a party will need to make it into Parliament so that it can receive resources to maintain operations. In this way, the resources available limits the possibility for parties to seek office in the long-term while staying outside Parliament. In contrast, parties in the less restrictive regulatory circumstances can stay out of Parliament and still receive financial support. This would allow them to pursue office in the long term. The regulation of public financing thus works on two levels but in the same direction: its more restrictive type discourages parties from forming and running alone as they have little chance to make it into Parliament on their own.

30. Having members also obviously influences how much electoral support a party has to begin with, but as already stated, this relationship is beyond the scope of this study.
31. A "strong" organization is one defined by a large membership, extensive network of local branches, and low levels of professionalization (van Biezen 2003).
32. Studies of party and party system institutionalization tend to equate "strong" parties with party systems of "strong" parties (Mainwaring 1999; Stockton 2001). However, as Randall and Svasand have argued, these two developmental processes can work against each another. If there is one highly institutionalized, but *not dominant,* party in any multiparty system, it can prevent the "institutionalization" of other parties in the system. This would lead to the inability of other parties to establish themselves, leading to a system of unstable parties (Randall and Svasand 2002, 8). While the concept of institutionalization involves more than simple organizational complexity, this complexity is one of its more tangible components.
33. This term is used following Poguntke (Pogunkte et al., forthcoming).
34. For a strong critique of the statistical studies dealing with economic development and democracy, see Rueschemeyer, Stephens, and Stephens (1992) and O'Donnell (1988).

CHAPTER 3

FORMATION, PERSISTENCE, AND CHANGE: PARTIES IN BULGARIA AND HUNGARY

This chapter examines the evolution of several parties in Bulgaria and Hungary in an attempt to validate the propositions about party behavior made in chapter 2. It provides some initial insights into the hypotheses dealing with the impact of electoral support, ideology, organization, and external events on the decision of individual parties to form and choose certain electoral strategies. It discusses the experience of the six political parties in the Bulgarian and Hungarian party systems chosen for detailed analysis: BEL, BSP, DPS, Munkaspart, FIDESZ and the SZDSZ. These parties were selected with two considerations in mind: their individual experiences of being inside or outside parliament, their participation in the government, and their ideologies. However, in an attempt to situate this discussion in the larger picture of party development in the two political systems, the chapter begins with a very brief and general introduction to the development of party politics in Bulgaria and Hungary during 1990–2005.

BULGARIAN AND HUNGARIAN PARTY POLITICS: GENERAL TRENDS

Bulgarian Party Politics*, 1990–2005

The democratic transition in Bulgaria started in November 1989 through what Linz and Stepan would call an internal coup within the Bulgarian Communist Party (BKP) (Linz and Stepan 1996,

338–339). The political vacuum created by the collapse of the communist regime presented an opportunity for the development of new political parties. However, unlike the situation in other Eastern European countries, no strong opposition movements had been created during the late 1980s. Thus, the majority of the 42 new political parties that formed before the June 1990 elections had no preexisting structures or organizations and, compared with the major opposition challengers in other Eastern European countries, they lagged behind in popular support (Karasimeonov 2002, 25).

With the largest opposition party, the Union of Democratic Forces (SDS), gaining only about 36 percent of the popular vote, the first democratic elections in Bulgaria clearly indicated that the BKP (renamed the Bulgarian Socialist Party) remained the most influential party in the country (table 3.1). Bulgaria thus became one of the few Eastern European countries that kept the revamped Communist Party in power through democratic elections. This "successor" party was thus probably more influential in the initial stages of democratization in Bulgaria than were similar parties in most Central European countries.

During the 1990s the political process in Bulgaria was dominated by the BSP on the left, and the SDS on the right side of the political spectrum. Although relatively unreformed until 1995 in terms of its lack of support for market reform and European integration, the BSP had, by the late 1990s, come to advocate a social-democratic platform and to support a pro-EU and pro-North Atlantic Treaty Organization

Table 3.1   Bulgarian election results, 1990 elections (Grand National Assembly)

Party/Alliance[1]	PR vote %	PR seats	SMD seats	Total seats
BSP (Bulgarian Socialist Party)	47.15	97	114	211
SDS (Union of Democratic Forces)	36.21	75	69	144
DPS (Movement for Rights and Freedoms)	8.03	12	11	23
BZNS (Bulgarian Agrarian National Union)	6.02	16	0	16
OF (Fatherland Front)	0	0	2	2
OPT (Fatherland Party of Labor)	0.6	0	1	1
SDP (Social Democratic Party)	0.72	0	1	1

[1] The tables included in the chapter list results for parties that either had more than 1 percent of the vote or had representation in parliament. For complete election results for Bulgaria and Hungary, see appendices B and C. For a list of the Bulgarian and Hungarian cabinets, refer to appendix D.

(NATO) foreign policy (Derleth 2000, 162; Murer 1995, 213; 2002, 392; Kumanov 1999, 123).

In late 1989, 11 newly founded opposition parties formed the SDS as single political entity but kept their separate organizations. The SDS thus cannot be classified as either purely a merged entity or an electoral alliance in the terminology used presently. However, as the 11 parties ran under a common label, behaved as a single political entity, and finally did merge their structures and leadership, the SDS will be treated as a single political entity in this book. The SDS claimed to be a "center-right" political formation, but in reality it included parties as diverse as the Bulgarian Social Democratic Party and the Bulgarian Christian-Democratic Party. The SDS suffered numerous defections and organizational challenges and finally transformed itself into a centrist-right political party in 1997 (Kumanov 1999, 156; Waller and Karasimeonov 1996; Karasimenov 2002). During the entire period of its existence, however, the SDS has firmly supported European integration and NATO membership for Bulgaria, which by the mid-1990s was complemented by a clearly center-right domestic political platform.

In addition, a myriad of smaller political parties struggled for "survival between the poles" (Karasimenov and Waller 1996, 140). The most important of these were the Bulgarian Agrarian National Union (BZNS), a historic peasant party that split into numerous factions during the 1990s; the DPS, a party that represented the Turkish minority; the Bulgarian Business Block (BBB), a populist party of "businessmen" that attracted substantial popular support in the mid-1990s but has since disappeared; and the social democratic BEL. The 1991 elections (See table 3.2) prompted a surge of political party activity. Of the 38 parties that contested elections, however, only 3 passed the 4 percent threshold mandated by the Bulgarian electoral law for seat distribution in parliament, and a quarter of the popular vote was thus "wasted" on unsuccessful parties. By the 1997 elections, however, Bulgarian parties seem to have achieved a stable pattern of interactions (see tables 3.3 and 3.4). The BSP and the SDS retained their dominant positions electorally, but both parties had to form electoral alliances with smaller parties to do so.

A major blow to the stability of the party system was delivered in 2001 with the entry of a major new contender, the National Movement Simeon the Second (NDSV). The NDSV's entry ended the "bipolarity" of the party system (Karasimeonov 2002, 54). The NDSV, which was built around the personality of the Bulgarian ex-monarch Simeon Sax-Coburg-Gotha, created a platform focused

Table 3.2   Bulgarian election results, 1991 elections (36th National Assembly)

Party/Alliance	Vote %	Number of seats	Seats %
SDS (Union of Democratic Forces)	34.36	110	45.8
BSP (Pre-electoral Union of the BSP, BLP, OPT, PKhZhD, KhRP, NLP "St. Stambolov," SMS, FBSM, SDPD, and "ERA-3")	33.14	106	44.2
DPS (Movement for Rights and Freedoms)	7.55	24	10
BZNS(e) (Bulgarian Agrarian National Union–United)	3.86	0	0
BZNS-NP (Bulgarian Agrarian National Union– "Nikola Petkov")	3.44	0	0
SDS-TS (Union of Democratic Forces–Centre)	3.2	0	0
SDS-L (Union of Democratic Forces–Liberal)	2.81	0	0
KTsB (Federation "Tsardon Bulgaria")	1.82	0	0
BBB (Bulgarian Business Block)	1.32	0	0
BNRP (Bulgarian National Radical Party)	1.13	0	0

Table 3.3   Bulgarian election results, 1994 elections (37th National Assembly)

Party/Alliance	Vote %	Number of seats	Seats %
Coalition of the Bulgarian Socialist Party, the Bulgarian National Agrarian Union "Alexander Stamboliiski" and Ecoglasnost Political Club	43.5	125	52.08
SDS (Union of Democratic Forces)	24.23	69	28.75
BZNS, DP (People's Union (NS) of the Bulgarian Agrarian National Union and the Democratic Party)	6.51	18	7.5
DPS (Movement for Rights and Freedoms)	5.44	15	6.25
BBB (Bulgarian Business Block)	4.73	13	5.42
DAR (Democratic Alternative for the Republic' Political Union)	3.79	0	0
BKP (Bulgarian Communist Party)	1.51	0	0
SNI (New Choice' Union)	1.49	0	0
PS (Patriotic Union)	1.43	0	0
FTsB (Kingdom of Bulgaria Federation)	1.41	0	0

Table 3.4 Bulgarian election results, 1997 elections (38ᵗʰ National Assembly)

Party/Alliance	Vote %	Number of seats	Seats %
ODS (Alliance of Democratic Forces—SDS, DP, BZNS, BSDP)	49.15	137	57.55
Democratic Left (Bulgarian Socialist Party, Ecoglasnost Political Club, BZNS-AS)	22.44	58	25.03
ONS (Alliance of National Salvation—BZNS-Nikola Petkov, DPS, Green Party, Party of the Democratic Centre, New Choice, Federation of the Bulgarian Kingdom)	9.44	19	9
EvroLev (Euroleft)	5.57	14	4.4
BBB (Bulgarian Business Block)	5.27	12	4.02
BKP (Bulgarian Communist Party)	1.3	0	0
OT (Alliance for the King)	1.12	0	0

on economic and financial issues, while its leader repeatedly advocated the abandonment of partisanship and unification around "historical ideas and values" (Harper 2003, 336). The transformation of the Bulgarian party system is illustrated in table 3.5. The NDSV itself emerged, virtually overnight, as one of the three major contenders for power, challenging the SDS and the BSP for governmental leadership. It also increased the electoral alliance possibilities in the party system and encouraged smaller parties to explore more options.

The destabilization of the party system continued at the 2005 elections. With voter turnout at an unprecedented low, the election returns sent seven parties to parliament and created the most unstable political situation in the 16-year history of Bulgarian democracy (table 3.6). Besides the main contenders—NDSV, DPS, BSP, and SDS—three new parties and alliances contested elections and made it into parliament. A new centrist alliance, the Bulgarian National Union (BNS), was forged, and it united the BZNS, the Internal Macedonian Revolutionary Organisation (VMRO), and the Union of Free Democrats (SSD), all three of which had previously been part of the SDS or the United Democratic Forces (ODS). Two parties were formed specifically for the 2005 election: Democrats for a Strong Bulgaria (DSB), a splinter of the SDS, and Ataka, a brand-new contender in 2005. There was also New Time (NV), which split from NDSV in 2003.

Table 3.5   Bulgarian election results, 2001 elections (39th National Assembly)

Party/Alliance	Vote %	Number of seats	Seats %
NDSV (National Movement Simeon the Second)	42.74	120	50
ODS (United Democratic Forces—SDS, BZNS-NS and DP, BSDP, National DPS	18.18	51	21.25
KzB (Coalition for Bulgaria—BSP and alliance)	17.15	48	20
DPS (DPS, Liberal Union, EuroRoma)	7.45	21	8.75
Gergiovden-VMRO	3.63	0	0
Coalition "Simeon II"	3.44	0	0
National Union for Tzar Simeon II	1.7	0	0

Table 3.6   Bulgarian election results, 2005 elections (40th National Assembly)

Party/Alliance	Vote %	Number of seats	Seats %
KzB (Coalition for Bulgaria—BSP and alliance)	30.95	82	33.98
NDSV (National Movement Simeon the Second)	19.88	53	21.80
DPS (DPS, Liberal Union, EuroRoma)	12.81	34	14.07
Ataka	8.14	21	8.93
ODS (United Democratic Forces—SDS BZNS, DP, Gergiovden, NS-BZNS)	7.68	20	8.44
DSB (Democrats for a Strong Bulgaria)	6.4	17	7.07
BNS (Bulgarian National Union)	5.19	13	5.70
Novo Vreme (New Time)	2.95	–	–
KR (Coalition of the Rose)	1.30	–	–
Evroroma	1.25	–	–

Hungarian Party Politics 1990–2003

The development of democratic politics in Hungary began significantly earlier than it did in Bulgaria. By the late 1980s several groups of dissidents began to challenge the authority of the Hungarian Socialist Worker's Party (MSZMP). The MSZMP itself was already a relatively reform-oriented communist party "which allowed more technocrats into its ranks than any other party in the Soviet bloc" (Bozoki 2002, 95). In early 1989 the Hungarian Parliament had passed a law on free association that allowed the "free establishment of parties" (Agh 1994, 224).

The first free elections in 1990 saw a mushrooming of political parties and the emergence of numerous serious challenges to the presumptive authority of the "successor" communist party, the Hungarian Socialist Party (MSZP).[1] About 100 parties formed before the 1990 elections, of which about 40 registered but only 11 managed to run national lists in the first free elections in 1990 (table 3.7) (Agh 1994, 226). The conservative Hungarian Democratic Forum (MDF), the liberal SZDSZ, and the historic Peasants' Independent Smallholders Party (FKGP) all ran ahead of the MSZP, making it the fourth-largest parliamentary party with less than 9 percent of the seats in parliament (Toka 1995b, 3235).

However, by the 1994 elections, the MSZP regained the top spot and established itself as one of the major political parties in the country. Party politics in Hungary since have continued to be dominated by these original main contenders with very few new challengers (Toole 2000, 280). By the mid-1990s, the center-left MSZP and the conservative FIDESZ had emerged as the two main poles in the Hungarian party systems, with the liberal SZDSZ and the conservative MDF, respectively, as their loyal government coalitional partners (tables 3.8 and 3.9).

Several of the original smaller parties—for example, the conservative Christian Democratic People's Party (KDNP), and the FKGP—continued their presence in political life. A few new parties appeared

Table 3.7 Hungarian election results, 1990 elections

Party/Alliance	PR vote %	SMD seats	Total seats	Seats %
MDF (Hungarian Democratic Forum)	24.73	114	164	42.49
SZDSZ (Alliance of Free Democrats)	21.39	35	92	23.83
FKGP (Independent Small Holders Party)	11.73	11	44	11.4
MSZP (Hungarian Socialist Party)	10.89	1	33	8.55
FIDESZ (Federation of Young Democrats)	8.95	1	21	5.44
KDNP (Christian Democratic People's Party)	6.46	3	21	5.44
MSZMP (Munkaspart)	3.68	0	0	0
MSZDP (Social Democratic Party of Hungary)	3.55	0	0	0
ASZ (Agrarian Alliance)	3.13	1	1	0.26
VP (Entrepreneurs' Party)	1.89	0	0	0
HVK (Patriotic Elections Coalition)	1.87	0	0	0

Table 3.8 Hungarian election results, 1994 elections

Party/Coalition	PR vote %	SMD seats	Total seats	Seats %
MSZP (Hungarian Socialist Party)	32.99	149	209	54.15
SZDSZ (Alliance of Free Democrats)	19.74	16	69	17.88
MDF (Hungarian Democratic Forum)	11.74	5	38	9.84
FKGP (Independent Small Holders Party)	8.82	1	26	6.74
KDNP (Christian Democratic People's Party)	7.03	3	22	5.7
FIDESZ (Federation of Young Democrats)	7.02	0	20	5.18
Munkaspart [ex-MSZMP] (Workers' Party)	3.19	0	0	0
KP (Republican Party)	2.55	0	0	0
ASZ (Agrarian Alliance)	2.1	1	1	0.26
MIEP (Party of Hungarian Justice and Life)	1.59	0	0	0

Table 3.9 Hungarian election results, 1998 elections

Party/Alliance	PR vote %	SMD seats	Total seats	Seats %
MSZP (Hungarian Socialist Party)	32.92	54	134	34.72
FIDESZ-MPP (FIDESZ-Hungarian Civic Party)	29.48	55	113	29.27
FIDESZ-MPP-MDF joint candidates	–	35	50	12.95
FKGP (Independent Small Holders Party)	13.15	12	48	12.44
SZDSZ (Alliance of Free Democrats)	7.57	2	24	6.22
MIEP (Hungarian Justice and Life Party)	5.47	0	14	3.63
Munkaspart (Workers' Party)	3.95	0	0	0
MDF (FIDESZ-MPP joint candidates)	–	15	15	3.89
MDF (Hungarian Democratic Forum)	2.8	2	2	0.52
KDNP (Christian Democratic People's Party)	2.31	0	0	0
MDNP (Hungarian Democratic People's Party)	1.34	0	0	0

by the mid-1990s, the most notable being the Hungarian Justice and Life Party (MIEP), which was an extreme right splinter of the MDF. However, at the 2002 parliamentary elections in Hungary, none of these smaller parties could surmount the election law barrier and make it into parliament (table 3.10) (Fowler 2003).

Table 3.10 Hungarian election results, 2002 elections

Party/Alliance	PR vote %	SMD seats	Total seats	Seats %
MSZP (Hungarian Socialist Party)	42.05	4373842	178	
FIDESZ-MDF joint list	41.07	4503303	188	
SZDSZ (Alliance of Free Democrats)	5.57	440050	19	
MSZP-SZDSZ (joint candidates)	0	13101	1	
MIEP (Hungarian Truth and Life Party)	4.37	245651	0	
OMC (Centrum Part, or Center Party)	3.9	224309	0	
Munkaspart (Workers' Party)	2.16	121503	0	

Parties Out of Parliament: GOR/BEL/BSD and Munkaspart

GOR/BEL: Struggling for Survival

The experience of the Citizens' Union for the Republic (GOR) BEL and BSD is a very good example of how a group of people with office ambitions can try to establish and maintain the identity of their group and ensure its existence in the party system by trying different formats and learning from its experience. Figure 3.1 describes the complex evolution of the GOR from being a faction within the Bulgarian Socialist Party to being an independent party, to forming an alliance with three other left-of-center parties (DAR, or Democratic Alternative for the Republic), to merging with one of them to form a new party (BEL), to suffering internal divisions and losing a faction, to forming another alliance (BEL-BZNS-BESDP), to merging again into a new party (Bulgarian Social Democracy, or BSD), and finally to forming an alliance (Coalition of the Rose). Although this evolution in fact involved the creation of three separate parties (GOR, BEL, and BSD), they will be discussed together as they represent the experience of a small group of politicians who have remained central in all three parties.[2]

Electoral Targets
According to statements of its leaders over the years, GOR/BEL/ BSD has been trying to get access to the executive branch of the Bulgarian government since its inception (Tomov 1993; *Capital* 1997a, 1997c; Zankov 2003a, 2003b). According to Roumen Zankov, the BEL deputy chairman in 2002–2003, "for BEL, social democracy is a practice, not just an idea." For his party, he claimed,

winning parliamentary presence is a way to ensure participation in the government, and that is only meaningful if it provides a possibility to

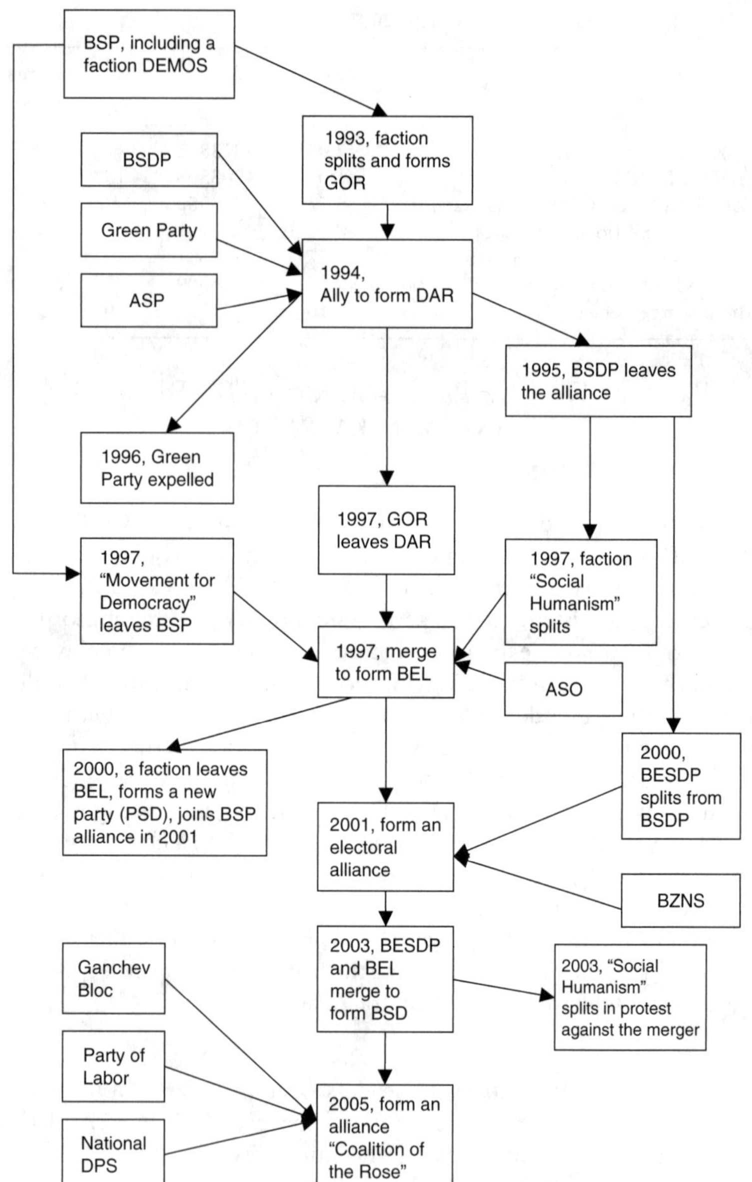

Figure 3.1   The evolution of GOR/DAR/BEL/BSD, 1993–2003.

influence policy-making . . . [A] political party that does not seek office is not a true political party but an educational society" (Zankov 2003a).

BEL is thus clearly a party seeking participation in the executive. It also seems to value office instrumentally, to use Strom's terms, as a way of influencing policies rather than as a source of office-related benefits (Muller and Strom 1999, 6). However, as Strom has argued, this does not impact the behavior and strategies of the party in its struggle for office, because it is still trying to achieve representation in the legislature (as a way to executive office).

Given its goal of participation in the executive, based on the discussion in the theoretical chapter, we can assume that GOR/BEL set their electoral target at each election as surpassing the electoral threshold. As the further discussion will note, the party has also been concerned with ideological positioning, but its dominant objective seems to have been to enter parliament.

GOR: Formation

GOR evolved from a faction within the BSP in the early 1990s. An interesting feature of the BSP was that it provided for "ideological platforms" or factions to develop within its membership (Krusteva 2003). One of these factions was the circle DEMOS led by Alexander Tomov, which left the BSP and founded GOR as a citizens' organization in 1993 because of "ideological incompatibility" with the BSP leadership. GOR proceeded to register as a political party in early 1994 and thus claimed a place in the Bulgarian party system.

At this time, GOR was not leaving a sinking ship. It is important to note that the split did not happen immediately following the quite narrow defeat of the BSP in the 1991 elections (see table 3.2). Instead, it came in 1993 at a time when the BSP's popularity was rising (Murer 2002, 387). In fact, the BSP swept the 1994 elections and formed a majority government.[3] Although there was no way for the "GOR-eans," as they were called, to know this back in 1993, opinion polls at the time had put the BSP in a favorable position. The formation of GOR as an independent party was clearly an electoral risk (GOR 1993, Tomov 1993). The process of GOR's formation and the party's electoral strategies are presented in figure 3.2.

GOR: Electoral Strategy in 1994

Realizing the challenges of running alone at elections, GOR immediately sought alliance partners (GOR 1993). Together with three other parties—the Alternative Socialist Party (ASP), the Bulgarian

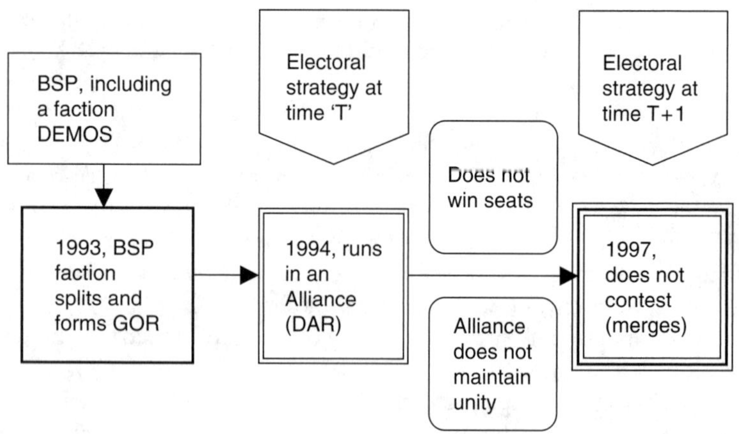

Figure 3.2   GOR, process of party formation and electoral competition, phases 1, 2, and 3.

Social Democratic Party (BSDP) and the Green Party (ZP)—GOR formed an electoral alliance, called DAR, in March 1994, six months before the scheduling of early elections.

GOR chose to seek easier representation in parliament using an alliance arrangement rather than to maintain its independence as a political formation. On their part, the other three parties were also searching for additional support. ASP was another, earlier splinter from the BSP. It was part of the SDS from 1991 to early 1993, when it was "expelled" from the alliance. BSDP and ZP split from the SDS in 1991, and both participated in separate alliances in 1991 but failed to get seats in parliament. Thus, the four parties saw forging an agreement aimed at the cooperation and consolidation of Bulgarian "social democracy" as the only way of achieving parliamentary representation. However, no merger was even considered, which demonstrated that the political parties were not ready to sacrifice institutional independence for electoral gains.

The alliance (DAR) gathered 3.79 percent of the vote in the 1994 elections and failed to make it into parliament (see table 3.3). The BSDP left DAR "temporarily" in early 1995, but never rejoined it, which probably contributed to the relatively poor performance of the alliance's candidates in the local elections in late 1995 (*Standart* 1995). Despite the obvious electoral failure, the alliance "expelled" one of its members, the ZP, in early 1996, and thus turned itself into a two-party alliance.

Electoral Strategy in 1997: Merger

By the beginning of 1997, the BSP government that had taken office in late 1994 had failed dramatically. It had allowed the country to go into the worst economic crisis since 1989, bankrupted a large segment of the population, and generally failed the "left-oriented" Bulgarians. The politicians in GOR decided to take advantage of the BSP's failure and disagreements among its leaders (Avramov 2002).

The failure of the one-party BSP government had demonstrated, in the view of GOR leaders, the BSP's inability to represent social democratic interests.[4] At this point, a large number of Bulgarians who were "leftist" by orientation and status could not possibly "associate the further development of the country with the Bulgarian Socialist Party" (Zankov 2003a). Neither did they see the BSDP—a natural candidate to represent social democratic interests—as being able to govern properly. After leaving DAR, the BSDP had gone back to being associated with the SDS—which was, by then, an openly Christian-democratic party. The BSDP thus "couldn't offer a social democratic alternative to the people" (Zankov 2003a). There was, as a result, in GOR's view, a social democratic political vacuum. However, as the 1995 local elections demonstrated, DAR (now a two-party alliance) could not achieve enough electoral support by itself.

Thus, in early 1997, GOR left DAR and together with Alternative Socialist Union (ASO, another earlier splinter of the BSP) and a splinter group from the BSDP formed a new party called Political Movement "Bulgarian EuroLeft."[5] GOR thus disappeared as a political entity after four years of independent existence and one electoral failure at the national level.

BEL: Formation

The new entity BEL claimed to unite the "true" social democrats in Bulgaria and clearly distinguished itself from the BSP (BSD 2003, 40; *Capital* 1997a). BEL attempted to represent the "the third way"—in both the ideological space and the party system of Bulgaria. Its position was clearly to the left and center-left in terms of social issues, but its foreign policy position supported European integration and NATO membership. In terms of party dynamics, BEL also tried to "challenge the bipolar nature of the party system," although it was neither the first nor the only party to do so in 1997 (Avramov 2002). Its electoral strategies are represented in figure 3.3.

BEL's behavior during 1997 clearly demonstrated that the GOR leadership, then in control of most of the leadership positions in the

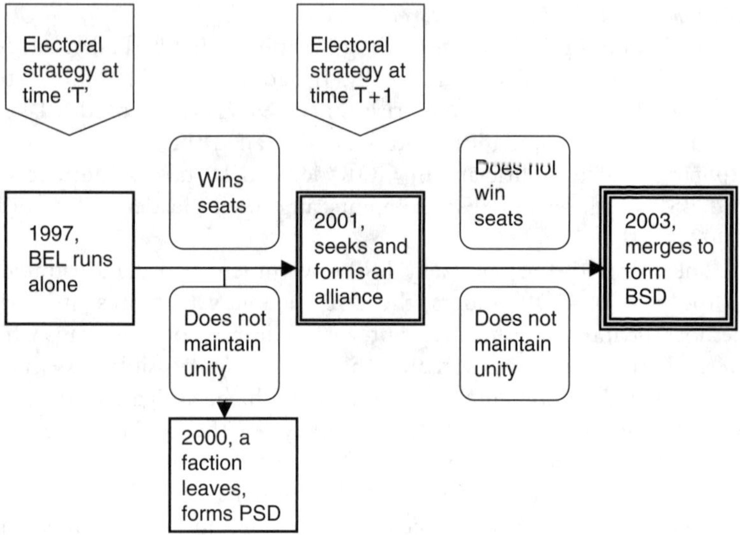

Figure 3.3   BEL, process of party formation and electoral competition, phases 1, 2, and 3.

new party, had learned from their previous experience in DAR. First of all, the GOR leadership realized that getting into office meant adapting its strategy and behavior to the institutional and political realities of the Bulgarian constitutional structures. Most immediate was the problem of surmounting the 4 percent vote barrier for gaining parliamentary seats (Kamov 1998). Moreover, their vote had to come from voters who were not only "leftist" by orientation but were also in favor of European integration and NATO membership. The recent failure of the BSP clearly presented a unique opportunity. However, to achieve broad support, BEL had to minimize the internal conflicts among its founding groups: GOR; the most recent defectors from the BSP; ASO; and one faction from BSDP. All of them had different political expectations and claimed to have contributed the most to the success of BEL (*Capital* 1997b).

Learning from their previous experience, the BEL members chose to merge these various political groups rather than just form an alliance, as DAR members had done in 1994. According to Kamov, the then BEL political secretary, this idea might not have had the support of some of BEL's founders, but the electoral success was a clear demonstration that a unified party was a better alternative to a loose alliance of several organizations (Kamov 1998).

Electoral Strategy in 1997: Running Alone
BEL rejected the idea of forming an alliance with the BSP or any other party as it was wary of cooperating with parties that could mar its image. According to BEL chairman Tomov, the party "would not tolerate being attached to the BSP or some other party" (*Capital* 1997b). However, this stance was possible largely because opinion polls had clearly indicated that BEL was the most likely of the small parties to surpass the 4 percent electoral threshold (*Capital* 1997c). In fact, it won 5.57 percent of the vote in 1997 and 14 seats in the Bulgarian Parliament. This marked BEL's "first big success" and the resurrection of Bulgarian social-democracy as an independent political force (BSD 2003, 30).

Electoral Strategy in 2001: Alliance
Despite BEL's success in the 1997 national and the 1999 local elections, and parallel efforts of the party to strengthen its organization, internal problems appeared by early 2000.[6] BEL chairman Tomov was accused of corruption and party finance fraud by a dissenting faction, and this accusation led to strong internal dissent and the eventual emergence of the first BEL splinter. However, as the national congress of the BEL reelected Tomov as leader in June 2000, his main opponents left the party and formed a separate political party called the Political Movement Social Democracy (PDS). As the PDS was led by popular politicians and enjoyed substantial support from the local branches, this split was a major blow to BEL's ability to gather electoral support (Mandzukov 2000a).

By early 2001, it was clear that BEL was in no position to claim anything close to its previous share of the vote. Even before the entrance of Simeon Sax-Coburg-Gotha into politics in April 2001, the party was only polling between 0.9 and 1.3 percent of the vote (NCIOM 2001). Afraid that it would not be able to gather even 1 percent of the vote, BEL formed a "hasty" electoral coalition with the BZNS and the Bulgarian United Social Democratic Party (BESDP) and managed to get just about 1 percent of the national vote (see table 3.5).

Interelection Merger: BSD
The poor showing led to the failure of the BEL-BZNS-BESDP alliance. However, BEL and the BESDP continued to work together; no future cooperation with the BSNZ was considered. In an effort to "unify social democracy in Bulgaria," BEL and the BESDP attempted to bring together various social democratic entities—parties, social

movements, labor unions, and other organizations—into a social alliance, rather than a structurally unified party organization (Zankov 2003a). In April 2002 they created the Confederation of Bulgarian Social Democracy.

Realizing that this was not enough in terms of an electoral strategy, in early 2003, BEL and the BESDP proceeded to merge into a new party, "Party Bulgarian Social Democracy" (BSD) (BSD 2003). Both BEL and the BESDP thus ceased to exist. The new party proclaimed itself to be "*the* unified social democratic party" in Bulgaria. However, as we shall see, the BSD united only two of the numerous social democratic parties that were active in the Bulgarian party system at that time.

Electoral Strategy in 2005: Alliance

By late 2003, the BSD had no realistic potential to surpass the electoral threshold at the national level, especially after the consolidation of other left parties around the BSP and the New Left (NL, discussed later in this chapter) (Karasimeonov 2002, 189). Thus, when it was time to contest elections in 2005, the BSD again sought to form an alliance and managed to attract three other formations into an electoral alliance called "Coalition of the Rose." The four parties united under this label had very little in common in terms of ideology: the alliance included the business-oriented Ganchev Bloc, a successor of the Bulgarian Business Bloc of the mid-1990s; National DPS, a splinter of the ethnic DPS; and the left-leaning United Labor Bloc. The only basis for the alliance was thus the shared desire of the party leaders to enter parliament and the hope that pooling their expected shared of the vote would allow them to do so (Staridolska and Gospodinova 2005). However, the alliance got only a little over 1 percent of votes, and the BSD stayed out of parliament again.

GOR and BEL were two political parties formed in an effort to realize the political ambition of its leaders. However, their electoral strategies seemed to have misfired, which led both parties to end their independent existence and brought about the ultimate marginalization of the newest merger, the BSD. Given its current outsider position in Bulgarian politics, GOR/BEL/BSD would probably not have been included in most studies of party politics in Bulgaria. However, in many ways, its experiences provide the most fascinating cases for the purposes of the question under study here. Chapter 4 will provide further examination of the factors that influenced GOR/BEL/BSD to form and the parties' choice of certain electoral strategies over the years.

Munkaspart: Staying the Course

Munkaspart is a hard-line Marxist party that was established in late 1989 and has maintained its existence in the Hungarian party system since then. While it regularly participated in local and regional governmental structures during the 1990s, it has never gained representation in the Hungarian Parliament. But in contrast to BEL, it has never changed its electoral strategy: Munkaspart has always contested elections under its own label. The name Munkaspart will be used to refer to the party under discussion to keep it separate from the communist MSZMP, although Munkaspart contested election in 1990 under the name MSZMP.

Electoral Targets

Munkaspart's goal, as defined by its deputy chairman, Janos Vajda, has always been the representation of the interests of the workers and poor people through the system of democratic government. Although in the early 1990s the party still maintained some elements of an anti-democratic communist platform, by the mid-1990s it had accepted the reality of a multiparty democracy and free-market economy (Vajda 2003; Swain 1991). Gaining representation in parliament thus became a natural goal for Munkaspart. Its electoral target has always been defined as surmounting the electoral threshold needed to gain representation in the Hungarian Parliament (4 percent in 1990 and 5 percent afterwards).[7]

Munkaspart: Formation

Munkaspart was formed in late 1989, after the transformation of the MSZMP into the MSZP. The MSZMP was already becoming too reform-oriented for some of its hard-line members, a trend that intensified with the formation of its "successor", the MSZP. The reform platform of the MSZP, adopted at its first Congress in May 1990, put the party closer to a social democratic, rather than to a communist, position (Bozoki 2002, 99). The hard-liners in the MSZP chose to form a new party under the old label, and attracted a substantial amount of the hard-line MSZMP members who disapproved of the "right-leaning" MSZP platform (Toka and Enyedi, 1994, 39; Vajda 2003). This process is represented in figure 3.4.

Both the official "successor" party—the MSZP—and Munkaspart asked people to reregister with them rather than to just continue their membership (as was done in other cases), and thus the new party lost a significant number of members. The MSZMP had 700,000

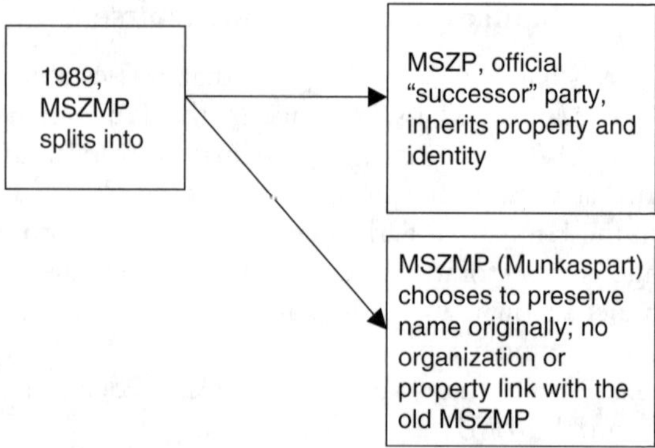

Figure 3.4   MSZMP split, 1989.

members in October 1988, but the MSZP claimed only 30,000 by the fall of 1989 (Bozoki 2002, 98). However, the MSZP inherited the property of the MSZMP, thus benefiting from its lineage, or as Munkaspart often complains, "The MSZP took the assets and left us Marx" (Swain 1991; Vajda 2003). Munkaspart claimed a membership of 100,000 by 1990, but the figure is considered an exaggeration (Toka 1995, 38).

Just like GOR/BEL in Bulgaria, Munkaspart also saw its role as representing the interests of the electorate that is "left" oriented and whose demands were not well represented by the official successor party (the BSP and the MSZP, respectively). According to Munkaspart, the MSZP was "moving more and more to the right" and did not adequately represent the interests of a large number of people who had been adversely affected by the economic reform in Hungary (Vajda 2003).

Electoral Strategies

Munkaspart competed in the 1990 elections but failed to surpass the 4 percent threshold needed to gain representation in parliament by a few thousand votes. It fielded 92 candidates and got 3.68 percent of the vote (see table 3.7). The failure to gain representation in parliament in 1990 was, according to the party's leadership, the blow of death for the party at the national level because, as Vajda notes, "Only parties that made it into parliament in 1990 have been able to stay in politics since" (Vajda 2003). The parliament raised the electoral threshold to 5 percent for the 1994 elections, thus making it even more difficult for Munkaspart to surpass it. The party gained 3.19 percent of the vote in the 1994 elections, 3.95 percent of the vote

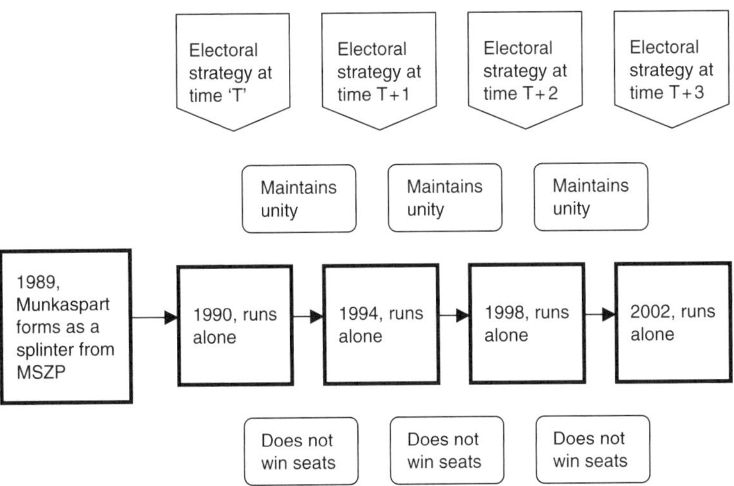

Figure 3.5 Munkaspart, process of party formation and electoral competition, phases 1, 2, and 3.

in the 1998 elections, and 2.16 percent of the vote in 2002 (tables 3.8, 3.9, and 3.10). For most of the period, however, Munkaspart has been the most prominent extra-parliamentary party in Hungary. As figure 3.5 shows, the party chose to run alone in all elections despite its failure to make it into parliament.

Since the early 1990s Munkaspart leaders have been envisioning cooperation with the MSZP or the Agrarian Alliance (a small left-wing alliance that ran in the 1990 elections), but the plan has not materialized. In fact, when asked this question in 2003, Vajda expressed a clear unwillingness to form electoral alliances, arguing that

> appearing in common electoral lists means giving up your face as a party . . . all small parties that have entered [electoral] coalitions have disappeared . . . for us preserving the party is more important than being in Parliament . . .

The experience of Munkaspart thus contrasts sharply with BEL's experience in Bulgaria and, in many ways, appears to contradict the expectations of the theoretical understanding of party behavior presented here. While electoral failure seems to have promoted a search for different electoral strategies in the case of GOR/BEL, and finally led to its demise, such failure has not had the same effect on Munkaspart. Munkaspart has maintained an impressively consistent presence in the party system without any major change in its organizational and electoral form. Despite the fact that both parties are involved in local and regional governments, BEL seems to be significantly more concerned with representation in parliament. A more detailed examination of the factors that have contributed to this divergence in the electoral strategies of the two parties will be provided in chapter 4.

Parties in Government: The DPS and the SZDSZ

DPS: the Limits of the Ethnic Vote

The DPS has been the most stable of the "smaller" political parties in Bulgarian politics. It has been present in all parliaments since 1990 and has played a balancing role in several Bulgarian governments. Although the DPS is currently trying to transform itself into a national, nonethnic party, for most of the post-1989 period it has been a de facto ethnic party representing a relatively well-mobilized minority.

Although the DPS has never had an openly stated ethnic platform and has always included ethnic Bulgarians in its membership and leadership, it has always represented the interests of the Turkish minority in Bulgaria. Its support has been concentrated heavily in the regions populated by this minority (Kumanov and Nikolova 1999, 134). As ethnic parties are banned by the Bulgarian Constitution, the DPS's ability to function freely in Bulgarian politics was challenged at numerous times in the early 1990s. By the late 1990s, however, it was clear that the constitutional provision could not prevent either the DPS or the other fledgling ethnic political parties from participating in the political process (Vassilev 2001).

By the end of the 1990s, however, the DPS realized that it could not expand its vote any more than it already had unless it reached beyond the Turkish minority (Dal 2003). Consequently, it formed electoral alliances with nonethnic parties in both 1997 and 2001. Moreover, the DPS has made a conscious effort to transform itself into a liberal party: it has tried to include more ethnic Bulgarian in its leadership and has joined the Liberal International (Gospodinova 2003; Tzachevski 2003, Karasimeonov 2002, 167–168).

Electoral Targets
The DPS's major goal has always been participation in the executive in all possible ways and at all possible levels of state administration. As Kasim Dal, deputy chairman of the party, put it, "Participation in

the government of the country is the only goal a real party can have"
(Dal 2003).

The DPS's aspirations to participate in its country's government were made clear from the very beginning of its participation in Bulgarian politics. However, back in 1991, when the DPS first became part of the governing majority in parliament, direct participation in the government was not possible because of strong nationalist feelings in the country. The Bulgarian public was "not yet ready" to see members of the Turkish minority in leading positions (Dal 2003; Vassilev 2001). However, the parliamentary support of the DPS parliamentary group was crucial for the survival of the 1991 SDS government. When the economic policies of the government began to hurt the interests of the Turkish minority, the DPS reconsidered its position and withdrew its support, thus contributing to the collapse of the government in late 1992 (Vassilev 2001, 51; Kalinova and Baeva 2000, 175). However, its experience clearly indicated that it could exert influence on the government by controlling a small but key number of seats in parliament.

The Berov government (1992–1994) that followed was formed using the DPS's mandate, and it even included a DPS representative, an ethnic Bulgarian, as a Cabinet minister. However, DPS influence over the government was minimal; the cabinet was officially a technocratic government that virtually relied on the BSP for support (Kalinova and Baeva 2000, 177–180). The two successive governments were majority coalitions not requiring the support or participation of the DPS. In 2001, the DPS was given two ministerial positions in the NDSV government, which the DPS considered a clear indication that it had been accepted as an equal partner in the political life of the country. By all accounts, the DPS is currently seen as a potential participant in any new government of the country (Gospodinova 2003).

Just like BEL and Munkaspart, the DPS values office instrumentally—not for the benefits of office per se, but because office provides a way to influence the country's policy in ways that favor DPS members and supporters (Dal 2003). A similar approach is sometimes seen as cynical in BEL's case because of the personal ambition of its leader Tomov (for which he had become notorious in Bulgarian politics). In contrast, non-DPS sources also claim that DPS leaders appear to be committed to advancing certain policies rather than simply gaining ministerial positions (Gospodinova 2003).

The DPS's electoral target from 1990 to 2005 has always been to surpass the electoral threshold that would allow the party to gain representation in parliament. However, as the 1991–1992 experience demonstrated, parliamentary representation was not enough for direct representation in government. Since then, and in an attempt to ensure its "coalitionability," the DPS has made sure to moderate its position on Turkish minority rights and to demonstrate its support for democratic politics and national integrity in any way possible. Still, surpassing the threshold remained the major target for the party until 2001.

DPS: Formation

As a political party, the DPS was founded in early 1990. It inherited the clandestine organizations of the "Turkish National Liberation Movement in Bulgaria," which were established in 1986 (Tatarli 2003, 9). The Turkish minority represents 9.24 percent of the population in Bulgaria. During the 1980s the BKP government had carried out repeated discriminatory campaigns against this minority, which culminated in its 1989 efforts to encourage the Turkish minority to leave for Turkey. But after the democratic changes in Bulgaria in late 1989, the Turkish minority mobilized politically and demanded full civil and political rights. The formation of the DPS as a vehicle to realize these demands in Bulgarian politics was thus the logical conclusion of the activities of the organization before 1989. The DPS never doubted the presence of an electoral demand for it, and once the one-party system was done away with, it moved quickly to register as a political party.

Electoral Strategy in 1990: Running Alone

Although the DPS was refused participation in the Round Table Talks that negotiated the first multiparty elections, it was able to contest elections in June 1990, when it ran alone and won 8.03 percent of the PR vote and 12 of the 200 SMD seats (table 3.1) (Vassilev 2001, 47). With 23 seats in the 1990 parliament, the DPS became the fourth-biggest parliamentary group in the Bulgarian Grand National Assembly. The DPS's electoral strategies in the 1990 and later elections are represented in figure 3.6.

Electoral Strategy in 1991: Running Alone

In 1991, the DPS continued to rely on the high level of political mobilization of the Turkish minority to provide its electoral support. But the party's entry into politics and the reestablishment of the civil rights of the Turkish minority in 1990 created a strong nationalist backlash among the Bulgarian public. Even the BSP used this issue in an attempt to broaden its appeal, making ethnicity a strong issue in

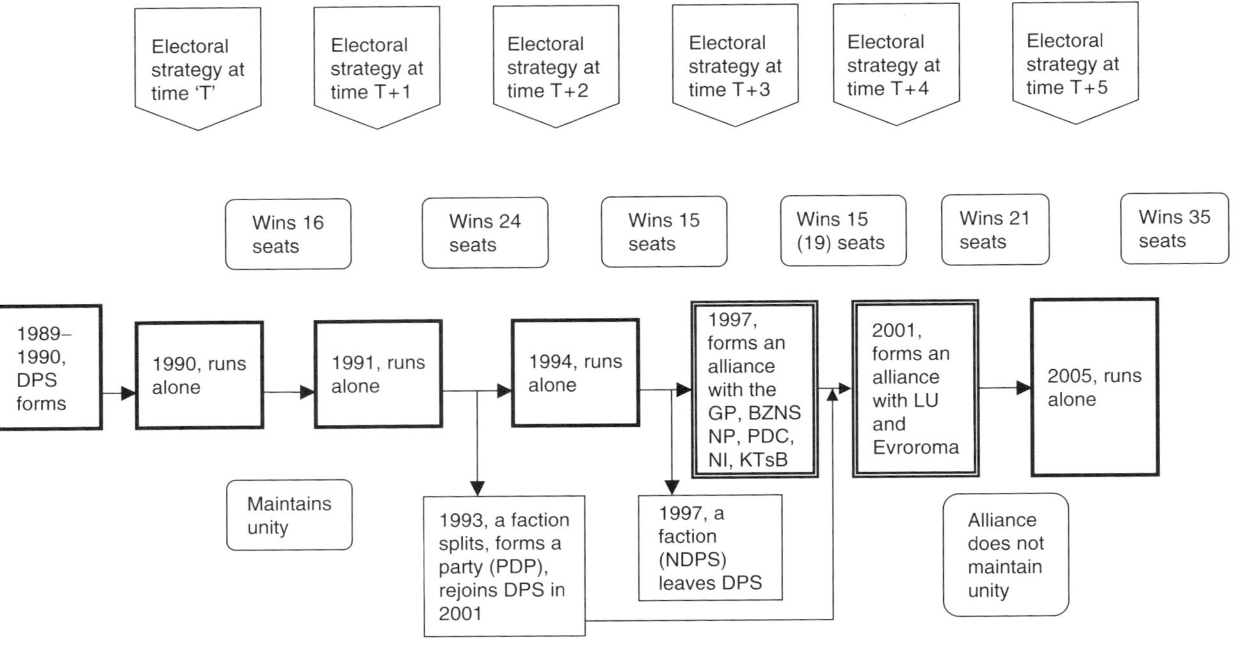

Figure 3.6 DPS, process of party formation and electoral competition, phases 1, 2, and 3.

the 1991 elections (Vassilev 2001, 38; Pirgova 2002, 94). In response to this backlash the DPS attempted to broaden its electoral appeal by endorsing civil liberties rather than just minority rights. The 1991 election results suggest that the nationalist campaign encouraged an even higher mobilization of the minority. In the second free elections the DPS increased its share to 7.55 percent of the vote (table 3.2). But because only three parties made it into parliament, it ended up with 10 percent of the total number of seats, making it the balancing power in parliament.

Electoral Strategy in 1994: Running Alone
The 1991–1994 interelection period witnessed the first challenges to the unity of the DPS. In 1993 a faction led by Mehmed Hodza left the DPS, citing disagreements with the party leader, Ahmed Dogan, and formed a new political party. In addition, another political party claiming to represent the Turkish minority—the Democratic Party of Justice—joined the competition for the minority's support. However, despite these challenges to its monopoly over political support for the Turkish minority, the DPS still contested elections on its own in 1994. Although the DPS claimed that neither of the two new parties had "any social basis," they managed to take away about 30, 000 votes from the DPS, decreasing its share from 7.55 to 5.44 percent of the vote in the 1994 elections (Tatarli 2003). The DPS thus came close to not surpassing the 4 percent threshold needed to gain entry into parliament for the first time in its existence (Karasimeonov 2002).

Electoral Strategy in 1997: the ONS Electoral Alliance
Following the 1994 elections, the DPS realized that the finite nature of its electoral support might make it difficult for it to gain parliamentary representation, especially in the presence of other competitors for the ethnic vote. As a result, the DPS began to look for alternative electoral strategies. In mid-1996 it participated in an early form of the ODS, an alliance formed to back a non-BSP presidential candidate. Despite the success of the presidential campaign and the election of an SDS presidential candidate, the alliance members disagreed over the order of candidates on the alliance's list when early parliamentary elections were scheduled in 1997. As a result, the DPS withdrew from the ODS and formed it own alliance, the Union for National Salvation (ONS) (Dal 2003).

The ONS was an alliance of the DPS, the ZP, New Choice Alliance (NI), two small centrist parties, and one royalist party. The alliance, which was supported by the Bulgarian monarch in exile Simeon

Sax-Coburg-Gotha, won 9.44 percent of the vote in the April 1997 elections. However, 4 of the 19 seats went to the ZP and NI, leaving the DPS with the same number of representatives as before. At the same time, the DPS alliance partners brought a minimal number of votes to the alliance, according to their own estimates, but received a disproportionately high number of seats (Dzudzev 2003). The DPS became increasingly unhappy with this alliance because it believed it had contributed the most to the campaign but had to give up too many seats to its electoral partners (Dal 2003).

Electoral Strategy in 2001: DPS-Liberal Union-Evroroma
The ONS members went their separate ways in the 2001 elections, citing various reasons, all of which clearly indicated dissatisfaction with the behavior of their partners. The deputy chairman of the ZP, for example, claimed that the DPS treated ZP members as respectful and equal alliance partners in the preelection and the immediate postelection periods, but during its term in parliament, it showed clearly that it continued to "care most about the rights and freedoms of one minority, ignoring the national interest of the country" (Dzudzev 2003).

So, when it came to contesting elections again, neither the DPS nor any of the other ONS members wanted to work with each other. The DPS, however, which seemed to be still searching for ways to increase its electoral support, sought the cooperation of two smaller and quite different parties—the Liberal Union and a party of the Roma minority (Evroroma). This time, the DPS seems to have played its cards right—it gave up no seats to its alliance partners and placed 21 representatives in the National Assembly.

Electoral Strategy in 2005: Running Alone
The DPS continued to search for a "liberal" image throughout the interelection period of 2001–2005. It became a full member of the Liberal Alliance in 2004, supported NDSV's bid to join the alliance, and helped it become an associated member in 2004. With the NDSV emerging as the DPS's stable partner after four years of coalition government, the DPS no longer needed small parties as alliance partners. A repeat of the 2001 alliance was not even considered. In early 2005, there was some discussion about possible joint NDSV-DPS lists for the June elections. However, both sides had reservations. According to the DPS chairman, Ahmed Dogan, "[R]unning alone is the easiest strategy for the DPS, but we are willing to [take a] risk [by allying with the other liberal parties NDSV and NV]" (Yanova 2005). Similarly, the NDSV leader Daniel Vulchev believed that the liberal parties

could do better if they ran alone (Yanova 2005). Both the NDSV and the DPS chose to run alone in the 2005 elections.

This decision seems to have been the right one for the DPS. Although the party had reportedly had some doubts about the stability of its electorate earlier in the year, the DPS supporters turned out to vote at a rate much higher than the overall rate of 55 percent for the whole country (BCEC 2005). As a result, the DPS emerged more powerful than ever from these elections, winning about 13 percent of the vote and about 14 percent of the seats, its best showing since 1990 (see tables 3.1–3.6). It proceeded to become a coalition partner in the three-party coalition that formed after the election, thus making its goal a reality yet again.

Overall, the DPS seems to have done very well over the years—it responded to decreasing electoral support by broadening its appeal and forming electoral alliances. But, in contrast to GOR/BEL, it has managed both to secure a stable share of the vote through these alliances and to preserve its leading position in them. In turn, it has chosen to run alone when there were reasons for the party to believe that this strategy would benefit it the most.

The SZDSZ: The Threat of Extinction

The SZDSZ was formed as a party in late 1988 and has been represented in all legislatures in post-1990 Hungary. However, its share of seats has decreased substantially over the years (see tables 3.7–3.10). It is considered part of the center-left coalition in Hungary and has participated in two MSZP-led governments.

The evolution of the SZDSZ is another example of a party's relatively consistent behavior with no major variations of electoral strategies (figure 3.7). However, unlike the Hungarian Munkaspart, the SZDSZ seems to have been able to achieve its targets and establish itself as an integral part of the Hungarian political system. In this regard, its experience is reminiscent of that of the DPS in Bulgaria. However, unlike the DPS, the SZDSZ has not sought alliance partners despite decreasing electoral support. But still, after the closeness of the 2002 elections, when with 5.57 percent of the PR vote the SZDSZ barely made it into parliament, the party might have to reconsider its electoral strategies.

Electoral Targets
The SZDSZ is, by all accounts, a party that seeks to participate in the executive branch of the government. According to Gabor Fodor,

a prominent leader and member of the executive committee of the party:

> The main goal of the SZDSZ has always been the establishment of the rule of law, democracy, human rights, and tolerance in Hungary; the straightening of liberal (in the social sphere) and centrist- liberal (in the economic sphere) values in society. . . . However, the real goal has been representation in Parliament and participation in the government of the country.   (Fodor 2003)

Peter Hack, one of the founding leaders of the SZDSZ, has expressed similar views about the aspirations of the party over the years. In addition, the party's participation in two governments along with the MSZP is a clear indication that participation in the executive is what the SZDSZ has been after. The electoral target of the SZDSZ thus has always been to surpass the electoral threshold needed to gain seats in the parliament.

Formation

The SZDSZ was formed as a successor of the dissident Network of Free Initiatives, whose roots go back to the 1970s and 1980s (Keri and Levendel 1995, 135; Toka 1995b, 36; Hollis 1999, 247). One of the first anticommunist proto parties created in Hungary, the SZDSZ was largely made up of intellectuals who espoused democratic ideas. At this point, proponents of democracy in Hungary had two strategies—the revitalization of historic parties (e.g., FKGP, KDNP) and the establishment of new ones. The SZDSZ members chose the second option, as they saw a demand for new political contenders in the system (Hack 2003). The SZDSZ became one of the more active proponents of change in the system during the Round Table Talks of 1989.

Electoral Strategies in 1990, 1994, 1998 and 2002: Running Alone

As elections approached in 1990, the SZDSZ enjoyed high popularity and so decided to run under it own label. It won 92 (of 386) seats in parliament and became the second-biggest parliamentary party in Hungary. However, it did not participate in the 1990 MDF-led government and assumed the role of the biggest opposition party instead (Keri and Levendel 1995, 135). Despite some bitter internal disputes over the leadership and the philosophy of the party during 1991–1992, and a 12 percent defection rate of its deputies during the term of the first parliament, the SZDSZ did not experience any formal splits and maintained its integrity (Toole 2000, 293; Pataki

1991, 1992; Lomax 1995). However, it failed to build a strong organization, relying instead on relatively loose networks of regional structures that were difficult to control (Pataki 1991, 15; Tamas 1999, 32–33). In 1993, the SZDSZ was strengthened by its incorporation of the Fodor-led liberal faction from FIDESZ (Racz and Kukorelli 1995, 259). The electoral strategies of the party at all elections are represented in Figure 3.7.

At the 1994 elections, the SZDSZ received a clear indication that its popularity was subsiding. Its share of the seats decreased by about 5 percent and it lost 23 deputies. Ironically, it remained the second-largest party in parliament, and so obtained its first chance to participate in government when the MSZP asked it to join in an attempt to broaden the government's legitimacy and share responsibility for reform (Hollis 1999, 262). The SZDSZ thus became a coalition partner of its former archrival, a decision that brought further internal disputes and leadership changes.

Although these problems were underscored by the 6 percent defection rate during the second term in parliament, the SZDSZ did not change its electoral strategy. It suffered a substantial setback in 1998, when it got only 24 seats in parliament, but it refused to change its approach to elections and party building (Hack 2003). It continued to have a relatively elitist approach to politics and to ignore the need to strengthen its presence in society.

In the 2002 elections the SZDSZ again contested the first round of elections on its own but managed to secure only 19 seats in parliament, barely getting the 5 percent of the PR vote needed to place its candidates in the legislature. However, due to the distribution of seats in parliament, the SZDSZ became a coalition partner in the government, as its 19 seats became crucial for the formation of a parliamentary majority and cabinet.

Thus, despite a consistent downward trend in its popular support, the SZDSZ has continued to run alone in elections.[8] Both Hack and Fodor have stressed that party independence has been extremely important to the SZDSZ, a claim that is definitely substantiated by the evolution of the party over the years. The main reason for this unwillingness to seek electoral alliances is the belief that small parties are always in a secondary position in such situations (Fodor 2003). However, the most recent election performance clearly demonstrated that although the SZDSZ has stayed intact (unlike other small parties in Hungary, such as the FKGP and KDNP), it has lost a substantial part of its constituency, suggesting that changes in its electoral strategy are needed (Hack 2003).

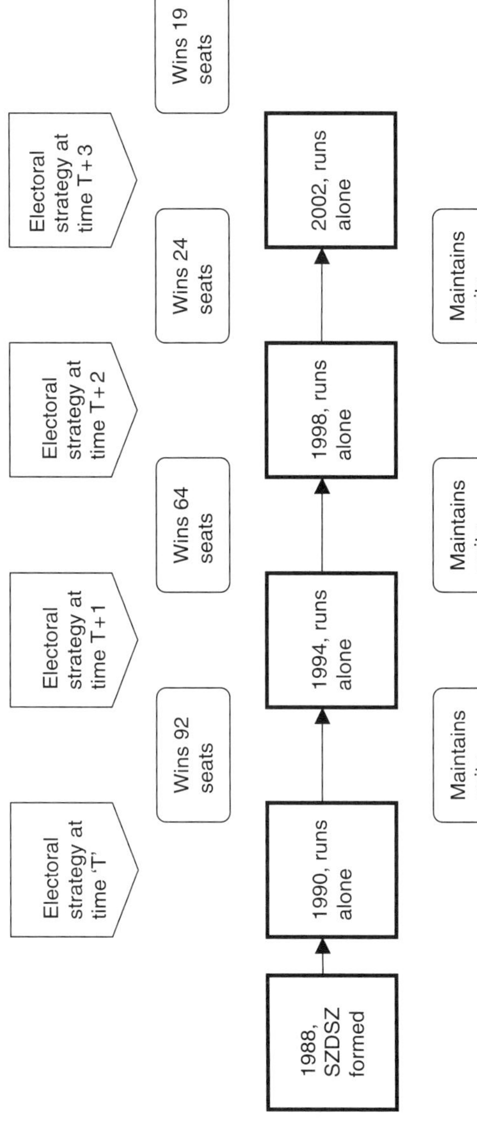

Figure 3.7 SZDSZ, process of party formation and electoral competition, phases 1, 2, and 3.

The behavior of the SZDSZ contrasts sharply with that of the MDF, another big party turned small, which is not discussed in detail here. The MDF followed a path of electoral success and failure similar to that of the SZDSZ—it went from dominating the first parliament to barely making the cutoff in 1998 (See tables 3.7–3.10). In response to this downturn and continuing unfavorable opinion poll rankings, the MDF chose different strategies in 1998 and 2002. In 1998, it sought an alliance and ran joint lists with the FIDESZ-MPP. In 2002, it started an official merger negotiation with the FIDESZ-MPP, with which it ran common candidates (see the following sections for a more detailed discussion of this issue).

In 2002, the MDF placed 24 of its candidates in parliament but the alliance was heavily dominated by FIDESZ-MPP (Szoke 2003; Fowler 2003). The FIDESZ-MPP/MDF alliance did not manage to secure a majority in parliament, making it possible for the MSZP-SZDSZ government to form. The MDF thus placed more people in parliament than the SZDSZ, but its alliance with the FIDESZ-MPP not only challenged its independence but also jeopardized the chances of both of them to be in government. The SZDSZ, on the other hand, secured its participation in government, but according to both Fodor and Hack, the 2002 election results posed to the SZDSZ a clear threat of party extinction and required it to re-formulate its approach to contesting elections and party building.

Parties in Control of the Government: The BSP and FIDESZ-MPP

The BSP: Allying for Glory

The BSP is the official "successor" party to the BKP. Unlike its counterparts in Hungary and other Eastern and Central European countries, the BSP did not formerly disband, but only changed its name and its members' documents. This move provided for organizational continuity and gave the BSP an organizational edge over the new parties in the political system in the early 1990s. With most of the opposition parties still in a very rudimentary stage at the time of the first democratic elections in 1990, the BSP thus did not find it too difficult to preserve its dominance over the party system.

Over the years, the BSP has governed the country directly only during 1990–1991, 1994–1997, and since the June 2005 elections, but it was a tacit and influential supporter of the Berov government during 1993–1994 (see appendix D for details). While clearly in opposition to the SDS government during 1997–2001, the BSP briefly participated in the 2001 NDSV government, and by late 2002 was in strong opposition to the Sax-Coburg–Gotha government.

By 2005, the BSP was clearly the most popular single party in Bulgaria, but this was not enough to allow it to come into control of the government. The BSP and its alliance partners won 82 seats (34 percent) in 2005, but this left it well short of the majority that polls throughout the campaign had predicted. Nonetheless, the party's plurality entitled it to a central role in the formation of the government (BCEC 2005).

The BSP has become notorious in Bulgarian politics for its tendency to form various electoral alliances, although the party has gained very little from its partners in terms of electoral support. The evolution of the BSP in more general terms is presented in figure 3.8.

Electoral Targets

There is no question that through the post-1990 period, the BSP has attempted to win control over the executive in Bulgaria, although in the early years the party sought to share the responsibility of government with coalitional partners. Despite its victory in the 1990 elections, the BSP seemed willing to "spread the blame for the impending economic crisis" (Birch et al. 2002). The party's attempts to shirk responsibility were unsuccessful, and the first BSP government (Lukanov government) had to resign after social unrest erupted in the country (Kalinova and Baeva 2000, 198).

However, since then, the Socialists have not shied away from governing alone. For our purposes, their electoral targets are then assumed to be winning a near plurality of seats in parliament. In fact, statements of BSP leaders and campaign platforms provide evidence that this was indeed the case. BSP campaigns were aimed at winning a majority of seats in parliament and the platforms of the party centered on the policies to be implemented if it came to govern (Krusteva 2003). In 1994, BSP chairman Videnov argued:

> We need a majority of seats in Parliament, we need as many partners and supporters in Parliament as we can have . . . The [early] elections will be meaningless if we have a 'balancing' party again.   (Videnov 1994)

Unlike the MSZP, when the BSP won a majority in 1994, it proceeded to form a de facto one-party government although it included members of its electoral alliance (Pirgova 2002, 198).

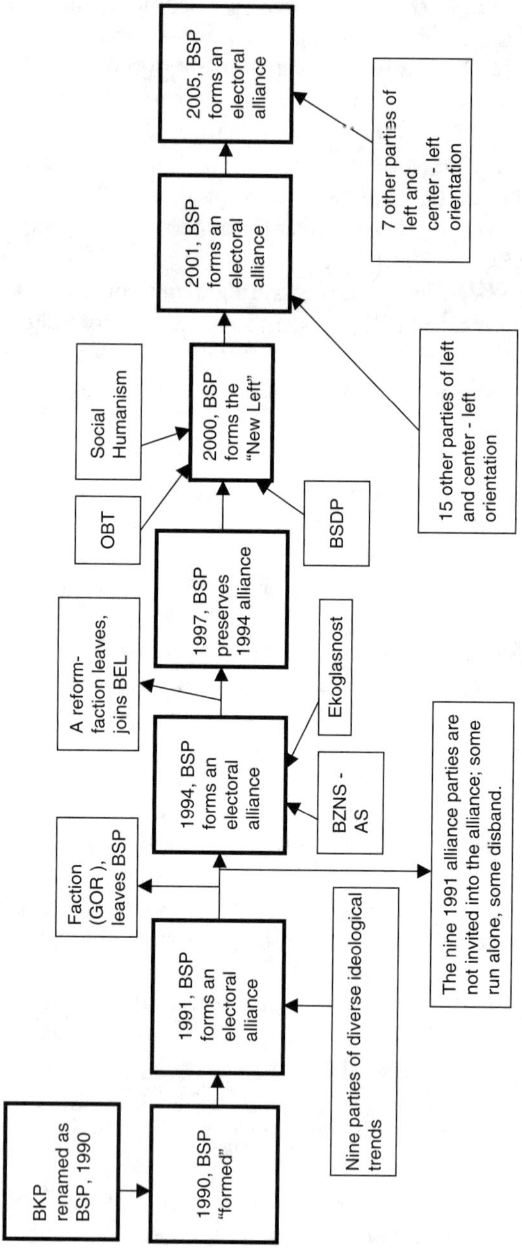

Figure 3.8 BSP, evolution 1990–2005.

The BSP has claimed that it needs power so that it can protect the interests of the "losers" of reform in Bulgaria by implementing a center-left platform (Krusteva 2003; BSP 1995, 1997, 2000, 2002). However, the BSP has a long tradition of using executive office to distribute various spoils and patronage appointments that has certainly left an imprint on the party. This makes it difficult to see the BSP as a party seeking office purely for policy influence. Nevertheless, the BSP has been motivated by a desire, instrumental or intrinsic, to control the executive, and has behaved so as to maximize the possibility of achieving that aim.

BSP "Formation" and Electoral Strategy in 1990
The BSP is the only one of the six political parties examined in detail here that did not form anew in the late 1980s or early 1990s. Instead, the party changed its name from the BKP to the Bulgarian Socialist Party (BSP) in early 1990. The BSP inherited the organization of the BKP and maintained its ideology relatively unchanged. Given the great popularity of the BSP at the time and the influence it still exercised over the electoral process, the party's decision not to form anew was hardly surprising. The BSP ran alone in the first democratic elections in Bulgaria (June 1990), won 114 of the 200 SMD seats and 97 of the 200 PR seats, and emerged as the majority party in parliament. The electoral strategies of the BSP are represented in figure 3.9.

Electoral Strategy in 1991: Electoral Alliance
Following the SDS's refusal to join in a coalition government in 1990 and share the responsibility for reform, the BSP formed a majority government. However, it was unwilling to implement any meaningful reforms, and this unwillingness led to an economic disaster in the winter of 1990, widespread social protests, and the resignation of the BSP Cabinet (Kalinova and Baeva 2000, 164). An expert government that included representatives of the three major parliamentary parties was formed in 1991 to carry out the first and most painful economic reforms in the country.

Sharing power and blame seems to have been a good step for the BSP; by late 1991, its popularity had declined but still remained at respectable levels. However, as winning a majority of the seats seemed uncertain at best, the BSP sought an alliance with other parties. At the 1991 elections, it formed an electoral alliance with, BLP, OPT, KhRP, NLP 'St. Stambolov,' and five smaller parties."[9] None of these parties was a serious competitor—the most popular of the alliance partners, the United Party of Labor (OPT),

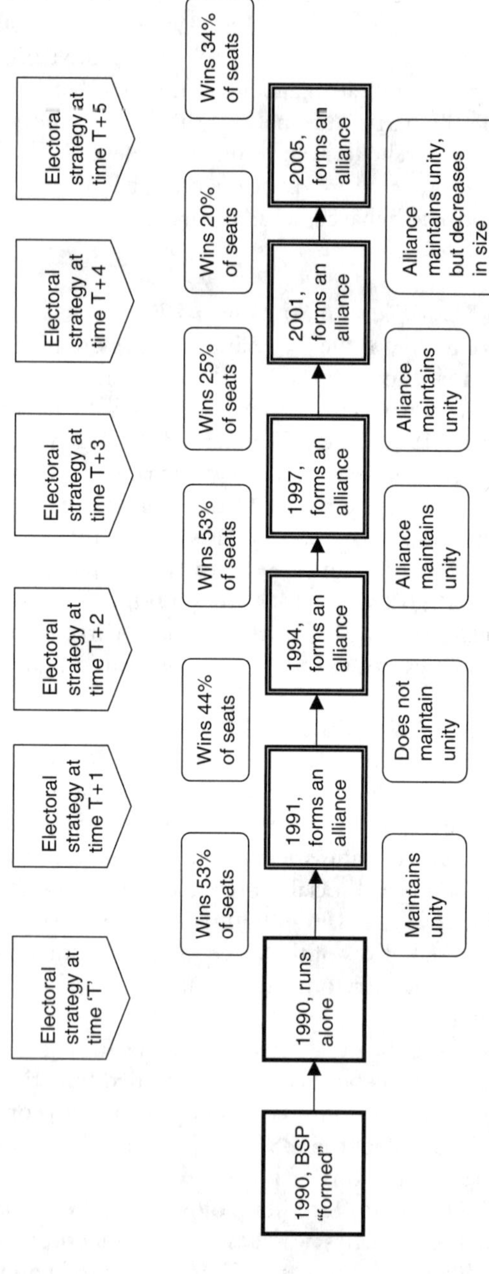

Figure 3.9   BSP, process of party formation and electoral competition, phases 1, 2, and 3.

had obtained 0.6 percent of the vote at the previous elections. Neither did any of them seem to show potential for the future. Inclusion of the OPT in the alliance was particularly surprising as the party had an openly nationalist ideology (Engelbrekt 1991). The alliance got 33.14 percent of the vote and 44.2 percent of the seats in parliament, which left the BSP a few seats away from being the plurality legislative party.

In hindsight, it would seem that the choice of an alliance strategy in this case was "hastily done" (Krusteva 2003). The official motivation, according to then BSP chairman Lilov, was the "unity of goals" of the alliance partners, namely, "to protect democracy and civil peace" (as cited in Engelbrekt 1991). The alliance certainly did not bring any electoral advantages to the BSP in terms of direct electoral support contribution. However, the alliance did provide a form of legitimacy for the BSP, at a time when the SDS and the DPS wanted to outlaw the BSP because it was the BKP's successor. Having other, "democratic" parties cooperate with the BSP lent it legitimacy as an equal participant in the democratic process. However, during the next elections, none of the 1991 alliance partners was included in the new BSP-led alliance.

Electoral Strategy in 1994: BSP-BZNS-Ekoglasnost Alliance
By 1994, the BSP was again the most popular party in the country and it certainly did not need additional support to win a majority of seats in parliament. Despite its popularity, the BSP formed an alliance with two other parties: one of the agrarian party factions, BZNS-Alexander Stamboliiski (BZNS-AS), and a splinter of the SDS, an environment-oriented party called Political Club "Ekoglasnost." The BSP's behavior at these elections showed some ideological consistency—both Ekoglasnost and BZNS-AS were left-leaning organizations that had similar policy objectives as the BSP. In addition, they both had a larger societal presence and stronger organizations than the BSP's 1991 alliance partners. The choice of an alliance strategy, even if not necessary, was certainly more prudent in terms of electoral benefits.

The nature of the electoral alliance was supposed to determine the distribution of governmental positions from 1994 to 1997. But, in reality, there functioned a one-party government in which the representatives of the smaller partners were dominated by the BSP. The participation of BZNS-AS in the BSP-led government is often cited as one of the reasons for the factional struggles and the final dissolution of the BZNS-AS in 1999 (Pirgova 2002, 203).

Electoral Strategy in 1997: Alliance
Following the dramatic failure of the BSP government in 1997, the BSP lost a substantial part of its electoral support. Seeking a broader electoral alliance now seemed a logical choice. However, the BSP was unable to attract more alliance partners—as it was the failed incumbent, making association with it was an electoral liability. The three alliance partners of 1994 signed another electoral agreement, formed the 1997 "Democratic Left" alliance, and contested the "predetermined elections" (*Capital* 1997b). Plagued by the "guilt" attributed to it for the economic crisis of 1996–1997 and various internal struggles between the BSP leadership and the alliance partners, the Democratic Left got only about 22 percent of the vote and 25 percent of the seats in the 1997 parliament (*Capital* 1997a).

Electoral Strategy in 2001: "Coalition for Bulgaria"
By late 2000, the BSP saw a possibility to make a comeback. The party had finally accepted a reform platform and elected reform-minded leadership. The SDS government had become quite unpopular, and BEL—a major competitor for the left vote in 1997—was suffering from internal dissent and was in no position to challenge the BSP successfully. However, the BSP seemed unable to benefit from this electoral situation. By late 2000, its popularity was barely over 13 percent (NCIOM, 2001). In an attempt to enlarge its electoral support, the BSP sought and formed its largest electoral alliance. In early 2001, 19 parties and organizations with socialist or social-democratic ideology formed an alliance called "Coalition for Bulgaria."[10] It should be noted that the electoral alliance built upon the already existing political union called the NL. Both the Coalition for Bulgaria and the NL were representative of the attempt to unify the Bulgarian "left" political space—a process that was paralleled by BEL as well.[11]

The members of the Coalition for Bulgaria included those of the NL and had either previously contested elections alone or had just formed. The new alliance defined itself as a broad, left-centrist electoral formation that had a single platform and would run common lists (Coalition for Bulgaria, 2001). The alliance won 48 seats in the legislature, of which 22 were distributed among BSP leaders.

There is no doubt that the majority of the expense of the electoral campaign of the alliance was met and the work carried out by the BSP's members and structures. There is also little doubt that the electoral benefit of forming the alliance was minimal for the BSP. In fact, the party experienced a lot of internal discontent over having joined the alliance, because local branches and members were dissatisfied working for the political benefit of other parties (Krusteva 2003). But the official reason the BSP gave for having formed the alliance was that it was to ideologically unify the left and to realize the "idea" of social democracy in Bulgaria (Krusteva 2003; Coalition for Bulgaria 2001). However, it seems much more realistic to suppose that the BSP decided to seek an alliance as a final attempt to build up electoral support. In addition, just as in 1991, the alliance allowed the party to further legitimize itself. This time, however, legitimacy came from abroad.

As already referred to in chapter 2, the PES and the Socialist International had been making conscious efforts to unite the various social democratic parties in Bulgaria since the mid-1990s. The BSP, then still relatively unreformed, was excluded from the early stages of this process. In fact, the BEL's creation in 1997 was supported substantially by PES because the European socialists saw BEL as the potential "democratic" center that could unite the social democrats in Bulgaria (Krusteva 2003; Avramov 2002; Zankov 2003).

However, by 1999, the BSP shed the last remaining features of its undemocratic past and clearly made the choice to support a pro-European position. It became part of the PES-organized unification processes and started to contest the focal place of Bulgarian social democracy with BEL. This process was paralleled by a decrease in electoral support for BEL, which made the BSP the only possible "unifier." As already discussed, BEL refused to be part of a BSP-dominated consolidation process, arguing that it had the original unifier status by virtue of its initial cooperation with PES (Zankov 2003).

The two processes of unification continued parallel to each other with BEL refusing to accept the BSP as a social-democratic party, and the BSP refusing to accept anything but an alliance on its own terms. The 2001 strategy was thus an attempt of the BSP not only to secure greater electoral support but also to gain the approval of PES and the Socialist International. By 2003, it seemed that the BSP's electoral strategy had worked—its acceptance process in the Socialist International was moving along and BEL's membership had been "frozen." In addition, the BSP was doing well internally. Despite the limited number of BSP members of parliament, the party was seen as *the* one important factor in the alliance and was clearly the most popular political force in the country as of late 2003.[12]

Electoral Strategy in 2005: 'Coalition for Bulgaria' Reduced
As the NDSV government was suffering increased criticism and the center-right was committing political suicide by continuing to fragment in 2004–2005, the BSP solidified its position as the most

popular political party in Bulgaria. BEL/BSD was no longer a threat, although one of the BSP partners in 2001—the United Labor Party—did abandon the BSP alliance in favor of a tie up with the BSD.

The BSP's stronger position allowed it to form an alliance with fewer members—it no longer needed the validation the previous broad alliance gave it. It signed an agreement with seven other parties, and thus significantly reduced the size of the alliance and the number of non-BSP people that were given top positions in the candidate lists (Vencislavova 2005). Thus, it managed to keep most of the 82 seats that the Coalition for Bulgaria won for itself. Only 4 mandates went to the alliance partners. By 2005, the BSP's tendency to form broad alliances with little benefit seemed to have been tamed a little. Nevertheless, even in 2005, nobody doubted that the bulk of the campaign work for the coalition was again carried out by the BSP and the majority of the support came from its members, which made the alliance redundant yet again.

FIDESZ-MPP: from an Alternative Youth Organization to a Conservative Party in Power

FIDESZ was one of the "new" democratic parties that were established in Hungary in the late 1980s. In 1990 FIDESZ was "little more than an anticommunist political club" with a liberal ideology and loose membership (Toka 1995b, 38; FIDESZ 1989). However, by 1993, advocating the "freedom of the individual to as great extent as possible" did not seem to be politically plausible, and FIDESZ moved to a more conservative position. By 1998 it had become the strongest conservative party in Hungary. FIDESZ (then FIDESZ-MPP) formed a conservative government with the MDF and FKGP in 1998 and remained in government until 2002.

Over the years, FIDESZ suffered from various internal conflicts but never split formally. Instead, it attracted a number of smaller political formations to its structures. The evolution of FIDESZ is presented in figure 3.10.

Electoral Targets
The goals of FIDESZ have evolved from a primary interest in parliamentary representation (1988–1994) into a clear desire to control the executive (1995 to the present). In its early years, FIDESZ continued in the tradition set by its original platform, which called for a change of the system through parliamentary means but did

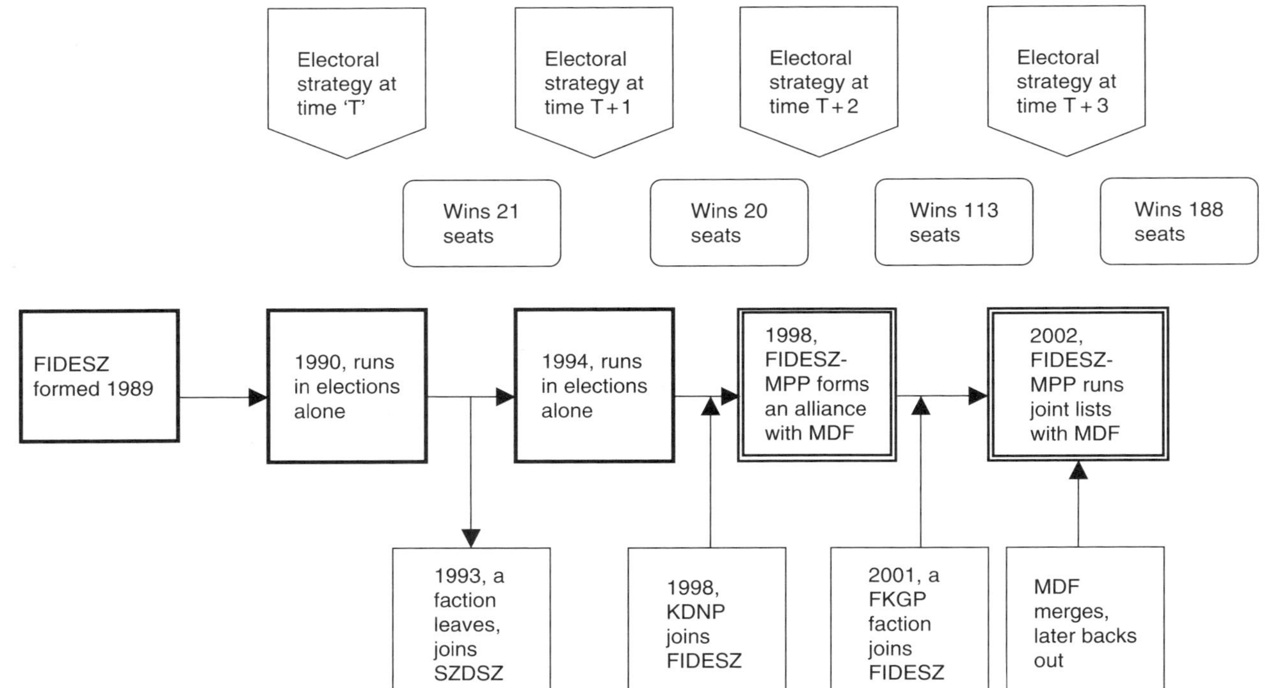

Figure 3.10 FIDESZ-MPP, process of party formation and electoral competition, phases 1, 2, and 3.

not envision any bigger role for the youth organization (FIDESZ 1989).

In many ways, the change in the party's aspirations was influenced by the reality that allowed FIDESZ to emerge as a potential contestant for control of the executive. The MDF's fragmentation during 1990–1994 created a political vacuum on the center-right that FIDESZ could fill (Kiss 2002, 757). After further fragmentation of the KDNP in 1997, FIDESZ was left with few competitors for the position of a leading political force on the center right. On its behalf, the youth organization had by then matured: it had removed the age requirement for membership in 1993 and changed its name to FIDESZ-MPP; its leaders had turned from hip young dissidents into savvy politicians who knew how to capitalize on popular political attitudes (Schopflin 2002).

Thus, the party's electoral target has been to acquire enough parliamentary seats so as to control the governing process in Hungary. To this end, according to the party president Tibor Navracsics, FIDESZ-MPP has tried to unite the conservative political parties in Hungary so that it can come to claim a majority of seats in the legislature and thereby control the executive (Navracsicz 2003). FIDESZ governed the country in a coalition with the MDF and the FKGP during 1998–2002 and did not hide its aspirations to continue to do so after the 2002 elections.

FIDESZ: Formation and Electoral Strategy in 1990
FIDESZ was created in 1988 as an alternative to the Communist Youth organization. It united young people who shared "basic principles of democracy," and when multiparty elections became a possibility, it evolved into a political party (FIDESZ 1989; Hollis 1999, 249). The party membership was limited to people under 35 years of age, a restriction that was removed in 1993. It contested the first democratic elections independently and won 5.44 percent of seats in parliament. Then still a liberal party, FIDESZ did not participate in the conservative MDF-FKGP-KDNP government of 1990–1994.

Electoral Strategy in 1994
During 1993 FIDESZ began to experience its first and probably most serious internal conflict. Part of the party's leadership was advocating a turn to a more conservative ideological position, a step that was bitterly opposed by some of the founding members (Racz and Kukorelli 1995, 259; Fodor 2003). The struggle was won by the conservative

faction, led by the FIDESZ chairman Orban, and the liberal faction left FIDESZ and joined the SZDSZ.

In 1994, FIDESZ contested elections on its own again. There had been earlier discussions and even a signed pact of electoral cooperation between the SZDSZ and FIDESZ; however, after the defection of the liberal faction this arrangement became untenable. The departure of FIDESZ liberals led to a sharp drop in the party's popularity, and by the 1994 elections FIDESZ was a conservative but "minor opposition force" (Racz and Kukorelli 1995, 259). The party won about 5 percent of the vote and formed the sixth largest parliamentary faction in the 1994 parliament (see table 3.8).

Electoral Strategy in 1998: Allying with MDF
In May 1995 FIDESZ changed its name from FIDESZ to FIDESZ-MPP to symbolize its transformation into a serious conservative political party. During the 1994–1998 interelection period, the development of FIDESZ was helped by the fragmentation of the other conservative parties. For example, the KDNP suffered internal conflicts and in 1997 disbanded their parliamentary faction, with most of their deputies joining FIDESZ (Toole 2000, 295). Overall, the FIDESZ parliamentary group grew by 60 percent during the 1994–1998 parliamentary term (Toole 2000, 294).

By early 1998, opinion polls could not predict a clear winner of the coming elections in Hungary. That there would be a coalition government after the elections was obvious. Opinion-poll results in early 1998 placed FIDESZ as having gained substantially from the previous round of elections, but it was still the second most-popular party in Hungary (the MSZP still maintained its dominance) (Reti 1998). FIDESZ then took an important decision that might have proven crucial for its future.

As it became clear that the MDF's popularity was not more than 2 percent and it would not be able to surpass the electoral threshold that would allow it to enter parliament on its own, FIDESZ decided to support MDF candidates. The MDF and FIDESZ-MPP ran joint lists in certain localities, thus effectively forming an electoral alliance. This arrangement allowed the MDF to place enough representatives in parliament and saved it from political marginalization (Navracsics 2003; Szoke 2003). At the same time, it provided FIDESZ-MPP with some parliamentary support that would have been lost otherwise. With the FKGP's 44 seats, the center-right managed to emerge as a narrow victor in the final distribution of seats in the 1998 parliament and proceeded to form a coalition government (Racz 2000, 336).

Electoral Strategy in 2002: FIDESZ-MPP/MDF Merger?
During the year leading to the 2002 election, FIDESZ-MPP decided to attempt to create a catchall conservative party that would unite all center-right formations of political significance in the country (Navracsics 2003). Parallel to this move, the fragmentation of the second-largest conservative party in the coalition, the FKGP, intensified. According to some, this process was carefully orchestrated by the FIDESZ-MPP leadership, which wanted "to create an exclusive position for itself on the right" (Ilonszki and Kurtan 2002). A scandal involving one of the FKGP governmental ministers ended with the expulsion of the party chairman from the party, the defection of about one-third of the deputies to the FIDESZ parliamentary group, and the creation of various factions within the FKGP.

FIDESZ-MPP thus had most of the conservative parties under its influence. With the FKGP in disarray, FIDESZ-MPP signed an electoral agreement with the revived KDNP (now within FIDESZ) and the MDF to run common lists at the local, regional, and national levels (Szoke 2003; Navracsics 2003). Some have even referred to this agreement as a merger between the two parties because the lists were under the name FIDESZ-MPP/MDF, and a future organizational merger was being planned at election time (Economist Intelligence Unit 2003).

The electoral alliance won 48 percent of the seats and became the largest group in parliament (see table 3.9). However, no other conservative parties made it into parliament, which prevented the formation of a center-right government. This development was seen by many as FIDESZ-MPP's undoing (Szoke 2003; Navracsics 2003). After the formation of the MSZP-SZDSZ government, the MDF deputies formed a separate parliamentary group and, despite FIDESZ's efforts, the party has refused to carry out the planned consolidation any further. In fact, according to MDF's vice-president Laszlo Szoke, the joint lists in 2002 were a mistake, and the MDF will do everything possible to preserve its independence in the future (Szoke 2003). The 2002 alliance thus seems to have been a failure for both FIDESZ-MPP and the MDF. The former realized the limits of being a broad, catchall party, and the latter the dangers of giving up its independence. In addition, both parties failed to realize their goals of controlling and participating in the executive.

Conclusion

This chapter has provided a description of the behavior of six selected parties over several different rounds of elections in two party-systems. It has presented some initial evidence that parties change their electoral strategies in ways that they believe will help them to realize their goals of legislative or executive office.

The BSP and FIDESZ (after 1995) have behaved in ways predicted by the model—as parties trying to gain control of the executive, they have tried to increase their presence in parliament through the formation of broad alliances. The DPS and the SZDSZ, realizing their ability to secure a place in the executive by being "balancing" parties in parliament, have chosen to stay independent as long as their electoral support was not under question. BEL and Munkaspart were formed when their leaders believed that their "mother" parties were not responding to the "demand" of the electorate that they could capitalize on.

However, the discussion has also pointed to some differences in the behavior of the parties. BEL and Munkaspart have been in a similar situation over the years—mostly outside parliament—but BEL has gone through numerous and various electoral strategies, while Munkaspart has chosen to stay independent and contest elections on its own. The Tomov-led faction within the BSP and the Fodor-led liberal faction within FIDESZ have chosen divergent paths in similar circumstances. The DPS seems to have reacted to a decreasing electoral support much faster than the SZDSZ. Thus, a more detailed analysis of the factors that have contributed to these decisions is clearly needed and will be presented in chapter 4.

Notes

*Some of the data and discussion in this section has previously been published in Spirova (2005).

1. Unlike other communist parties in the region, the MSZMP did not simply rename itself but de facto dissolved and asked its members to reregister with a newly founded party, the MSZP. In this way, the party not only established a clear break with the past but also experienced the most dramatic decline in membership compared with other parties in a similar situation in the region (Toka 1995).
2. In many ways, the evolution of GOR/BEL/BSD reflects the realization of the political ambition of one politician, Alexander Tomov, who has been the leader of all formations. At the time of BEL's creation as

a political party in 1997, his personal political ambition was seen as the major driving force for the creation of the party as well as its predecessors (*Capital* 1997a; Staridolska and Gospodinova 2005).

3. All post-1989 Bulgarian cabinets are listed in table 1 of Appendix D.

4. In addition, the BSP was suffering from internal dissent, which in early 1997 resulted in the resignation and departure of several reform-minded politicians—Elena Poptodorova, Nikolaj Kamov, and Filip Bokov, among others. They indicated their willingness to associate themselves with GOR (BSD 2003, 40).

5. Although BEL did not get a chance to register officially as a party before the elections (due to their early scheduling), it did so immediately afterwards, and will thus be treated as a new "party."

6. At this point, BEL (following the example of the BSP) allowed the creation of internal "platforms" (factions) in an effort to maintain democracy and unity in the face of absence of complete agreement. After the 2000 split, this article of the party code was eliminated.

7. Representation in parliament is paralleled by an attempt to represent workers' interests through any form of participation in local governments. Thus, participating in several local government coalitions, particularly in the northern and eastern regions of Hungary, has been enough to keep the party viable even in the face of its inability to surpass the national electoral threshold (Vajda 2003).

8. In the case of Hungary, the specifics of its mixed electoral system allow for two types of electoral alliances—appearing together in a single list in its PR part and running common candidates in the SMD part, or reaching agreements to support each other's candidates in the second round of the SMD part while running independent lists for the PR part of the competition and separate candidates in the first round. For the purposes of the current study, the concept of electoral alliance is limited only to the first type of alliance as it is the one that involves a change in labels. The SZDSZ has signed agreements for second round alliances; it has never (unlike other Hungarian parties) run common lists.

9. These parties are listed in appendix B but most of them remained insignificant for Bulgarian politics.

10. The alliance, as current commentaries argued, was a sign of desperation among BSP leaders (Mandzukov 2000b). It had to agree to give up more than half of the leading positions on the alliance district lists of candidates, while the total electoral support brought by the 18 organizations was estimated to about 2 to 3 percent of the vote. For example, the NCIOM reports about 13 percent electoral support for the BSP and about 2 percent support for the rest of the alliance partners in March 2001 (NCIOM 2001).

11. The NL was formed in early 2000 by four parties—the BSP, one of the parties that had inherited the original BSDP, the United Labor

Party (OBT), and the Social Humanism movement that had left BEL. The basis for the formation of the NL was the natural process of unification of the fragmented "left" (social-democratic) political formations: "The New Left was a political formation . . . that tried to develop and advocate a unified 'leftist' policy in Bulgaria . . . to build on what existed and gradually evolve into a common ideology (Krusteva 2003)." Originally, there had been discussion of merging the four founding members of the NL in a way that the Bulgarian Social Democrats did later, but the idea was only favored by the smaller partners and has yet to materialize (Krusteva 2003).

12. Whether the other 18 alliance partners will benefit from the alliance beyond getting one seat in the 2001 legislature each remains to be seen. The previous BSP alliance partners—the BZNS-AS and Ekoglanost—disappeared from political competition largely because of their cooperation with the BSP, a fact that BEL was quick to point out while discussing its refusal to join in the alliance. One of the current alliance partners, the Communist Party of Bulgaria (CPoB), seemed to be well aware of the BSP's tendency to overpower its partners. Consequently, the CPoB only joined the alliance after it had signed a very strict agreement for the distribution of places on the candidate lists and of seats in Parliament (Vanev 2003).

Explaining Formation, Persistence, and Change: Bulgarian and Hungarian Trends

This chapter provides a detailed analysis of the party behavior described in chapter 3. It presents some qualitative tests of hypotheses H1, H2 and H3 by examining the impact of electoral success and failure and the expectation of electoral volatility on the formation and evolution of political parties; of hypotheses H5 and H6 by investigating further the relationship between party ideology and party electoral strategies; and of hypothesis H9 by examining the links between organizational trends and party behavior. Finally, the chapter provides some insights into the external events that have impacted the choice of electoral strategies of the political parties. As a larger systemic consideration is clearly needed for the test of these proposed relationships, the present discussion incorporates the experience of other parties within the two systems as well.[1] However, the primary focus on the behavior of the six original parties is preserved.

Electoral Support and Party Electoral Strategies

Expectations

H3 proposed that office-seeking parties form only when they have reason to believe that they will enjoy enough electoral support to obtain office. In the absence of direct evidence of this support (such as from opinion polls), parties will use the expectation of electoral volatility as a proxy for such evidence.

Further, the hypotheses suggested that, once formed, parties will choose electoral strategies that promise to give them the chance of winning office. The choice of electoral strategies will be made before each election, with a consideration of previous performance and current electoral popularity. Thus, although developments in interelection periods will complicate matters, we can expect that electoral failure at previous elections will encourage parties to seek alternative strategies, and success will encourage parties to preserve the same strategy.

Observed Behavior: Expected Electoral Support and Party Formation

Of the six parties discussed in detail, five were formed before the first democratic election in each system, and they used the original expansion of electoral demand to establish their electoral presence. GOR was formed in 1993 at a time when its "mother" party was enjoying high popularity, which made the decision on its formation riskier. However, GOR's choice of an alliance electoral strategy at its first election in 1994 is an indication that the party had realized the limitations of its electoral support and tried to preempt the electoral risk by forming the DAR alliance.

An examination of the pattern of new entries into the party systems in Bulgaria and Hungary reveals that the largest number of new entrants into each party system was recorded during the first two rounds of democratic elections. This finding supports the propositions in H3 that periods of high expected electoral volatility should see a higher number of new entrants. For the present purposes, using Simon Hug's distinctions, new entrants are defined as parties that had not contested elections on their own before—they could be either brand-new parties or splinters of others. Mergers and alliances are not considered new entrants here (Hug 2001, 13–14).

In both Bulgaria and Hungary, the number of new parties that have entered the party system since the early 1990s has been relatively small—one or two new parties do so at each election round (table 4.1). The major difference has been in the level of support they receive. The new entrants in Bulgaria have gained at least twice as much of the vote as those in Hungary. Several events in the two systems deserve further explication—the high number of new party entries in the 1991 elections and the 2001 entry of the NDSV in Bulgaria, and the entry of the Centrum Part (Center Party, or CP) in the 2002 elections in Hungary.

Table 4.1   "New" Parties in Bulgaria and Hungary, 1990–2005

		First election	Second election	Third election	Fourth election	Fifth election	Sixth election
BU	Number and % of parties with more than 1% of the vote	2 (50)	5 (50)	2 (20)	1 (14)	2 (25)	3 (30)
	Vote %	44	12.59	5.28	5.57	46.37	20.2
HU	Number and % of parties with more than 1% of the vote	8 (80)	2 (18)	1 (11)	1 (16)		
	Vote %	84	4.14	1.34	3.9		

In 1991, three of the five new parties/alliances that entered the electoral competition in Bulgaria were SDS splinters: SDS-Center, SDS-Liberals, and BZNS–Nikola Petkov (BZNS-NP). These new entries were a direct result of the fractionalization of the SDS during 1991. This process started in early 1991 when the policy positions of the "big" members of the SDS (parties that enjoyed high membership, i.e., the BSDP, the BZNS-NP, and the ZP) and the "powerful" groups (small formations with popular leaders) started to diverge significantly (Karasimeonov 2002, 125). As a result, the three "big" parties originally decided to form a "centrist" SDS, but finally contested elections as three separate entities. Although they formally established alliances with other smaller splinters, *de facto*, the SDS-Center *was* the BSDP, and the SDS-Liberals was heavily dominated by the ZP.

One of the major reasons for the determined independence of the BSDP, the BZNS-NP, and the ZP was the expected high approval from the SDS supporters. According to an opinion poll in April 1991, the BSDP contributed 27 percent of the support for the SDS, the BZNS-NP 24 percent, and the ZP around 8 percent (Ribareva and Nikolova 2000, 52–53). In other words, these were the strongest constituents of the most popular political formation in Bulgaria. While other factors certainly contributed to the SDS split, the mistaken belief that they enjoyed high enough support to make it into parliament was crucial in the decision of the BSDP, the BZNS-NP and the ZP to leave the SDS and form their own alliances. Opinion polls right up to election night continued to list their support as being over the 4 percent threshold, which made the final election results shocking for most (see table 3.2 for results).

Probably, the most surprising and consequential entry into the Bulgarian party system has been that of the NDSV in 2001. The appearance of this political competitor in April 2001 and its electoral triumph three months later are certainly unique in the political development of the post-communist systems. It is the only case of a party that entered the political competition at a relatively late point in time aspiring to control the executive, and achieved its goal at the first try. The great popular support that the personality of the Bulgarian ex-monarch Simeon Sax-Coburg-Gotha used to enjoy in the country was the major factor in this success, but the reason he chose to enter politics at this time was the expectation of high level of volatility in the country as of early 2001.

As already mentioned in chapter 3, by early 2001, the SDS and its government were suffering a substantial drop in popularity (compared with the 1997 election). However, the BSP, which would logically have been the party to benefit from this high disapproval of the incumbent, was doing even worse according to opinion polls (NCIOM 2001). Three months before the elections, the largest percentage of the electorate (27) in Bulgaria had not made up their minds about their electoral preferences, and the second largest group expressed no intention of voting (table 4.2) (NCIOM 2001).

Although the support for royalist political formations (Federation "Tsardom Bulgaria," or KTsB) was not high either, the situation was

Table 4.2 Support for parties in Bulgaria, February–March 2001. Answers to the question: "Which party would you vote for if elections were held today?"

Party	February %	March %
SDS	15.3	17.0
ODS	6.8	7.9
BSP	15.8	13.6
DPS	3.9	3.9
BEL	1.3	1.4
Gergiovden	2.1	1.0
VMRO	1.6	0.6
BBB	0.9	0.5
KTsB	3.9	7.4
Another party	2.7	2.2
Not decided	25.7	27.2
Will not vote	20.0	17.3

Source: NCIOM 2001.

very suitable for a major entry into the system, a move that Simeon Sax-Coburg-Gotha seemed to have been waiting to make for some time (in 1997 he had supported the ONS, and in earlier elections had not hidden his political preferences). After the declaration of his intention to contest elections as part of a political party and participate in the republican government of the country, his electoral support jumped to 34 percent and the projected voter turnout increased by 8 percent (NCIOM 2001). The ex-monarch's political entity swept the elections in June 2001 by gaining 42.74 percent of the vote.[2]

The NDSV's creation and its entry into the system provide a clear empirical example of the propositions of the model. As a party that wanted to control the executive, the NDSV needed to control at least a plurality of the seats in parliament. To achieve this objective, the party in turn needed the willingness of the electorate to abandon the established dominant parties (SDS and BSP). In 1997, the SDS was the party that led the country out of the BSP-government crisis leaving no room for a monarch-led formation. By 2001 however, neither of the two major parties in Bulgaria was enjoying great popularity, which allowed for a much more certain electoral support for the NDSV.

Turning to the Hungarian parties, the emergence of FIDESZ as a major contestant for control of the executive in 1998 was in many ways a result of a similar process—except it was an existing party that could capitalize on the absence of a strong party on the center-right in the system. In Hungary, no new entrant into the electoral competition since the MDF in 1990 has managed to gain control of the executive at its first election. However, considerations of electoral support seem to have motivated the founders of CP and its entry at the 2001 elections in Hungary. One of the main reasons for the CP's creation in 2001 was the fact that, according to opinion surveys, only about 50 percent of the Hungarian electorate supported the two major parties (MSZP and FIDESZ), and about 15 percent of the Hungarian electorate was in the middle of the ideological spectrum—that is, they embraced an ideology that was neither left nor right (Kupa 2003). Hoping to capitalize on this situation, the CP contested elections in 2001 and managed to get 3.86 percent of the vote.

Observed Behavior: Electoral Performance and the Choice of Strategies

Next, we turn to an examination of the behavior pattern of already established parties to examine their choice of strategies following success/failure to achieve electoral targets. Of the six parties discussed in detail in chapter 3, Munkaspart, BEL, and the BSP are the ones that have failed most often in achieving their targets. Munkaspart has never made it into parliament, which could have allowed it access to the executive at the national level. BEL has failed to do the same two out of the three times it has contested elections; and the BSP has failed to gain control of the executive in three out of the five times it has tried to do so. FIDESZ has only failed once as a party seeking control of the executive, and the DPS and the SZDSZ have never failed to make it into parliament and have only once not been invited to participate in the executive.

Overall, parties have clearly responded to electoral success and failure, which provides some confirmation for the relevant hypotheses. Faced with a shrinking electoral demand by 2001, BEL sought an alliance in 2001 and a further merger in 2003, which contributed to the consolidation of the party system. BEL expressed strong concerns with electoral performance and a realization that if the party were to continue its political activities, it needed to unite with others so as to capture the social-democratic vote (Zankov 2003a; Avramov 2002). Similarly, following failures in the 1997 and 2001 elections, the BSP has attempted to increase its electoral presence by allying with other similar parties in the NL and in "Coalition for Bulgaria." After its failure in 2002, FIDESZ-MPP has chosen to continue the consolidation of the center-right in Hungary and to look for alternative ways to increase its electoral support. The party has expressed a clear understanding of the fact that it needs to able to attract more votes if it is to achieve its goal of control of the executive at the next elections (Navracsics 2003). The DPS and the SZDSZ seem to realize the threat of decreasing electoral support—the DPS has chosen to preempt it by allying with others, while the SZDSZ has not. However, SZDSZ leaders have shown an understanding that a change is certainly needed by the next elections if the party is to keep its parliamentary representation (Fodor 2003).

At first glance, Munkaspart is the one party that contradicts H1 and H2. Despite repeated electoral failure, it has chosen to stay independent and not ally or form coalitions with any party. Its behavior contrasts sharply with that of BEL and even more so with the behavior of the CPoB, which has been in a situation similar to that of Munkaspart. The CPoB is a legislative-office-seeking party that formed in 1995 and united hard-line Marxists. It contested elections in 1997 as part of a small leftist electoral alliance, but failed to gain any representation in parliament. As a result, when the BSP formed the Coalition for Bulgaria, the CPoB joined the coalition and has become one of its most active members (Krusteva 2003; Vanev 2003). Although the coalition members were fearful of a BSP dominance of the alliance, they saw cooperation with the BSP as their best option. The CPoB sent one representative to parliament through the coalition lists in 2001 and one in 2005.

The difference in the behavior patterns of the CPoB and Munkaspart might not be so striking if we take into account their different evaluation of parliamentary representation. Munkaspart has tried and has been able to secure an active place in local and regional politics, while the CPoB has carried much more limited and unsuccessful local political campaigns (Vanev 2003). For CPoB, representation in parliament has been the key to further existence and activities (Vanev 2003). Thus, the difference in the electoral strategies of the two lends some support to the proposition in chapter 2 that certain parties will compensate for parliamentary representation with other forms of political participation.

An examination of the pattern of behavior of a larger number of parties in Bulgaria and Hungary allows us to look for further evidence of the empirical applicability of the theoretical propositions. For the present purposes, of particular interest are parties that have tried and failed to gain representation in parliament and their choice of electoral strategies at the next elections. All parties that have gathered more than 1 percent but less than 4 or 5 percent of the vote in Bulgaria and Hungary are examined. Tables 4.3–4.9 list all parties of interest, their electoral strategy and electoral support at each election, and their electoral strategy at the next one.

In Bulgaria, at the 1990 elections, there are no parties that match these criteria. Parties seem to have either made it into parliament or got a minuscule percentage of the vote. This can be explained partly by the early scheduling of elections: despite the high number of parties competing, only 22 parties of a total of 42 managed to get any votes (see appendix B, table 1), and only four got more than 1 percent of the votes.

In the 1991 elections, seven parties failed to cross the 4 percent threshold but got more than 1 percent of the vote (table 4.3). Of them, one had been in the previous parliament (BZNS), three were splinters (SDS-Center, SDS-Liberals, BZNS-NP) of a party (SDS) that had been in parliament, one had got less than 1 percent of the vote in the 1991 elections, and two were new parties.

By the 1994 elections, three of these seven parties were still using the same strategy as in 1991(BBB; Bulgarian National Radical Party, or BNRP; KTsB). Two of them had just been formed before the 1991

Table 4.3 Bulgarian parties outside parliament (1991–1994) with more than 1 percent of the vote: 1991 electoral strategy and percent of the vote, and 1994 electoral strategy

Party	1991 electoral strategy	1991 performance, % of the vote	1994 electoral strategy
BZNS	Runs alone	3.86	Seeks and joins an electoral alliance
BZNS-Nikola Petkov	Runs alone	3.44	Seeks and joins an electoral alliance
BSDP, as part of SDS-Center	Seeks and forms an alliance	3.2	Seeks and joins a broader alliance
Green Party, as part of SDS-Liberals	Seeks and joins an alliance	2.81	Seeks and joins a broader alliance
KTsB (Kingdom of Bulgaria Federation)	Runs alone	1.82	Runs alone
BBB (Bulgarian Business Block)	Runs alone	1.32	Runs alone
BNRP (Bulgarian National Radical Party)	Runs alone	1.13	Runs alone

elections, and none of the three had even come close to crossing the threshold that year. This might suggest that defeat in the 1991 elections was not seen as a failure, perhaps because the parties were newcomers to politics and needed to establish themselves.

The situation for the other four was quite different. All four competitors had had parliamentary representation before, and three of them had chosen a different strategy, hoping to achieve representation again. For them, the 1991 failure seemed to be an important indication of the potential of these electoral strategies, and all four changed strategy by the 1994 elections.

In the 1994–1997 period there are several parties that are of interest (table 4.4). Of the five alliances/parties that failed to gain representation in parliament, three had previously participated in parliament: DAR (discussed in detail in the section, "Parties Out of Parliament: GOR/BEL and Munkaspart"); New Choice Union (SNI, an alliance of splinters of the SDS); and the Patriotic Union (an alliance of six parties, some previously part of the 1991 BSP coalition). The other two—the BKP and KTsB—had never had legislative representation before 1994. Of the five alliances/parties, only one—the BKP—continued its 1994 electoral strategy in 1997. The members of the other four joined in new alliances, hibernated, or merged. Of the 12 parties that contested the 1994 elections as members

Table 4.4 Bulgarian parties outside parliament (1994–1997) with more than 1 percent of the vote: 1994 electoral strategy and percent of the vote, and 1997 electoral strategy

Party	1994 electoral strategy	1994 performance, % of the vote	1997 electoral strategy
BSDP (within DAR)			Splits, one faction merges, another faction seeks to ally
ZP (within DAR)	Form electoral alliance	3.79	Seeks an alliance
GOR (within DAR)			Merges
ASP (within DAR)			N/A
BKP (Bulgarian Communist Party)	Runs alone	1.51	Runs alone
Center for New Politics (within New Choice Union—SNI)	Form electoral alliance	1.49	Seeks a broader alliance
Rally for Democracy (SD)(within New Choice Union—SNI)			Hibernates
Six parties within PS—Patriotic Union	Form electoral alliance	1.43	One runs alone, two seek alliances, three hibernate
FTsB (Federation "Tsardom Bulbargia")	Runs alone	1.41	Seeks an alliance

of alliances, only one chose to run alone in the next elections. The others changed their strategies in the predicted manner.

In 1997 parties in Bulgaria seemed to have learned from previous experience. Alliance formation seemed to have been quite popular, and the percentage of wasted vote was at its lowest (table 4.5). There are only two parties of current interest—the BKP and the Alliance for the King (OT). Both of them ran alone in 1997, failed to enter parliament, and did not contest the 2001 elections in the same format: the BKP did not run in elections, and the OT joined another royalist formation in 2001.

Failure also seemed to have had an effect on the behavior of the parties that failed to cross the 4 percent threshold in 2001 (table 4.6). Of the seven parties (five of which were united in two alliances), all changed

Table 4.5 Bulgarian parties outside parliament (1997–2001) with more than 1 percent of the vote: 1997 electoral strategy and percent of the vote, and 2001 electoral strategy

Party	1997 electoral strategy	1997 performance, % of the vote	2001 electoral strategy
BKP (Bulgarian Communist Party)	Runs alone	1.3	Hibernates
OT (Alliance for the King)	Runs alone	1.12	Disbands

Table 4.6 Bulgarian parties outside parliament (2001–2005) with more than 1 percent of the vote: 2001 electoral strategy and percent of the vote, and 2005 electoral strategy

Party	2001 electoral strategy	2001 performance, % of the vote	2005 electoral strategy
Gergiovden	Alliance	3.63	Joins a broader alliance (ODS)
VMRO			Joins a broader alliance (BNS)
Alliance "Simeon II"	Runs alone	3.44	Hibernates
National Union for Tzar Simeon II	Runs alone	1.7	Hibernates
Bulgarian Euroleft			Merges
BESDP (United Social-Democrats)	Alliance	0.98	Merges
BZNS			Joins a broader alliance (ODS)

their strategies: VMRO, Gergiodven, and the BZNS all joined bigger alliances that are now successful—the three parties are represented in parliament after the 2005 elections. The royalist parties—Alliance Simeon II and National Union for Tzar Simeon II—chose to hibernate, which was a predictable strategy. The parties had benefited significantly from the 2001 entry of Simeon Sax-Cobug-Gotha by winning votes as copycats and had no real political presence of their own (Staridolska and Gospodinova 2005). BEL and BESDP merged, as already discussed, in an attempt to avoid further failures. Thus, all parties of interest reacted in the predicted way.

Table 4.7   Hungarian parties outside parliament (1990–1994) with more than
1 percent of the vote: 1990 electoral strategy and percent of the vote, and 1994
electoral strategy

Party	1990 electoral strategy	1990 performance		1994 electoral strategy
		PR vote %	Seats %	
MSZMP (Hungarian Socialist Workers' Party, or Munkaspart)	Runs alone	3.68	0	Runs alone
MSZDP (Social Democratic Party of Hungary)	Runs alone	3.55	0	Runs alone
VP (Entrepreneurs' Party)	Runs alone	1.89	0	Runs alone
HVK (Patriotic Elections Coalition)	Runs alone	1.87	0	Disbands

An examination of the pattern of party behavior in Hungary reveals
a somewhat different process. In the 1990 elections, there were four
parties that are of interest (table 4.7). Of the four, all were new
(although the status of Munkaspart can be debated), and three of them
preserved their electoral strategies at the next election. One (Patriotic
Election Coalition, or HVK) changed strategy as expected, given its
failure to achieve representation. The other three, however, chose to
run alone again despite clear indications that they were unable to surmount the electoral threshold.

In 1994 there were five parties that meet the criteria of interest.
All five parties, none of which had had parliamentary representation
before (table 4.8), ran alone. Three of them chose to do so again
in 1998, while two disbanded and exited the electoral competition. Of the three that persisted, one was a new party and the other
two—Munkaspart and the MSZDP—had already faced failure twice,
which makes their behavior more surprising. There was no cooperation or electoral coordination between Munkaspart and the MSZMP
despite their common absence of electoral success and their relative
ideological closeness.

In 1998–2002, there were only three parties that gained more
than one precent of the vote but less than 5 percent (table 4.9).
Of them, two parties had representation in parliament previously.

Table 4.8 Hungarian parties outside parliament (1994–1998) with more than 1 percent of the vote: 1994 electoral strategy and percent of the vote, and 1998 electoral strategy

Party	1994 electoral strategy	1994 performance		1998 electoral strategy
		PR vote %	Seats %	
Munkaspart (ex-MSZMP)	Runs alone	3.19	0	Runs alone
KP (Republican Party)	Runs alone	2.55	0	Disbands
ASZ (Agrarian Alliance)	Runs alone	2.1	0.26[1]	Disbands
MIEP (Party of Hungarian Justice and Life)	Runs alone	1.59	0	Runs alone
MSZDP (Social Democratic Party of Hungary)	Runs alone	0.95	0	Runs alone

[1] Seat won in by-election.

Table 4.9 Hungarian parties outside parliament (1998–2002) with more than 1 percent of the vote: 1998 electoral strategy and percent of the vote, and 2002 electoral strategy

Party	1998 electoral strategy	1998 performance		2002 electoral strategy
		PR vote %	Seats %	
Munkaspart	Runs alone	3.95	0	Runs alone
KDNP (Christian Democratic People's Party)	Runs alone	2.31	0	Merges
MDNP (Hungarian Democratic People's Party)	Runs alone	1.34	0	Merges

Both of them chose strategies as predicted by the model by merging with FIDESZ. Munkaspart, just as in all the previous elections, chose to run alone, refusing to cooperate with any of the other parties, and failed to achieve its electoral goals.

The theoretical propositions also suggest that parties that do well in each election will choose to maintain their current format for the next election. This argument calls for an examination of the choice of electoral strategies of parties that achieve their goals in the previous election. Table 4.10 presents the Bulgarian parties of interest here.

Table 4.10 Parties in parliament in Bulgaria (1990–2001): Electoral strategy and performance, and electoral strategy at following election

Election year	Political party	Electoral strategy	Percent of the vote	Electoral strategy at following election
1990	BSP	Runs alone	47.15	Forms an alliance
	SDS	Runs alone	36.21	Runs alone
	BZNS	Runs alone	8.03	Runs alone
	DPS	Runs alone	6.02	Runs alone
1991	SDS	Runs alone	34.36	Runs alone
	BSP	Runs in alliance	33.14	Runs in alliance
	DPS	Runs alone	7.55	Runs alone
1994	BSP, BZNS, AS Ecoglasnost	Run in alliance	43.5	Run in alliance
	SDS	Runs alone	24.23	Runs in alliance
	NS (BZNS-M, DP)	Run in alliance	6.51	Runs in alliance
	DPS	Runs alone	5.44	Runs in alliance
	BBB	Runs alone	4.73	Runs alone
1997	SDS, DP, BZNS, BSDP and VMRO (ODS)	Run in alliance	49.15	SDS, DP, BZNS, BSDP run in same alliance, VMRO forms a new alliance
	BSP, BZNS-AS, and Ecoglasnost (DemLev)	Run in alliance	22.44	BSP forms a broader alliance, BZNS-AS disbands, Ecoglasnost joins another alliance
	DPS, BZNS-NP, ZP, Party of the Democratic Centre, New Choice, FTsB 9 (ONS)	Run in alliance	9.44	DPS, ZP, and FTsB seek new alliances, NI and PDC disband, and BZNS-NP merges
	EuroLeft (BEL)	Runs alone	5.57	Joins an alliance
	BBB (Bulgarian Business Block)	Runs alone	5.27	Splits in two, both splinters run alone
2001	NDSV (National Movement Simeon the Second)	Runs alone	42.74	Runs alone, a splinter splits and runs alone (NV)
	ODS (United Democratic Forces)—SDS, People's Union: BZNS-NS and DP, BSDP, National MRF	Run in alliance	18.18	SDS, DP, BSDP run in same alliances; BZNS-NS, and National MRF run in other alliances; a splinter from SDS forms a new party

(Continued)

Table 4.10   (*Continued*)

Election year	Political party	Electoral strategy	Percent of the vote	Electoral strategy at following election
	"Coalition for Bulgaria" (BSP, OPT, CPoB, BSDP-2+)	Run in alliance	17.15	BSP, CPoB, and five others run in same alliance, OPT leaves and joins a smaller alliance
	DPS (DPS–Liberal Union–EuroRoma)	Run in alliance	7.45	DPS runs alone, Evroroma runs alone

For the most part, parties behave as expected given their electoral targets and electoral performance. The BSP is one of the parties of interest during 1990–1991. Although it had achieved control of executive office in 1990 by running alone, in 1991 its popularity was being challenged by the SDS and it decided to form an alliance. As already discussed, this alliance was aimed more at achieving democratic legitimacy than at increasing electoral support. In contrast, the SDS, which had lost the 1990 elections but enjoyed increasing electoral support in 1991, not only did not look for alliance partners but did little to prevent its split. The other two parties behaved as expected—having achieved their electoral targets in 1990, and enjoying consistent support, they again ran alone in 1991.

The behavior of the parties in 1991–1994 supports the propositions that previous performance is a major factor in the choice of electoral strategies. The SDS and the DPS had contested elections on their own in 1991. By 1994 both had experienced splits, and despite clear indications that their popularity was declining, the two chose to run alone again. In contrast, the BSP, having failed to achieve its target in 1991, formed a smaller but more beneficial electoral alliance.

In the 1994–1997 period, parties' behavior exhibited a less solid but still relatively consistent pattern. The two parties—the BSP and the SDS—sought to achieve a plurality of seats, and both behaved as expected. The 1994 winner (BSP) preserved its 1994 alliance strategy, and the SDS decided to form a broad alliance that incorporated five parties of similar ideology in its attempt to win a majority of seats. That the BZNS-Mozer (BZNS-M) and the Democratic Party (DP), which had previously contested elections in an alliance by themselves (NS), decided to join the SDS led alliance is surprising. The NS had won legislative representation with a comfortable margin in 1994 and there was little reason to suspect that it would not do the same in 1997 (Kutov 2004). However, the decision of the BZNS-M and the DP was part of a larger process of unification of the right that happened in the interelection period partly under external influence, which will be discussed later. The DPS's decision to ally can be attributed to the drop in its support at the 1994 elections. The BBB's persistence was expected as the party had achieved its goal of legislative representation and was still enjoying relatively high levels of support.

More surprising is the behavior of some of the smaller Bulgarian political parties during the 1997–2001 period. The major parties behaved as could be expected: the SDS and the BSP formed or preserved their alliances in light of the threat by a major new entry in 2001; the DPS abandoned its 1997 alliance and sought a new one, a decision that was partly motivated by its desire to increase its own seats in parliament; the BEL's decision to seek an alliance is explained by the drop in its popularity during the interelection period. However, the exits of the VMRO and the ZP from the ODS and ONS alliances, respectively, and the formation of two BBB splinters are quite surprising in light of the theoretical model of party behavior suggested here.

VMRO was one of the members of the ODS alliance in 1997 and the ZP was part of the ONS alliance. For VMRO, the 1997 electoral alliance was the first opportunity to gain parliamentary representation, and for the ZP the ONS alliance was the first successful alliance since 1990 (all previous alliances with its participation had failed to make it into parliament). In 2001 both parties understood that they would most likely not make it into parliament if they left their respective alliances. Still they both did so and contested the elections in smaller alliances that did not promise to deliver immediate electoral benefits (Dzudzev 2003, Murdzov 2003).

When asked about the choice of electoral strategy in 2001, the leaders of the two parties cited their dissatisfaction with the way they had been treated by the dominant parties in the alliances as the main reason. Both Dzudzev (ZP) and Murdzov (VMRO) argued that preserving the independence and honor of ZP and VMRO as "parties" was more important than the immediate reward of legislative seats. Neither expressed any regrets about leaving the ODS and ONS alliances, respectively, despite the alliances' electoral failures in 2001. These two cases present a clear indication that electoral benefits are not the only determinants of party behavior. Similarly, the appearance of a splinter from the BBB in 2001, at a time when the party was not enjoying great support, also contradicts the expectation that a concern with immediate electoral rewards will dominate the decision making of political parties.

However, in 2005, both VMRO and the ZP sought alternative electoral strategies, which indicated a desire to find alternative ways to legislative office. The ZP joined the Coalition for Bulgaria, and VMRO joined the SSD and the BZNS-NS to form a new alliance, BNS. However, the BNS was clearly a different alliance than the ODS had been—the VMRO chairman became cochairman of the alliance and "equality of partnership" became one of the founding principles of the BNS (BNS 2005). The BNS sent 13 members to parliament, three of whom were VMRO leaders. The ZP's strategy was similar—it also sought a broader alliance that would bring them legislative seats. However, the BSP's policy toward its alliance partners had changed, as discussed in the previous chapter. In 2005 the BSP was no longer willing to "give up" leading places in its candidate lists for the benefit of the small parties that were part of the alliance. The ZP leader was given a nonelectable place in the lists, and the ZP remained outside parliament yet again.

The electoral strategies of the parties of interest in Hungary are presented in table 4.11. For the most part, parties in Hungary seem to behave as expected: those that achieve their electoral targets tend to choose the same electoral strategy again, and when they change strategy, it is mostly in the direction of alliance/merger. However, a few cases are striking. During the 1990–1994 period, the MDF experienced a major split that led to the creation of a new party—the MIEP. The MDF's fragmentation during its first parliamentary term certainly does not fit with the expectation of rational electoral behavior and has been called a clear example of "lack of political learning" (Benoit 1999, 136). The split and the formation of the neo-fascist MIEP in 1992 occurred despite clear indications of lack of electoral support for the party (Minkenberg 2002). However, a major factor in this decision was the expulsion of the MIEP leader Ivan Csurka from the MDF structures after strong ideological divergence between the MDF majority and the extremist faction (Hollis 1999, 287).

Similar concerns are raised by the FKGP's continuous fragmentation during the 1990–2002 period, as well as the appearance of several KDNP splinters in the 1994–1998 period. Both parties had achieved a parliamentary presence on their own in the past and had participated in the executive, but groups within them split during the respective periods and chose to run alone. If the original splits might be attributed exactly to a desire to benefit from the electoral success

Table 4.11 Parties in parliament in Hungary (1990–1998): Electoral strategy and performance, and electoral strategy at following election

Election year	Political party	Electoral strategy	Percent of the seats	Electoral strategy at following election
1990	MDF	Runs alone	42.49	Runs alone; one faction splits and runs alone
	SZDSZ	Runs alone	23.83	Runs alone
	FKGP	Runs alone	11.4	Runs alone, factions split and run alone
	MSZP	Runs alone	8.55	Runs alone
	FIDESZ	Runs alone	5.44	Runs alone
	KDNP	Runs alone	5.44	Runs alone
1994	MSZP	Runs alone	54.15	Runs alone
	SZDSZ	Runs alone	17.88	Runs alone
	MDF	Runs alone	9.84	Runs in alliance
	FKGP	Runs alone	6.74	Runs alone
	KDNP	Runs alone	5.7	Mergers
	FIDESZ	Runs alone	5.18	Runs alone
1998	MSZP	Runs alone	34.72	Runs in alliance
	FIDESZ-MPP and	Runs in alliance	29.27	"Merge"
	MDF	Runs in alliance	12.95	
	FKGP	Runs alone	12.44	Factions split and run alone
	SZDSZ	Runs alone	6.22	Runs alone
	MIEP	Runs alone	3.63	Runs alone

of the party, that the trend continued after the downturn in their electoral performance and their 1998 failure to enter parliament cannot be explained by electoral considerations. The final result of this process, though—the incorporation of most of the politicians belonging to some KDNP and FKGP factions into FIDESZ-MPP—does provide some support for the expectations that parties will only remain in existence as along as they promise to help politicians get elected.

Overall, the propositions of the model about party choice of electoral strategies find some support in the behavior of Bulgarian and Hungarian parties. An examination of the evolution of parties in Bulgaria and Hungary points to several conclusions regarding hypotheses 1, 2, and 3.

Previous and anticipated electoral support play a role in the decisions of office-seeking parties to form; periods of high expected volatility seem to conducive to formation of new parties; parties that seek to control the executive form when the expectations of volatility is at extreme levels, thus providing support for H3.

Electoral support also appears to play a role in decision by parties, once formed, to choose certain electoral strategies. The overall number of office-seeking parties that fail in the system seems to decrease over time. When their running alone does not provide them with the benefits they are after, rather than continuing to do so, parties seek alliances and/or mergers. Parties seem to learn from experience and adapt their electoral strategies so that they either do better or disappear.

Unfortunately, there is very limited data to test H2—in both Hungary and Bulgaria there have only been a handful of proper mergers, or mergers in which both parties end their previous existence to form a new one (BEL and BSD in Bulgaria), one merger of a party within another party (KDNP within FIDESZ) and one attempted "proper" merger (MDF-FIDESZ-MPP). Of the four instances, only the KDNP had not tried allying with FIDESZ before merging. Although no meaningful conclusions can be reached, there is a resistance to mergers evident in the two systems. The trend is particularly obvious in Bulgaria, where parties seem more than willing to form alliances, but mergers remain a rare occurrence despite a fragmented system.

However, the inability of expected and previous levels of electoral support to explain the behavior of parties in a substantial number, although not the majority, of party choices indicates the need for an examination of the role of other factors, a subject to which this chapter turns next. Finally, and quite obviously, there also seems to be a systemic effect—parties in Hungary run alone at a much higher rate than do parties in Bulgaria. Factors that work on a systemic level— electoral laws and regulations of party financing, for example—clearly need to be incorporated into the understanding of the process of party formation and electoral competition.

IDEOLOGY AND PARTY ELECTORAL STRATEGIES

Expectations

The empirical implications of H5 suggest that, when parties are uncertain about the adequacy of their electoral support and their ideological space is "crowded," they will be discouraged from entering this space on their own. The hypothesis also suggests that an increased number of competitors within a party's ideological family should encourage alliances or even mergers among them. Further, if ideological concerns do govern party behavior, parties should be picking partners that stand close to them in ideological terms when forming alliances.

Observed Behavior

According to all five of the newly formed parties examined in detail (BEL, Munkapsart, DPS, SZDSZ, and FIDESZ), ideological opposition to the established parties was a major factor in their decision to form. Again, GOR/BEL's case is particularly important due to its late arrival.

According to GOR leaders, at the time of their original decision to leave the BSP, the latter's positions on various issues of the economic and political development of the country were "nostalgic for the old type of government, [favoring] price control, control over the banking sector, etc." (BSD 2003). At this point, the BSP's economic platform and policy positions still supported state economic planning and price controls as well as opposition to NATO membership and European integration and cooperation (Murer 2002, 388; Dainov 1999, 160–161). In contrast, politicians in GOR were reform minded and Europe oriented, and for them the policy positions of the BSP as a still unreformed socialist party were untenable (GOR 1993; BSD 2003).

> Social democracy presents a plan for social development that differs substantially from the platform of the BSP. The BSP is not a social democratic party, but a party of democratic socialism.   (Zankov 2003b)

There were already several social democratic formations in Bulgaria at this time, which made an independent existence for GOR implausible. Simply joining the BSDP was not an option for GOR members. But, according to them, the BSDP was in no position to represent social democratic interests on its own. The BSDP had repeatedly associated themselves with a right-wing political formation—the SDS—and campaigned on the issue of anticommunism only, which made it "not a true social-democratic alternative." The behavior of the BSP and the BSDP created a real "niche" for a social democratic party (Zankov 2003a). Following this reasoning, GOR formed the political coalition DAR.

Ideological considerations also seem to have played a factor in GOR's 1997 decision to initiate a merger with part of the BSDP, ASO, and a new BSP splinter into a new political party (BEL), and in BEL's 2003 decision to merge with the BESDP in the formation of the BSD. The BSP's decision to form the NL and the Coalition for Bulgaria in 2000 and 2001 was also driven by a concern with "unifying the ideological space" in the face of ideological fragmentation (Krusteva 2003). Similar motivations were expressed by FIDESZ in Hungary when explaining its decision to cooperate with the MDF and to incorporate the KDNP and some FKGP splinters into their structures in 1998 and 2002 (Navracsics 2003).

> We [FIDESZ and MDF] have shared value systems and are very close to each other and it is only natural to try and unite in a catch-all center right formation.   (Navracsics, 2003)

Ideological uniqueness is one of the reasons that the SZDSZ consistently competed in elections alone and did not to consider any other electoral strategies. However, the CP's appearance in the 2002 elections made the first inroad into SZDSZ support and caused some disturbance among the SZDSZ leadership (Kupa 2003; Fodor 2003).

H6 proposed a distinction between ethnic parties and nonethnic parties in their ability to maintain control of their "ideological" space. Unfortunately, with only one ethnic party present in the two party systems, it becomes close to impossible to establish any meaningful conclusions in this regard. The example of the DPS, however, does lend some support to this hypothesis. The DPS was quick to establish itself as *the* party of the Turkish minority and has managed to preserve a relative monopoly over its electorate through the years. Although it has had two challengers over the last fourteen years, neither of them became a major threat, especially when compared with the situation in other ideological families of the Bulgarian party system. However, when competitors appeared (the Party of Democratic Change, or PDP, in 1993 and the National Movement for Rights and Freedoms, or NDPS, in 1997) the DPS realized the potential danger of their presence and attempted to integrate them back into its structures right away.

While these trends seem to indicate clear support for ideology as a factor in the decision making of parties, it does not seem to be enough to consolidate ideological trends completely. The pattern of behavior of all parties in the two systems, especially in Bulgaria, provides further mixed support for H5 and H6. Hungarian parties, or at least the ones that "matter," have shown consistent ideological positions and relative stability, especially toward the end of the period under examination. Table 4.12 presents the ideological distribution

Table 4.12 Ideological distribution of Hungarian parties with more than 1 percent of the vote (1990–2002)

Year	Marxist[1]	Socialist	Agrarian	Conservative	Liberal	Extreme right/ nationalist
1990	Munkaspart	MSZP MSZDP	FKGP ASZ	MDF KDNP	SZDSZ FIDESZ VP	HVK
1994	Munkaspart	MSZP MSZDP	FKGP ASZ	MDF KDNP FIDESZ	SZDSZ KP	MIEP
1998	Munkaspart	MSZP	FKGP	[MDF, KDNP, FIDESZ] MDNP	SZDSZ	MIEP
2002	Munkaspart	MSZP		[FIDESZ-MDF]	SZDSZ CP	MIEP

[1] The ideological classification was done following Hollis 1999 and Kitschelt et al. 1999.

of Hungarian parties with more than 1 percent of the vote at the four rounds of elections. Parties that are of the same ideological trend and run in a common alliance are in parentheses.

Since the mid-1990, the FIDESZ/MDF/FKGP and the MSZP/ SZDSZ political blocs have been stable and dominant in Hungarian political life. In fact, as already discussed, the center-right bloc has come close to merging into a single party after realizing that, as the FIDESZ-MPP party director put it, "There are only so many conservative votes in Hungary" (Navracsics 2003). However, the presence of three "FKGP" parties outside FIDESZ at the 2002 elections (see appendix C, table 4), and the fractionalization of the KDNP over the years (1998, particularly) are indications that ideological unification is not the only electoral strategy in Hungary either.

In Bulgaria, the ideological fragmentation is more pronounced. Table 4.13 provides the ideological distribution of Bulgarian parties with more than 1 percent of the vote (or participating as independent entities in alliances with more than 1 percent of the vote) over the five rounds of elections. Parties that are of the same ideological trend and run in a common alliance are in parentheses. Despite an expressed commitment to ideological principles and a stated desire to unify their

Table 4.13 Ideological distribution of Bulgarian parties with more than 1 percent of the vote (1990–2005)

Year	Socialist/ Marxist[1]	Agrarian	Center Left/Social-democratic	Center-right	Ethnic	Royalist
1990	BSP	BZNS		SDS	DPS	
1991	BSP	BZNS-NP BZNS-E	[Green Party, Ecoglasnost] BSDP	SDS BBB	DPS NRP	KTsB
1994	BSP BKP	BZNS-M BZNS-AS	[GOR, BSDP, Green Party] SNI PS Ecoglasnost	SDS DP BBB	DPS	FTsB
1997	BSP BKP	BZNS-M BZNS-AS BZNS-NP	BEL BSDP PDC SNI	[SDS, DP] BBB	DPS	FTsB OT
2001	[BSP, OPT, CPoB]	BZNS-M BZNS	[BEL, BESDP] BSDP BSDP-2	NDSV [SDS, DP] [Gergiovden, VMRO]	DPS NDPS	CSII NOSII
2005	[BSP, CPoB]	BZNS-M BZNS	BSD, BSDP	NDSV, NV, [SDS, Gergiovden, DP], DSB, [SSD, VMRO]	DPS NDPS Ataka	—

[1] The ideological classification was done following Kitschelt et al. 1999 and Karasimeonov 2002.

respective ideological spaces, fragmentation is clearly a pattern that persists within all ideological families, and does not appear to subside with the passage of time.

Since 2001, there seems to be a tendency for unification of the left and further fragmentation of the right in Bulgaria. The SDS has had three major formal splits since then: the SSD, the Bulgarian Democratic Union-Radicals (BDS-Radicals), and the DSB[3] are the new parties that emerged from these splits. The NDSV has had one splinter, New Time (NV). The formation of new parties as SDS splinters is particularly counterintuitive as the SDS has been experiencing declining electoral support since 2001 and has faced increased competition from the NDSV for the center-right ideological space.[4]

However, both the SDS and the SSD argued that ideological considerations were the most important factors that influence them in their coalitional decision making. The SDS maintained that the party's ideological principles limited its possible alliance partners to only these parties that were on the right of the political spectrum (Mladenov 2003). However, when asked about allying with the BDS, SDS deputy chairman Mladenov openly said that because of a personal confrontation between BDS leader Bakurdziev and the SDS leadership, no cooperation was possible (Mladenov 2003). No meaningful cooperation of the center-right was achieved in the 2003 local elections in Bulgaria, and the appearance of more SDS splinters has in many ways predetermined the emergence of the BSP as *the* one strong political force in Bulgaria.

On the left, the political "space" is more consolidated, although previous trends continue. The parallel "unification" processes around the BSP and the BSD, and the absence of any cooperation between the two have already been discussed. However, with the decline of the BSD support and the NL's increased activity, the consolidation of the left seems a reality (Karasimeonov 2002, 188).

In the "center," agrarian parties have traditionally been the most prolific in terms of producing factions and splinters. Of the 303 parties in Bulgaria, 21 are different agrarian (BZNS) parties. Of them, six contested the 2001 elections independently of each other (see appendix B, table 5), and most of them were in alliances with other, nonagrarian parties. Despite this obvious fragmentation, one of the BZNS leaders, Georgi Pinchev, argued that "we have always and will always choose our partners depending on how close our ideologies are" (Pinchev 2003). However, his party did not hesitate to split from BZNS-M in 2000 and contest elections in an alliance with BEL in 2001.

The behavior of political parties in Bulgaria and Hungary presents mixed support for the propositions that ideological considerations play an important role in the decision of parties to form and choose certain electoral strategies. Evidence suggests that parties do consider ideological factors when deciding to form, run alone, ally, merge, or disband. However, based on both party leaders' statements and the pattern of behavior, parties seem to allow other considerations to override objective facts that there can only be a limited number of successful parties within one ideological group. This seems to be more pronounced in Bulgaria than in Hungary.

ORGANIZATIONAL STRENGTH AND PARTY ELECTORAL STRATEGIES

Expectations

H9 and its empirical implications suggested that at party level, we should observe that parties do make an effort to develop organizationally, and that, when taking the decision to form, run alone, ally, or merge, they take into account the organizational strength of other parties in the system. Within the party system, we should observe the gradual consolidation of the number of parties competing in elections as, presumably, with the passage of time, the party organizations grow stronger and new entrants are discouraged.

Observed Behavior*

Attitudes toward Organizing

To evaluate the empirical evidence in support of the role that organization development plays in party evolution, we start by examining the claim that organization does matter to parties in Bulgaria and Hungary, by investigating the attitudes of party leaders to attract new members and build organization. The general view in the discipline has been that post-communist parties have no organizations to speak of, do not even attempt to attract members, and hire professionals to carry out party work instead. Citing an SZDSZ party leader, van Biezen argues that in East Central Europe, expanding membership is seen as an old-fashioned phenomenon belonging to a different era (van Biezen 2003, 115). In general, parties tend to stress attracting votes rather than members. However, a closer scrutiny of the attitudes of party leaders reveals a more complex picture.

The leaders of both the Bulgarian parties examined in detail and of most other Bulgarian parties interviewed expressed views that strongly valued building party organization and attracting membership. Many of the party leaders talked about the dichotomy between parties based on "electoral presence" and parties based on organizational structures. However, with one exception, they all agreed that the time of the parties of the "electoral presence" kind was over. For example, Georgi Pinchev, BZNS chairman, argued that

> . . . after 1989, some parties influenced the electoral process not so much because of their regional structures, but because of their messages (the so-called "electoral influence"). The victories of the SDS in both 1991 and 1997, and of NDSV in 2001 are examples of this trend.

But this period is over. From now on, especially given the lower voter turnout in recent elections, the role of the organizational structures and the membership will be more and more important. (Pinchev 2002)

Similarly, Milan Milanov, organizational Secretary of SSD, claimed that "Bulgaria has witnessed the creation of some so-called electoral parties but further development in this direction is not possible." Milanov argued that it would be extremely dangerous to allow personalities (such as the ex-monarch and current Prime Minister Simeon Sax-Coburg-Gotha) to become more important than party structures. Organizational development becomes the "only solution" if such trends are to be countered (Milanov 2002).

The BSP seems to share similar attitudes toward the issue of organization and membership. Although the BSP still has the strongest and most extensive organizational structures of all Bulgarian political parties, it has to be remembered that in 1990 the party had close to a million members and has since experienced a drastic drop in membership. However, it has recently begun to realize that it can no longer rely on its traditional supporters only and has made efforts to attract new, younger, members. This is evident in the presence of these issues in the political report of the party commitment at the last two congresses while such points were absent in 1995 and 1997 (BSP 1995; 1997; 2000; 2002). The party has also tried to "democratize" its view of membership. According to Krusteva, the BSP's attitude toward membership has evolved to stress not so much what she called "solid membership," but rather to maintain a membership base and build around it a periphery of supporters and sympathizers (2003).

In an even stronger argument, Miroslav Murdzhov, deputy chairman of VMRO, attributed his party's better performance in certain regions of the country in the 2001 elections to the better organizational work done there. However, unlike the SSD and the BZNS, VMRO argued that organizational development was not the only path to success. For VMRO, whose structures and hard-core membership are solid, presence in the media has begun to emerge as another way to evolve politically. However, Murdzhov stressed that this could be done only because of the extensive organizational networks that had already been created (Murdzhov 2003).

The SDS's attitude toward extensive organization has evolved since its formation. Because of the anticommunist nature of its members and supporters, building a strong organization was initially impossible as people associated it with the BSP. Besides, the SDS's coalition character made building a unified structure and membership impossible (Waller and Karasimeonov 1996, 134–162). However, after the transformation of the SDS into a party in 1997, the need for organization building has been well understood (Mladenov 2003).

The DPS expressed probably the strongest concern with local structures and members. One of its priorities over the last few years has been the development of organizational structures in all regions of the country. In addition, Kasim Dal, DPS vice-chairman, maintained that the party had a very close connection with all the party members and supporters, and valued their opinions and attitudes (Dal 2003).

The only party whose leaders expressed ambivalence toward building its image through organizing was BEL. Its deputy chairman, Roumen Zankov, argued that BEL, like most young parties, tended to follow the example of the BSP and tried to cover the whole territory of the country with its structures. However, BEL had realized that there were other means of winning elections, and from now on, the party would put its energy into formulating the policies it advocated and presenting these to the electorate in an attractive way (Zankov 2003a).

In contrast to most of the Bulgarian party leaders, politicians in Hungary argued that building organization has not been a dominant strategy of their parties during the 1990s. More attention was paid to media presence and electoral campaigns. However, there seem to be indications that things are changing in Hungary as well.

According to Navracsics, FIDESZ-MPP did not consider building an organization to be a useful strategy for winning elections until 2002. Instead, it had decided to become a "catchall media party," a tendency that found expression in the incorporation of various other center-right groups within FIDESZ as well.[5] However, the 2002 elections demonstrated that things have to change. With electoral turnout (74 percent) and political mobilization at its highest, and with all center-right organizations incorporated under FIDESZ's leadership, the party still did not manage to win the elections. The realization that they "cannot expand the vote" any further called for a change of electoral strategies, one of which was the stress on building organizational structures and attracting membership (Navracsics 2003). In addition, since 2002, FIDESZ-MPP has started building "civic circles" in an effort to mobilize people not only as voters but as members and activists as well.

With the obvious exception of the MSZP, which retains its organizational priorities from earlier times, the leaders of all other parties expressed similar views. Both Hack and Fodor, for example, argued that the electoral campaigns of the SZDSZ (and others) had become mostly "media and money oriented." However, they both saw such campaigns as a problem for the SZDSZ and argued that unless the SZDSZ started to recruit members and sympathizers more actively, there was little future for the party (Fodor 2003; Hack 2003).

The tendencies in the other smaller parties in Hungary have been similar. Vajda of Munkaspart, for example, expressed regrets that his party did not have a bigger and stronger organization. But he saw organizing as only one of the two key policies of his party—having a media presence was equally important for electoral success in his view (Vajda 2003). Similarly, Kupa of the new CP argued that his party, which was originally founded by 25 people as an "elite party," had been debating whether or not to open up its structures to other people and ordinary members (Kupa 2003). CP has decided to go the "third way" and build its electoral presence through societal work as a whole rather than just activities within a membership organization.

The MDF expressed probably the strongest support for organization building as a means to electoral success. Party vice-president Szoke saw the absence of organization building as one of the biggest problems of his party. That "party organization translates into electoral success" has been demonstrated by the MSZP and FIDESZ (since 2002) (Szoke 2003).

Bulgarian and Hungarian Parties: Organizational Trends
An examination of several indicators of organizational development provides further mixed support for the belief that parties build organizations as a way to achieve their respective goals. For the purposes of comparison, this discussion employs measures of organizational development as used by van Biezen and Toole (van Biezen 2003; Toole 2003). It discusses data on membership, extensiveness of organizational structures, and levels of professionalization.

The Bulgarian political parties demonstrate levels of organizational development that support the relatively high concern with organization building expressed by their leaders. Membership figures for the Bulgarian parties are reported in table 4.14. The data presents membership figures reported at the parties' respective congresses or conferences during 2002 and 2003.

Similar to trends in organization in other post-communist systems, the "successor" party in Bulgaria, the BSP, has the highest membership among Bulgarian parties. But its membership of over 200,000 people is also the highest among its counterparts in the other countries and certainly above the MSZP membership. Of the post-1990 parties, the DPS has the highest membership, around 59,000 people as of late 2002. While figures for some of the other parties might be exaggerated, the level of organization building among the newest parties, the SSD and the NDSV, clearly demonstrates a concern with organizational structure. Both parties have memberships of around 19,000 after only about a year of existence.

Political parties in Bulgaria report membership figures that are somewhat higher than membership figures in Hungary (presented in table 4.15). Membership figures for Hungarian parties are even

Table 4.14   Bulgarian parties: Number of members

Party	Membership
NDSV	19,000
SDS	35,000
BSP	210,000
DPS	58,000
DP	7,000
Green Party	5,000
CPoB	29,000
BEL	18,000
BZNS	30,000
RDP	3,000
SSD	17,600
VMRO	12,000
Total:	**443,600**
Parties in parliament only	**352,000**

Table 4.15   Hungarian parties: Number of members

Party[1]	Members
MSZP	39,000
SZDSZ	16,000
MDF	23,000
KDNP	10,000
FKGP	60,000
FIDESZ	15,600
Total:	**163,600**

[1] *Source*: van Biezen 2003, pp. 110–112. Numbers validated by interviews as well (Kupa 2003; Vajda 2003; Fodor 2003; Szoke 2003; Navracsics 2003; van Biezen 2003).

Table 4.16 Members-to-electorate ratios in Bulgaria and Hungary

Country	M/E ratios
Bulgaria	5.15%
Hungary	2.8%

lower as of 2002–2003 because of the fragmentation of the KDNP and FKGP (Hack 2003; Toole 2003).

Two measures are used to compare party membership across parties and across systems: the ratio of members to electorate (M/E) and the ratio of members to voters (M/V) (Mair 1997, 186; van Biezen 2003, 111–112; Toole 2003, 104; Szczerbiak 2001, 111). Both of these measures are used to evaluate the extent to which membership in political parties is common among politically active people. The M/E ratio represents the percentage of the registered voters in a given country who are also members of a selected number of parties, usually the ones represented in parliament. The M/V ratio compares the number of votes each party receives with the number of members it has. For comparison purposes the M/E and M/V ratios for Bulgaria are calculated for parties represented in parliament only. The M/E ratios for Bulgaria and Hungary are presented in table 4.16.

The M/E ratio for Bulgarian parties is 5.1 percent, almost double that of parties in Hungary and all other Central European countries.[6] Although Bulgarian parties are still far below average Western levels of party organization—Toole (2003) cites 10.4 percent as the average M/E ratio for Western European countries—Bulgarian parties demonstrate distinctly higher levels of membership than any of the Central European countries, including Hungary. Hungarian parties, in contrast, exhibit much lower levels of membership that are more in line with the general pattern of post-communist party development.

The M/V ratio of each of the Bulgarian parliamentary parties is presented in table 4.17. These figures are not as straightforward as they should be, because all four parties ran with an alliance partner(s) in the 2001 elections. The BSP ran within the Coalition for Bulgaria, the SDS ran with the DP and BZNS-M, the DPS ran in its own alliance with four other parties, and the NDSV ran on the same ticket as two other political parties. The membership figures of the Democratic Party (DP) and the CPoB were thus included in the membership figures of the SDS and the BSP, respectively. The M/V ratio is

Table 4.17 Members-to-voters
ratios for major Bulgarian parties,
2001 elections

Party	M/V ratio
BSP (incl. CPoB)	30.60%
DPS	16.93%
NDSV	0.97%
ODS (incl. DP)	4.21%

Table 4.18 Members-to-voters ratios
for major Hungarian parties, 2002
elections

Party	M/V ratio
MSZP	2.6%
FIDESZ/MDF	1.65%
SZDSZ	5.11%

calculated using the results at the 2001 elections. For the Hungarian figures (presented in table 4.18), membership of both the MDF and FIDESZ was included in the calculations of their M/V ratio.

Of the seven parties in the two systems for which the measure was calculated, the NDSV shows the least extent of encapsulation of its electorate. Members do not even constitute 1 percent of the people who voted for the NDSV. However, the appropriateness of this measure is questionable as the NDSV did not even register as a party until almost two years later, and membership reflects developments as of mid-2003. For all practical purposes, it can be said the NDSV won 42 percent of the vote in 2001 with no members. However, this was highly unusual and can almost certainly be attributed to the extreme nature of the pro-NDSV vote in 2001. This partly nostalgic, partly protest vote was a one-time phenomenon, as the NDSV's dismal showing at the 2003 local elections demonstrated. Nevertheless, it is important to note that even the NDSV, the most "electoral" and personality-driven of the parties in Bulgaria, felt it necessary to start an active organization-building campaign. By mid-2003, two years after its conception and less than a year after formally registering as a party, it had a membership of about 19,000.

FIDESZ-MPP/MDF has the second least-encapsulated vote: 1.65 percent of its votes came from members, and in this case the measure is highly illustrative of the tendencies of membership-building present within FIDESZ and the MDF. However, while low membership figures might be typical for parties of this type, the low encapsulation of the MSZP's vote is quite surprising. With only 2.3 percent of its vote coming from members, the MSZP is quite atypical among the successor parties in the region. The BSP has an M/V ratio of about 30 percent, the successor party in Poland 9.3 percent, and the successor parties in the Czech Republic have M/V ratios of 11.55 and 24.30 percent (van Biezen 2003, 141; Toole 2003).

The SDS in Bulgaria and the SZDSZ in Hungary show relatively similar levels of encapsulation—around 5 percent of their votes came from members in the respective elections. Besides the BSP, the DPS in Bulgaria also has a relatively high degree of organizational encapsulation of voters with about 17 percent of its votes coming from members. Of the new parties in both Bulgaria and Hungary, it seems to be the one most concerned with gaining popularity through organizing.

Overall, the M/E and M/V ratios in Bulgaria and Hungary seem to support the claim that organization building is more popular among the Bulgarian parties than among the Hungarian parties. Although it is difficult to use these figures as evidence to support H7, there is enough evidence to suggest that parties in Bulgaria have at least made efforts to attract members that are comparable to trends in some Western European countries. The M/E ratios of Bulgarian parties are of similar levels as the M/E ratios of parties in Ireland, Portugal, and Germany, and are way above the party membership levels in the United Kingdom, the Netherlands, and France (Mair 1996). An examination of several other indicators of organizational development might provide more evidence in this regard.

Another measure of the organizational complexity of political parties is the extent to which they have developed their organizational structures across their country. A high extensiveness of organization (usually measured as percentage of territory covered) can be considered evidence that parties do develop organizations, thus supporting H9.

In line with the previous discussion, the Bulgarian parties have structures that seem to be more extensive than the structures of parties in Hungary. Bulgarian parties report local branches in the majority of the municipalities of the country. The DP, BEL, and the ZP report the least extensive networks—they have local clubs in 140 (50 percent), 146 (52 percent), and 130 (48 percent) of 280 municipalities, respectively. The BZNS and VMRO report higher levels of reach. Both parties have branches in around 200 municipalities (71 percent). The youngest and most active in terms of organization building, SSD, reports active branches in 218 municipalities (78 percent) (Milanov 2003). Even the regionally bound DPS reports branches in 223 (79 percent) municipalities (Dal 2003). The BSP, the SDS, and the CPoB have active primary organizations in all of the 280 municipalities in the territory of the country (Vanev 2003; Stoianova 2003; Krusteva 2003).

Hungarian parties seem to have less extensive structures than parties in Bulgaria. As of 2003, CP does not have structures outside the capital, Munkaspart and the MDF have structures in about 15 percent of localities of the country: the SZDSZ, in about 25 percent; FIDESZ, in about 45 percent; and the MSZP, in about 80 percent. In 1997, the FKGP and the KDNP had structures in 55 percent and 25 percent of localities, respectively (Kupa 2003; Vajda 2003; Fodor 2003; Szoke 2003; Navracsics 2003; van Biezen 2003). None of the Hungarian parties reports branches in all municipalities.

It appears that in this regard, again, the behavior of the Bulgarian parties indicates that they are more interested than Hungarian parties in building organizations in an attempt to secure electoral support. While comparisons are difficult, owing to the different administrative structures of the two countries, Bulgarian parties still seem to report more extensive structures and to be making efforts to increase their reach. This conclusion is further corroborated by a comparison of the levels of professionalization of the parties in the two systems.

The level of professionalization measures the number of paid professionals per member and is viewed as an indicator of the relative importance attributed to party organization by parties. The measures indicate that Bulgarian parties are less professional than parties in Hungary. In Bulgaria, there are, on average, one paid professional for every 1,736 party members, while the Hungarian parties employ one professional for every 1,395 members (Toole 2003).

Overall, organizational tendencies provide mixed support for H9. Most parties do seem to exhibit an understanding that organization matters and make some effort to put that belief into practice. Differences in organizational trends seem to be driven by system-level factors and by ideology and the age of parties. Bulgarian parties surveyed seem to represent a higher level of organizational development than their Hungarian counterparts. Older and left-of-center parties also seem to demonstrate a stronger concern with organization building, while liberal and newer parties value media presence and newer communications techniques more.

Organization and Electoral Strategies

The most direct implication of H9 though is the proposed relationship between the organizational strength of any party in relation to that of its competitors and its choice of an electoral strategy. Do parties take organizational factors into consideration when they make alliances? Does the organizational development of established parties discourage potential parties from forming? The discussion devoted to the first question will be relatively limited to parties in Bulgaria because, as we have seen, alliances with different partners are more common in Bulgaria than in Hungary. Further, given the higher level of organizational development in Bulgaria, we should be able to obtain a clearer pattern of the relationship between organization and party stabilization.

Parties in Bulgaria maintain that they prefer better-organized parties when they form electoral alliances. The BSP, for example, requires all prospective alliance partners to provide an updated list of local structures and members, and requires their own branches to verify this information for both local and national elections. The BSP only backs a potential partner if the local organizations are deemed dependable (Krusteva 2003).

The DPS is not as clear as the BSP in its preferences for stronger parties. In 1997, for example, the DPS chose the ZP as an alliance partner party because of the ZP's organizational superiority in certain regions at that time. As the DPS did not have branches in some of the regions of the country, it used the ones created by the ZP to gain electoral support (Dal 2003; Dzudzev 2003). However, by 2001, ideological motivations were more important, and the DPS chose parties that strengthened its "liberal" image. At the same time, the DPS also developed its own structures further and thus did not need ZP support any more.

BEL does not value organization very much for itself, nor does it consider the organizational strengths of its potential partners when forming alliances. For it, ideology plays the most important role in selecting allies (Zankov 2003a, 2003b). However, most other parties interviewed did express a preference for better-organized alliance partners, within the limits imposed on their choice by the ideological proximity principle.

The SDS maintained that it chose alliance partners for both ideological and organizational reasons. For example, in 1997, the SDS included its partners—the DP and the BZNS-M—because these parties trusted their local branches to provide for a better-synchronized election campaign (Mladenov 2003). The SSD argued that it would only choose "serious right-wing parties, not parties made up of five people" as prospective allies (Milanov 2003). VMRO rejected one of the SDS splinters in 2001 as an alliance partner because "it had no organizational structures" (Mandzukov and Gospodinova 2001). Pinchev of the BZNS argued that organizational characteristics of a party are very important in his party's decision with whom to ally at elections. However, organization ". . . is not the decisive element . . . ideology is" (Pinchev 2003).

An indication of the importance of organization for the evolution of individual parties and the party system as a whole is the trend in factionalism in individual parties. In both systems, the successor parties have been both the best organized and the least fractionalized. In Hungary the MSZP has not only had no formal splits, but has suffered the fewest defections over the years (Toole 2003, 293). In Bulgaria, as discussed in earlier sections, the BSP has suffered three splits, but has still been by far the most stable of the major parties in the country. In addition, one of the BSP splinters has since returned to the party alliance (Karasimenov 2002; Krusteva 2003).

Another example of the importance of organization in a party's decision to form is provided by the FIDESZ liberal faction's decision to join the SZDSZ in 1993. The decision of Gabor Fodor and the liberal faction of FIDESZ to split in 1993 is in many ways reminiscent of GOR leader Tomov's decision to leave the BSP in 1993. Both Tomov and Fodor were popular politicians who had come to disagree with their parties' ideological positions. What the two of them chose to do, however, differed substantially. Tomov (and his allies), who claimed to represent a social-democratic ideological position, could have joined the existing and then relatively strong BSDP. This move would have strengthened the BSDP and allowed it to do better in elections. Instead, Tomov chose to form a new party, then allied with the BSDP for the elections in DAR, and later parted ways with it altogether to seek his own political realization in BEL.

Fodor, on the other hand, chose to join the SZDSZ. It was not an easy decision as the SZDSZ had been FIDESZ's opponent before and was an already well-established party. However, Fodor argued, that starting a new party made little sense as "there already was a liberal party" (Fodor 2003). To build a new one was a challenging task that required organization and finances that he could not count on. Fodor thus ran as an SZDSZ-supported candidate in 1994, and later became one of the most popular and respected leaders of the SZDSZ.[7]

In this case, Tomov seems to have disregarded the existence of an already-existing organizational structure and not to have been deterred by it in his decision to build a new party. This decision, which seems to be indicative of a more general tendency in the Bulgarian party system, might help shed some light on the second question raised by H9. Do better-organized parties deter new parties from forming and running alone at elections, and do better-organized parties promote a stabilization of the party system? A more detailed examination of the systemic indicators of fragmentation might provide more evidence and some answers to these questions.

Several indicators of the size and competitiveness of the Bulgarian and Hungarian party systems are reported in table 4.19: the number of parties running in elections, the number of parties with more than 1 percent of the vote (office-seeking parties), the number of effective electoral parties (ENEP), the number of parties represented in parliament, and the effective number of parliamentary parties (ENPP). For comparison purposes some averages for the Eastern European region are presented as well.[8]

There are several observations to be made. First, there are more parties contesting elections in Bulgaria than in Hungary, but at the same time the Bulgarian parties seem to be less successful than parties in Hungary. The absolute number of parties running in elections is consistently high in Bulgaria, and, more importantly, the number does not seem to decline over time. The number of parties contesting elections has varied between 38 and 56 over the years, with the highest number of participants in the most recent parliamentary elections,

Table 4.19   Party systems in Bulgaria and Hungary (1990–2002)

Indicator	Election	First	Second	Third	Fourth	Fifth
Parties	Bulgaria	42	38	49	41	56
	Hungary	28	34	28	19	n/a
Office-seeking	Bulgaria	4	10	10	7	8
parties	Hungary	11	10	9	6	n/a
ENEP	Bulgaria	2.75	4.197	3.88	2.89	4.54
	Hungary	6.71	5.50	4.47	2.837	n/a
	East European average	5.5	5.6	4.6	4.1	n/a
Parliamentary	Bulgaria	6	3	5	5	4
parties	Hungary	7	6	6	4	n/a
ENPP	Bulgaria	2.42	2.41	2.73	2.53	2.92
	Hungary	3.79	2.89	4.08	2.21	
	EE average	4.00	3.7	3.7	3.8	

which were held in 2001. This contrasts significantly with the situation in Hungary where the number of parties running in elections has not only been lower overall, but has also decreased significantly from the first to the most recent elections (Bielasiak 2003; Lewis 2001a). Further, the number of office-seeking parties in Bulgaria, while not higher in the beginning, has similarly not declined over the years. In contrast, the number of office-seeking parties in Hungary has gone down by almost half.

Second, the number of parties that "matter" in Bulgarian politics also does not exhibit stable trends. Until the fourth round of elections, the "effective" numbers of electoral parties in Bulgaria were relatively lower than the respective numbers in Hungary. But the effective number peaked again during the fifth election to a level significantly above that of the same indicator for Hungary, and somewhat above the Eastern European average. This implies that until 2001, the popular vote in Bulgaria had been concentrated in a few political parties, but fractionalized again in 2001.

Finally, the number of parliamentary parties and the ENPP in Bulgaria is similarly low. With the values of the latter measure between 2.41 (in 1991) and 2.92 (in 2001), the Bulgarian Parliament remains among the least fractionalized parliaments in Eastern Europe. In this regard, the Hungarian party system seems to perform similarly.

Overall, the specifics of Bulgarian party-system development provide somewhat mixed support for the link between individual party organization and the fractionalization of the party system as a whole. Bulgarian parties seem to enter the political process relatively easily—whether through forming anew or splitting from existing parties—thus contradicting the expectations of H9 that organizational strength deters formation of new parties. More importantly, this trend does not seem to decline substantially over time. Given that the Bulgarian parties were better organized by 2003 than they were in the beginning of the period under study, this observation seems to reject H9.

However, new parties in Bulgaria seem to have little chance of successfully challenging the established parties. A higher level of organizational development is thus not necessarily associated with fewer incentives for politicians to break away and start new parties. However, it seems to prevent *successful* entries in the party system by making it more difficult to match the organizational strategies of the established parties.[9]

Hungarian parties' pattern of behavior further complicates the picture. At first glance, the developments over time provide clear support for H9. The number of parties, the number of office-seeking parties, and the number of effective parties decrease consistently over time. This would be in line with the expectation that as parties "age," they establish themselves better organizationally and provide fewer incentives for new parties to form. However, as discussed, parties in Hungary have traditionally not organized very well, suggesting that the apparent link between organization and consolidation might be spurious. On the other hand, the second peak of electoral activity in 1998 might indicate that the absence of organizational strengthening allowed for new challengers to emerge as well.

The evidence of the role party organization plays in the decisions of parties to form, run alone, ally, merge, or disband is thus inconclusive. Support for the proposition does seem to exist at party level—some parties organize better than others and seem to suffer less fractionalization; most parties take organizational factors into consideration when splitting, allying and merging, but there seems to be little effect on the party system as a whole. These conclusions, however, are based on substantial within-system but small across-system differences, which probably confounds the analysis. The system-level test of the model (presented in the next chapter) provides a further test of H9.

External Shocks, Random Events, and Party Electoral Strategies

Parties in Bulgaria and Hungary have often chosen their electoral strategies under the influence of external forces. Party leaders have been expelled by their parties and forced to form new ones; whole parties have been expelled from alliances and forced to seek alternative electoral strategies; European and American actors have intervened to help parties break away or merge into new ones. While there is no systematic effect that we can observe, some more discussion of the evidence that this happens is warranted.

The discussion of party evolution in chapter 3 has already presented some evidence of this type. MIEP's creation in 1992 was a direct result of the expulsion of its leader from the MDF. Expulsions of partners from alliances and parties have been a relatively common practice in Bulgarian party politics as well. The SDS has repeatedly "expelled" various members in an attempt to preserve ideological harmony and to get rid of "trouble-makers" (Karasimeonov 1996, 145–149). The SDS expelled the leaders of the BSDP, the BZNS-NP, and the ZP, and thus significantly helped them in their choice of alliance partners in 1991.

The emergence of BEL (1997) and the NL (2001) in Bulgaria occurred under the strong influence of the PES and the Socialist International. By 2003 PES was not as directly involved in BEL's work. But, according to BEL leaders, the decision to merge the BEL/BESDP alliance partners and form the BSD was taken partly because imminent European integration (expected in 2007) necessitated the unification of Bulgarian social democracy (Zankov 2003b).

Unfortunately, the very nature of this process makes examples of it difficult to discern. Various methodological issues prevent the systemic examination of the influence of this factor.[10] However, a closer examination of party development in Bulgaria provides at least another major example of European actors intervening in party politics in individual countries.

Earlier sections referred to the 1997 decision of the BZNS-M and DP political union (NS) to join with the SDS in a new alliance (ODS).[11] The discussion also referred to an apparent contradiction of some of the hypotheses explored here. However, the decision to seek and form an alliance was a result of substantial outside influence. In 1996, the Konrad Adenauer Foundation, with the EPP's support, gathered all Bulgarian center-right parties on Lake Como, Italy, to "convince them that together they can do more" (Kutov 2004; Mladenov 2003; *Capital* 2001b). On its behalf the International Republican Institute had earlier convinced the Bulgarian center right to hold primaries for the presidential elections and in other ways encourage the consolation of the center-right (*Capital* 2001b).

The importance of the EPP's approval became further evident in the 2001 elections when the "conservative" parties in Bulgaria were threatened by the NDSV's entry. The NDSV's membership of the EPP became a hotly debated issue, and the EPP's support was presented as "European" support for the incumbent SDS (*Capital* 2001a; Terziev 2001).

The EPP and PES have been active in other political systems as well—for example, they held meetings in Poland in 1992 and in Slovenia in 1996, just before elections in these two countries. Similarly, international recognition has been used as a legitimating force by FIDESZ and the MDF in Hungary. However, direct intervention was not observed in other cases than those in Bulgaria (*Capital* 2001a). Even so, given the increased interest of European transnational parties and institutions in the domestic politics of the new accession countries, more interventions of a similar kind have probably occurred (Delsoldato 2002).

Conclusion

This chapter has provided further validation and the first test of the proposed model of party formation and electoral competition in the post-communist world. It examined the behavior of political parties in Bulgaria and Hungary to find empirical evidence at party level to support or reject hypotheses 1, 2, 3, 5, and 9. It has done so by investigating the reasons behind the choice of electoral strategies of the six parties discussed in detail in chapter 3, and other parties in the two systems during five rounds of elections in Bulgaria and four rounds in Hungary.

The discussion has provided mixed support for the hypotheses. There is sufficient evidence to claim that electoral support, ideology, and organization play a role in the parties' decision making. However, there are indications that we need to look at the system level to find an explanation of some of the choices parties have made over the years. First, not all behavior can be explained by party level factors discussed here. While electoral support seems to be a strong predictor of party electoral strategy, we find mixed support for ideology, and, particularly, organization, as strong determinants of party decisions. Again, information from individual parties largely confirms the hypotheses, but the general pattern of party behavior points to different conclusions. Second, parties in Hungary seem to choose to run alone at a generally higher rate than parties in Bulgaria, irrespective of their motivations, electoral support, and ideology. Chapter 5 will thus pick up where this one has left off and discuss the impact of system-level variables on the party choice of electoral strategies.

Notes

*Some of the data and discussion in this section has previously been published in Spirova (2005).

1. For the present purposes, the discussion is limited to parties with 1 percent of the vote. I assume that these are the parties with true office ambitions, and as such are of interest here. This assumption is clearly questionable, as many parties that have less than 1 percent of the vote do have office motivations. However, these parties will

have, most likely, at least at one electoral point been above the one percent threshold, which allows me to examine their behavior. The one percent threshold is arbitrary but does seem to divide the parties in both Hungary and Bulgaria in a way that reflects their position and ambitions in the system. Most studies usually do not consider parties that are outside parliament; however, Rose and Munro have also used the 1 percent threshold to define parties of importance in the post-communist world (Rose and Munro, 2003).

2. The NDSV did not register as a party until late 2002, but it behaved as one in the election and afterwards. Thus, here it is considered to have been a party from April 2001.

3. Two additional factions split and formed political parties, but did not come to play any importance in Bulgarian politics.

4. According to early 2004 opinion polls, none of the center-right political parties could get more than 10 percent of the popular vote if elections were held then (NCIOM 2004).

5. In the 2002 elections, FIDESZ-MPP became familiarly known as the "voice-mail" party after its dominant electoral campaign technique (Hack 2003).

6. Van Biezen reports M/E ratios of 3.21 and 1.5 for the Czech Republic and Poland, respectively (van Biezen 2003).

7. The current situation of the two politicians and political parties further speaks of the wisdom of this decision. By 2003, both Fodor and the SZDSZ were doing significantly better than Tomov and the BSD. Although Fodor will probably never become the SZDSZ chairman, Tomov has enjoyed the leadership position in all parties of which he has been a member.

8. Measures are calculated following Taagapera and Shugart (1989, 79). ENEP $= 1/\Sigma p_i^2$, where p is the proportion of the vote for each party I; ENPP $= 1/\Sigma p_i^2$ where p is the proportion of the seats won by party i. Country indicators are calculated with data from the *Political Transformation and the Electoral Process in Post-Communist Europe Project*, available at http://www.essex.ac.uk/elections/. Averages for Eastern Europe are from Bielasiak 2003.

9. However, the latest developments in Bulgarian politics might change this trend. The share of the vote that went to "new" parties increased substantially in 2001—most of it went to the NDSV but several other new parties also did well (ENEP of 4.54). The subsequent fraction-alization of two of the big players—the SDS and the NDSV (both parties experienced major splits within their parliamentary groups by late 2003)—might also contribute to drastically changed dynamics of party competition in the next round of elections that will allow newer competitors to do better.

10. Self-selection limits the cases in which we observe European involve-ment in party life to the countries that are in the process of accession,

and which in addition have a pan-European counterpart and belong to a relatively fragmented ideological family. In cases where we observe no European involvement, we might have one of several real situations: there is no interest on behalf of the European structures; there is no need for it because the ideological space is consolidated enough; or European involvement has a different form—for example, the fragmentation of the ideological space might have been prevented by the potential threat of European disapproval.

11. In fact, this alliance was part of a longer and larger process that had begun in 1996. In 1996, before the presidential elections in Bulgaria, all center-right political formations in the country united in their support for one presidential candidate in an attempt to prevent a BSP candidate from winning.

Explaining Formation, Persistence, and Change: Post-Communist Trends

The discussion in chapter 4 pointed to some clear indications that factors at the system level influence the behavior of political parties and their decision to form, run alone, merge, or ally. This chapter discusses in detail the way that regulations of party financing and the electoral systems in Bulgaria and Hungary seem to have constrained the parties in their evolution, and then provides a system-level test of the model.

The party-financing regulations in Bulgaria and Hungary provide two different examples of party-financing provisions. Hungary provides direct public subsides to all parties with more than 1 percent of the vote, while Bulgaria only finances parliamentary parties. Similarly, the electoral arrangements in the two systems are very different—the Hungarian Parliament is elected using a mixed system with a 5 percent threshold for its PR part, while Bulgaria uses a purely proportional system with a 4 percent threshold for all contestants. The two systems provide an appropriate testing ground for the hypotheses about the relationship between electoral arrangements and party development.

PARTY FINANCING

Regulation of Party Public Financing in Hungary and Bulgaria

Public Financing of Parties in Hungary

The public funding of political parties in Hungary is established by the *Law on the Operation and Financial Functioning of Political Parties,* adopted in 1989 and amended in 1990. It has not been changed since, which shows, as Ilonszki has argued, the general satisfaction of the main political actors in Hungary, the parliamentary parties, that they are "relatively satisfied" with the system or could not come up with a more beneficial system (Ilonszki 2005).

According to the stipulations of the law, the budget allocated to funding political parties is used in two distinct ways: 25 percent of it is allocated to parliamentary parties only and the rest is divided among all political parties that have gathered at least 1 percent of the vote in the first round of parliamentary elections (*Law on the Operation and Financial Functioning of Political Parties,* Section 5 1989). An original stipulation that these funds can only constitute 50 percent of the party's total budget was "quietly" repealed in 1990 because it left many parties in financial uncertainty (Okolicsanyi 1991, 13). Money is disbursed through annual subsidies, which makes the Hungarian provisions among the less-restrictive party-financing laws.

Public Financing of Parties in Bulgaria

Direct party financing in Bulgaria has similarly been regulated by the *Law on Political Parties.* Until 2001, funding was provided for electoral campaigns only (*Law on Political Parties* 1990). However, the amount and the method of disbursement were not precisely defined by the law and, as a result, funding has varied from election to election. In 1990 all political parties running in elections were given equal subsidies to run their campaigns. For the 1991, 1994, and 1997 elections, funding was provided in the nature of loans to parties that ran in elections. However, the loans had to be returned if the party failed to place any candidates in the legislature. In effect, direct party financing was limited to parliamentary parties only and advantaged them over the extra-parliamentary ones (Smilov 2001; Kostadinova 2005).

In 2001 there were no subsidies for electoral campaigns since the new law on political parties provided for direct annual subsidies instead. The *Law on Political Parties* was "the first serious attempt to regulate public funding" (Kostadinova 2005, 6) and mandated funding along lines very similar to the ones in Hungary. Annual subsides are currently given to all parties in parliament and biannual subsidies to *all parties* with more than 1 percent of the vote in parliamentary elections (*Law on Political Parties* 2001). In addition, the law also mandates that the state provide premises to all political parties that received more than 1 percent of the vote at the previous elections. For most of the period under consideration, Bulgarian parties have only received election campaign subsides; parties outside parliament have had no financial support from the state except for the 1990 elections and no parties had any campaign support in 2001. The Bulgarian system of party financing thus falls within the most restrictive category.

Party Financing Regulations and Party Electoral Strategies

Expectations
The empirical implications of H7 and H8 suggested that office-seeking parties within systems that allow for the public funding of extra-parliamentary parties would be encouraged to seek office in the long run. This will, in turn, allow parties to choose to remain out of parliament in situations when getting representation might call for a sacrifice of their autonomy. In addition, the availability of campaign resources will increase the likelihood of parties running alone in elections.

Observed Behavior
The direct financing of parties has played an important role in the development of political parties in Hungary—for both parliamentary parties that receive the lion's share of state money and for extra-parliamentary parties (Lewis 1998, 140). There is no doubt that the "well established and electorally successful parties" have benefited from this system of state financing more than the smaller and less successful parties (Ilonszki 2005, 12). However, the latter have certainly been able to secure more financial resources than their counterparts in more restrictive systems.

The funding of parties that do not make it into parliament but receive more than one percent of the vote clearly makes it easier for some parties in Hungary to persist in the system. For a party such as Munkaspart, this has been a very important factor in its ability to persist in the system and carry out its functions at the local level. Despite not getting representation in parliament, Munkaspart continues to receive funding from the state. As of 2003, it was receiving 75 million HUF (about $392,000) annually from the state, which provided for half of its budget, while the other half came from membership fees. In Munkaspart leader Vajda's opinion, the party could not exist without state funding, but it received far from enough. In contrast, "the big parties" that did not need state financing benefited the most from the funding provisions (Vajda 2003). Similar views were expressed by a CP leader, who argued that without state money, the newly founded party (that also has no members to pay dues) could not maintain its office and personnel (Kopa 2003).

In contrast, Bulgarian parties outside parliament received no funding from the state until 2001. That year some parties considered the promise of state money a strong enough incentive to join in electoral alliances so as to try to surpass the 1 percent threshold (Kostadinova 2005, 10). As already discussed, the 2001 alliance between BEL and the BZNS was, in the opinion of both, circumstantial. By the BZNS account, however, they formed an alliance because they understood that they could not surpass the 1 percent threshold each alone, which they thought would lead to the loss of state property they already possessed (Pinchev 2003). Similarly, in 2004, the Radical Democratic Party (RDP), a small extra-parliamentary party in Bulgaria with legislative ambitions, expressed a willingness to ally with smaller parties at future elections so that it could receive and keep state funding and property. It appeared that achieving legislative representation was no longer as important for smaller parties so long as they could finance their operations and continue their work at the local level (Petrov 2004).

This anecdotal evidence in support of party financing as a factor in the choice of party electoral strategies is supported by the examination of Hungarian and Bulgarian parties' electoral strategies presented in the last chapter. Hungarian parties seem to choose to "run alone" at a significantly higher rate than Bulgarian ones do. There is, then, some preliminary support for H7 and H8, and a clear need for a systemic examination of the effects of party financing regulations on party evolution.

Electoral Institutions

Electoral Systems in Bulgaria and Hungary

The second system-level factor that has emerged as a substantial influence on party formation and choice of electoral strategies in Bulgaria and Hungary is the type of electoral system in place in the two countries. These systems will be discussed in turn.

The Electoral System in Hungary

Hungary has introduced and maintained one of the more fascinating mixed electoral systems in the post-communist world. Introduced in 1989, it borrowed heavily from the German system and combined elements of both the SMD and PR systems in a conscious attempt to achieve a balance between the two and encourage the formation of a strong party system (Hack 2003). Voters have two votes, but the system is virtually made up of three interrelated parts: SMD with a run off, PR regional lists, and national PR compensatory lists (Benoit 2001).

About half of the seats in the legislature are elected using the SMD method—the country is divided into 186 single-member districts in which individual candidates compete and voters choose their most preferred candidate. If no candidate wins an absolute majority at the first round, all candidates with more than 15 percent of the vote, "but at least the three strongest candidates," can proceed to the second round in which the candidate with plurality of votes wins (Toka 1995b, 47).

Candidates in the PR part are elected from regional lists. The country is divided into 20 electoral districts, each electing between four and 28 MPs to make up a total of 152. In this part, candidates are elected through party lists using the Hagenbach-Bischoff formula. The system also employs the two-thirds rule, which prevents parties whose remainders are less than two-thirds of the district quota from using these votes to gain seats in the redistribution. The seats that remain unassigned are then transferred to the national compensatory lists.

To further preserve the proportionality between votes and seats, national lists were created to compensate the parties whose candidates won votes in the first round in the SMD districts but did not proceed to the second and the parties whose votes were unused in the regional districts. However, these unassigned seats (58 or more, depending on how many were transferred from the regional lists) are distributed only to parties with more than 5 percent of the vote (4 percent until 1994) in the multimember districts.[1]

In addition, the system makes qualifying for running in elections relatively difficult by interlocking the qualifications for having regional and national lists. A party needs to have nominated candidates in at least one quarter of the districts of the county to be able to run a regional list; it further needs to have seven regional lists to have a national list. Running a national list is thus relatively difficult (Toka 1995b).

The Electoral System in Bulgaria

Bulgaria has used two separate electoral systems since 1990. That year a combination of majority SMD and PR electoral system was used. In fact, this mixed system, which was loosely based on the Hungarian one (Birch et al. 2002, 116), allowed for half of the seats to be filled using majority SMD list and the other half using PR lists. However, the Bulgarian mixed system also allowed for independents to win seats and did not create any further links between the two parts of the system. Candidates could run both in a single-member district and on a party list. Although it was a mixed system, in reality it was more like a mechanical combination of the two systems rather than a mixture of the two (Tzenova 2004).

As agreed upon at the Round Table Talks, this system was only to be used for electing the Grand National Assembly. A new electoral system was adopted by that Assembly and remained in use, virtually unchanged, until 2001, although several minor amendments were made during the 1990s (Tzenova 2004, 157). The system introduced 31 regional districts in which parties ran regional lists but the distribution of seats was based on the national level results using the D'Hondt formula. Seats were allocated only to parties that surpassed a 4 percent national threshold (*Law on the Election of Members of the National Assembly* 1991).[2] This system created the possibility of translation of votes into seats that substantially distorted regional results and benefited the winning parties. Theoretically, it could advantage the winning party with up to 11 seats (Tzenova 2004).

Despite some efforts to lower the threshold to 3 percent, this "relatively unusual" system remained in effect until 2001, when a new electoral law was introduced (Birch et al. 2002, 121). The national debate on how to improve the system included suggestions to raise the threshold and to introduce special requirements for electoral alliances, but proved inconsequential. The main features of the electoral procedure in terms of threshold, counting method, and distribution method remained unchanged in the 2001 law. Some minor changes in the registration mechanisms and the already discussed changes in the funding of political parties were the only meaningful alterations (Tzenova 2004).

Electoral Systems and Party Electoral Strategies

Expectations

The empirical implications of H4 suggested that, at the system level, we should see a higher number of office-seeking parties in systems with lower thresholds, and less party proliferation in systems with higher thresholds. Over time, given no major change in the electoral system, we should observe a more rapid decrease in the number of office-seeking parties running in elections in the higher threshold systems. Although an isolated discussion of the experience of parties in two systems does not provide us with enough variation to test hypotheses, party development in Bulgaria and Hungary should provide some important insights into the nature of the proposed relationship.

Observed Behavior: Hungary

According to one of the creators of the Hungarian electoral system, ex-SZDSZ leader Peter Hack, the system was created in a conscious effort to provide people with a "real democratic choice" by limiting the number of political parties and forcing them to establish grassroots organizations. In his view, the system has managed to do the former: it has preserved the number of parties at a relatively low level and discouraged new entries, but it has failed to encourage strong party organization (Hack 2003).

In the early 1990s there were fears that voters and parties would have difficulty understanding the "fabulously incomprehensible," electoral system in Hungary and behaving strategically so as to allow it to have its intended effects (Toka 1995b, 44). However, by the 2000s, the Hungarian electoral law seems to have had its desired effect: voters do act strategically, and parties seem to have coordinated their strategies as well, which leads to a decrease in the number of parties (Duch and Palmer 2002).

The Hungarian electoral system clearly punishes small parties. Not only is the translation of votes into seats biased toward larger national parties, but even participating in elections is impossible for some of the smaller parties (Benoit 1999, 135). This seemed to be having an effect as early as the second election in 1994, although some parties appeared to disregard the incentives of the system (136).[3] In fact, in terms of the number of parties, the Hungarian party system has become more stable than the Bulgarian one only during the last round of elections. A reexamination of some of the indicators of party-system fragmentation that were presented in table 4.19 and a comparison of the Hungarian indicators with those of other Central European states (table 5.1) reveal that until 2002 the respective numbers for the Hungarian party system were usually very close to those for the other Central European states, and in some case above the Bulgarian levels and even above the Eastern European averages. However, by 2002, the anticipated effect of the electoral system seems to have become a reality.

Table 5.1 Some indicators of party system fragmentation: Bulgaria, Czech Republic, Hungary, and Poland

Indicator	Election	First	Second	Third	Fourth
Electoral parties	**Bulgaria**	42	38	49	41
	Czech Republic	15	20	16	10
	Hungary	28	34	28	19
	Poland	110	34	12	16
ENEP	**Bulgaria**	2.75	4.197	3.88	2.89
	Czech Republic	3.13	6.21	5.33	4.72
	Hungary	6.71	5.50	4.47	2.84
	Poland	13.80	9.80	4.59	4.50
	EE Average	5.5	5.6	4.6	4.1
Parliamentary parties	**Bulgaria**	6	3	5	5
	Czech Republic	4	6	6	5
	Hungary	7	6	6	4
	Poland	30	8	6	7
ENPP	**Bulgaria**	2.42	2.41	2.73	2.53
	Czech Republic	2.06	3.35	4.15	3.71
	Hungary	3.79	2.89	4.08	2.21
	Poland	10.86	3.87	2.95	3.59
	EE Average	4.00	3.7	3.7	3.8

But clear examples of "failures to learn" are still present in the Hungarian system. Although the number of small parties and independent candidates "has been steadily decreasing with each election" (Benoit 2001, 487), new parties do continue to emerge. In 2002, new parties ran alone. These included the CP and several FKGP factions. The final merger of the MDF and FIDESZ-MPP did not materialize after the 2002 elections, which led to an expectation of a return to a more fragmented party system. In fact, by 2005, it was clear that Hungary would maintain at least four major parties in parliament.

It will be unfair to underestimate the impact of the Hungarian electoral system, however. This system has clearly contributed to a different nature of party dynamics than that most other systems. In the context of this research, the presence of the second round makes it possible for parties to strike agreements between rounds after the electoral results are partially known. This allows parties to remain independent contesters but secure seats through the support of other parties half way in the electoral process. It also prevents larger parties from forming alliances with smaller parties that do not bring electoral support.

On the other hand, the system also encourages two divergent types of behavior. As small parties are disadvantaged by the interlocking nature of the system, they are sometimes pressed to join electoral alliances or merge with other parties. Examples are the alliances of the MDF with FIDESZ in 1998 and 2002 and the KDNP's merger with the latter. However, the system also clearly rewards parties that have a distinct electoral position. Such parties are more likely to be seen as valuable allies and invited to join alliances during the negotiations that go on between the two rounds of elections. Parties are thus encouraged to remain independent, and the SZDSZ's decision to do so has proven to be a wise one as it has been a valuable coalition partner in several governments. This dichotomy in the system was clearly expressed by the MDF leader Kupa who described the MDF's dilemma in 2003 as the choice between merging further and staying independent.

Overall, the Hungarian electoral system has clearly impacted the behavior of political parties, sometimes in conflicting ways. By uniquely combining and interconnecting SMD with a runoff and PR, the system has created constraints that Hungarian parties have found difficult to ignore.

Observed Behavior: Bulgaria

The Bulgarian electoral system is much simpler than the Hungarian and, in general, much more permissive. It is purely proportional and has a lower threshold (4 percent compared with 5 percent in the Hungarian PR part). In addition, and unlike other electoral systems in the region, the Bulgarian system provides no disincentives for parties to form alliances. The same electoral thresholds apply to all competitors that run under a single label, and no distinctions are drawn between *apparantement* and non-*apparantement* arrangements (*Law on the Election of Members of the National Assembly* 1991). In contrast, the electoral systems in the Czech and Slovak Republics, Poland, and Romania employ higher thresholds for electoral contestants that are alliances, and the electoral laws in Latvia and Estonia (since 1998) ban *apparantements* (Pettai and Kreuzer 2001).

The PR system was introduced because, with its relatively low threshold and D'Hondt formula, it promised to preserve significant proportionality in the system and to allow the representation of smaller parties in parliament. (Konstantinov 2001; Panev 2000). However, in many ways, it has brought counterintuitive results. As evident in table 4.19, there have been between three and five parties elected to parliament under this system. The real multiplicative effect of the PR system has been the creation of a multitude of small parties that usually do not manage to make it into parliament. In fact, researchers have seen this as an absurd situation and called repeatedly for a change of the electoral system (Konstantinov 2000; Yanova 2000; Panev 2000).

The leaders of the small Bulgarian parties often blame the 4 percent threshold of the electoral system for their inability to gain representation in parliament. Similarly, they consider it a major reason for the many and diverse electoral alliances that the smaller parties have formed over the years (Dzudzev 2003; Pinchev 2003; Kutov 2004; Zankov 2003a, 2003b; Murdzov 2003). Naturally, few of them saw the very existence of their parties as a direct result of the multiplicative effect of the system. In fact, it is the relatively permissive nature of the system that at least partly explains the presence of 300 parties in Bulgaria and the fact that a significant number of them do run in elections (see table 5.2).

The level of wasted vote in Bulgaria is another indication of the misjudged political potential of the parties in the country. Encouraged by the low threshold, splinters appear often and choose to run in elections alone, which leads to a substantial vote wastage. Table 5.2 presents the level of vote wastage in Bulgaria and compares it with that of Hungary.

The amount of wasted vote in Bulgaria varies more significantly from election to election than does the Hungarian indicator, and unlike the Hungarian one, does not display a clear directional trend. The difference in the number of electoral contestants among which the wasted vote is split is even more substantial: in Hungary it declines from 13 in 1990 to nine in 2002, but in Bulgaria it increases from 22 in 1990 to 27 in 2001 (and reaches 38 in 1994).

Table 5.2   Wasted Vote in Bulgaria and Hungary

Indicator[1]	Election	First	Second	Third	Fourth	Fifth
Percent of	Bulgaria	2.59	24.96	15.59	9.9	14.48
wasted vote[2]	Hungary	15.8	12.66	11.41	11.31	—
Number of parties	Bulgaria	22	30	38	29	27
splitting the	Hungary	13	13	10	9	—
wasted vote[3]						

[1] *Political transformation and the electoral process in post-communist Europe* project; Trud 1991 for Bulgarian results in 1990.
[2] Hungarian results are calculated using the PR part of the vote only.
[3] Includes *all* parties that received votes.

The electoral systems in Bulgaria and Hungary are certainly not the only factor that explains the differences in the behavior pattern of their political parties. However, based on both interview data and aggregate patterns, the systems clearly emerge as a major factor. It appears that the Hungarian mixed system strongly discourages small parties as illustrated by their declining number, but not to the extent predicted; some of the smaller parties persist and turn out to be encouraged by the electoral system to remain independent entities rather than ally or merge. In contrast, the much more permissive Bulgarian PR electoral system encourages small parties and has been seen as a contributing factor to the proliferation of unsuccessful parties in the party system over the years and their proclivity to form disparate alliances at election time. Coupled with the consequences of party financing, this factor clearly points to the need of a system-level analysis of the behavior of political parties and the constraints on their choice of electoral strategies. It is to this task that this chapter turns next.

TESTING THE MODEL AT SYSTEM LEVEL: TWELVE POST-COMMUNIST SYSTEMS

Model Overview and Operationalization of Variables

Having shown some preliminary evidence about the importance of system factors in parties' decision to form and their choice of electoral strategies, the chapter now turns to the final test of the proposed understating of party behavior. It uses system-level data from 12 post-communist states to test hypotheses 1, 3, 4, 6, 7, and 8. It does so by estimating a statistical model that conceptualizes the number of parties in each system as a function of the expectation of electoral volatility (H3), the extent of ethnic heterogeneity in the country (H4), the level of the electoral threshold (H6), and the nature of party financing (H7 and H8). To capture the temporal element of the model (H1), and to indirectly test the impact of party organization, the model also includes a variable representing the elapsed time since the first democratic election. The equation of the proposed model can be presented in the following way:

$$\text{Number of parties} = \alpha + \beta 1 \text{ electoral volatility} + \beta 2 \text{ ethnic heterogeneity} + \beta 3 \text{ threshold} + \beta 4 \text{ party funding} + \beta 5 \text{ number of election} + e$$

Dependent Variable: Number of Parties
Similar examinations of party system dynamics usually operationalize the dependent variable as the "number of effective parties" in the system (Roper 2003; Bielasiak 2003; Reich 2001; Cox 1997, among many others). The effective number of parties is a quantitative measure that produces a value that takes into account both the number of parties that compete in elections and the relative vote shares of each. This value is calculated using the following formula (Taagapera and Shugart 1989, 79):

$$\text{ENEP} = 1/\Sigma p_i^2,$$ where p is the proportion of the vote for each party i.

However, the focus of this study is not on how well parties do in elections per se, but on how and why parties decide to compete in elections. For the purposes of the present research, whether a party does well or not—in terms of seats and votes—is only of consequence for the party's choice of electoral strategy at the next election. This is why using the ENEP measure is not appropriate here. Instead, following Ordeshook and Shvetsova (1994) and Hug (2001), the model will use the absolute number of parties with more than 1 percent of the vote at each election and in each system as a measure of the dependent variable. In this case, however, and in opposition to the preceding discussion in this book, *a party* is defined as an electoral competitor; that is, electoral alliances are treated as parties.[4]

The number of parties at every election and in each system is the unit of analysis; all elections, including the founding ones, in each of the following countries are included in the data set: Bulgaria, the Czech Republic, Estonia, Hungary, Latvia, Lithuania, Poland, Romania, Russia, the Slovak Republic, Slovenia, and the Ukraine. A total of 44 observations are included in the sample. Values of the dependent variable vary from four to 25 with a mean of 11.34 and a standard deviation of 3.9 for all countries and all periods. The complete data set is provided in appendix E. Data on this variable is from the *Political Transformation and the Electoral Process in Post-Communist Europe* project at the University of Essex, supplemented with data from Munro and Rose (2003), and, where possible, verified by national elections statistics.

In general, all democratic elections since 1989 have been included in the sample; except for the post-Soviet states, the Czech and Slovak republics, and Slovenia, where only the post-independence elections are included. While most studies tend to exclude the founding elections because of their unique nature, they are important to this study and have been included. Authors (Cox 1997; Taagapera and Shugart 1989) often refer to these elections as abnormal as they happened in periods of extreme politics; however this characteristic is present only in the extreme values of some of my independent variables (e.g., expected electoral volatility). In fact, the nature and number of parties in the founding elections are very important factors for the further development of the party system because in many cases the parties that succeed at the first elections are the ones that come to dominate politics later on (Reich 2001, 1244; 2004).[5]

Independent Variables: Expected Electoral Volatility
Electoral volatility is usually measured as the percentage of difference of votes secured by each party over two elections (Przeworski 1975; Pederson 1979).[6] It is used widely in studies of party system development and party system institutionalization (Bielasiak 2003; Mainwaring 1999, 68–69). However, it is a measure of the actual volatility, while here we need a variable to capture the *expectation* of volatility. As this cannot be measured directly, following Hug (2001), I use the percentage change in inflation as a proxy for dissatisfaction with the political system.

While other indicators of economic problems can be used (unemployment or GDP per capita), the change in inflation (of consumer prices) gets at the most basic implication of economic problems, namely how much people can afford to buy (Reich 2001, 1250). To capture the general spirit of the time surrounding each election, the variable is measured as the yearly change in consumer prices, as reported by the IMF International Financial Statistics database. The variable can take both positive and negative numbers and varies between -93.67 and 770, with an average of 54.69.

As H3 suggested, the variable *inflation* is expected to correlate positively with the number of parties in the system; in other words, the more drastic the price rise (a higher positive number), the higher the expected electoral volatility and the higher the number of parties that might see a political opportunity and decide to form and run alone.[7]

Independent Variables: Ethnic Heterogeneity
The level of ethnic heterogeneity is measured by Rae's Index of Fractionalization, using the formula: $FI = 1 - \Sigma g_i^2$ where g is the proportion of population belonging to ethnic group *g*. The index can vary from 0 (least fragmented or least heterogeneous) to 1 (most fragmented or most heterogeneous). For this study, the measure was calculated using data on all ethnic groups listed in the *CIA World*

Factbook. Values vary from 0.06 (for Poland) to 0.57 (for Latvia); all values are listed in appendix E.

The variable *ethnicheter* is expected to correlate positively with the dependent variable. The higher the heterogeneity, the higher the number of parties that can have an ethnic base, and thus the higher the number of parties in the system that will have stable electoral support and can be expected to form and run alone in elections.

Independent Variables: Electoral Threshold

There are different ways that electoral thresholds can be measured. Studies have used the legal threshold (Moraski and Lowenberg 1999) and the "effective" threshold (Lijphart 1994, 25–29; Perea 2002). The legal threshold is the one legislated by the electoral law at the national or district level, while the "effective" threshold includes both the legal threshold and district magnitudes.[8] The legal threshold is used here. While the "effective" threshold might be a more precise measure of how much support a party would need to win a seat, this information is unlikely to be available to parties while making their choice of electoral strategies. Following Moraski and Lowenberg (1999), the variable *threshold* is measured as the percentage of the vote that a party needs to get at national level in order to gain seats in the legislature. The variable takes values from 0 to 5, with a median value of 5, but enough variation to allow for analysis.[9]

The *threshold* variable is expected to negatively influence the number of parties competing in elections. The higher the threshold, the more difficult it is for each individual party to achieve its electoral target on its own, and the more discouraged it will be to form or run alone in elections.

Independent Variables: Funding of Political Parties

As there is very little research on the effect of party funding on party development, and none that uses a quantitative measure and distinguishes among the different types of funding, the current operationalization of the variable is my own. Using data from the most comprehensive database on party financing, the *IDEA Handbook on Political Parties Financing*, I categorize the regulation of party financing in each country and at each time period in four distinct categories that reflect the discussion in chapter 2. The values of this variable for each country and election period are reported in table 5.3.

Measured in this way, the variable *funding* is expected to positively influence the number of parties in the system. As H7 and H8 suggested, the presence of financing for extra-parliamentary parties both

Table 5.3 Party financing, variable categories

State funding[1] provided for:	Value assigned	Countries
No parties	0	Ukraine, Latvia, Lithuania, Estonia (1992)
Parties in parliament only	1	Bulgaria, Poland, Romania
Parliamentary and extra – parliamentary parties (based on previous performance)	2	Bulgaria (2001), Czech Republic, Estonia, Hungary, Lithuania (2000), Slovakia, and Slovenia
All parties competing in current elections	3	Russia

[1]*Source*: IDEA Handbook on Political Parties Financing, Roper 2002 and 2003, and Smilov 1999 and 2001.

encourages parties to seek office in the long run and provides reasons to believe that electoral support will remain stable until election day. As a result, parties are encouraged to form/run alone at a higher rate than when financing is not present, thus increasing the overall number of parties in the system.

Independent Variables: Number of the Election
To capture the temporal dimension of the model suggested by H1 and indirectly by H9, a simple variable signifying the number of the election is included in the model. The variable takes the value of 1 for the first democratic election in each country, 2 for the second, etc. In countries such as the Czech Republic, where the first election after independence did not coincide with the first democratic election, the number reflects the number of the election overall. The variable *election* is expected to influence the number of parties competing in elections negatively over time; unsuccessful parties should leave the electoral competitions and new entries should be discouraged as the established parties become stronger organizationally.

Model Estimation

Several possible statistical techniques can be used to estimate the model. Studies that use the number of parties as dependent variables have often employed "count" models. Count models estimate the "number of times that something has happened" (Long 1997, 217). For example, this method was used by Hug in his analysis of the number of new parties in the system (2001). However, as Hug himself argues, the assumptions of the count model are violated by the temporal and spatial dependency of the number of parties emerging at each election in each country. As a result, he decided against the use of the count model and estimates an OLS regression and an MLE, or maximum likelihood estimation, regression of a transformed variable finding little difference between the two (Hug 2001, 182).

With this consideration in mind and due to its own limitations, this study uses a pooled cross-sectional (panel) linear regression to estimate the model at the party system level. Pooled cross-sectional models include data from several systems over several years. This allows me to test for temporal as well as spatial effects, which are especially important here, given that one of the underlying assumptions of the model is that parties will learn from their experience over time and adapt their strategies to political and institutional constraints (Stimpson 1985, 914).

The use of a panel data set, however, violates the assumption of OLS regression of independent error terms. In fact, with data arranged in panel format, there is a danger that the error terms will be correlated contemporaneously and within panels. Contemporaneous correlation arises when the observations are correlated across panels (Beck and Katz 1995). For example, the numbers of parties in the Czech and Slovak republics might be related to each other because of their common experience. In addition, the number of parties in each system might be correlated based on the characteristics of each system. Finally, first-order serial correlation is also usually present between consequent observations (Beck and Katz 637). However, these are correctable with the use of appropriate estimation techniques—in this case, given the specifics of the data and model, linear (Prais-Winsten) regression estimation with panel-corrected standard errors and panel-specific autocorrelations will be used. The method specifies that there is both heteroscadasticity and autocorrelation, and estimates the coefficients within these limits. According to Beck and Katz (1995), this method performs better than any existing methods (Parks method, for example) in estimating efficient coefficients.

Results and Discussion

The results of the model estimation are reported in table 5.4. Several observations had to be dropped because of unavailability of data. Overall, the model performs quite well, with an R-squared of .86. However, a substantial amount of its explanatory power is due to the autocorrelation allowed.[10] Even so, all variables are significant at the

Table 5.4 Linear (Prais-Winsten) regression with panel-corrected standard errors estimates

Group variable: panel	Estimated covariances = 78
Time variable: year	R-squared = 0.860
Number of obs: 37	Wald chi2(5) = 61447.03
Estimated autocorrelations = 12	Prob > chi2 = 0.0000
Estimated coefficients = 6	

Variable	Coefficient	Panel-corrected standard error	P-value	[95% conf. interval]	
Inflation	− .007	.003	0.009	− .008	− .005
Ethnicheter	5.715	1.572	0.000	2.004	8.859
Threshold	− 1.916	.782	0.014	− 2.869	− .913
Funding	.679	.393	0.084	.110	.878
Election	− 1.128	.573	0.049	− 1.418	− .729
Cons	21.007	2.725	0.000	15.665	26.348

.10 level, most at the .01 level, and except for one, the coefficients are all in the predicted direction. In addition, there is no significant correlation between ethnic heterogeneity, funding, and threshold (correlation coefficients are between .15 and .30), which indicates that their effects are, in fact, independent of each other.

Inflation and the Number of Parties
The results point to a significant relationship between the percentage change of inflation in each country and the number of parties competing in elections. However, they predict a negative change in the number of parties associated with a higher positive increase in the inflation rate. This result is against the hypothesized direction, but is not surprising. As mentioned before, inflation rates might not be the best measure of expected electoral volatility for the purposes of this study. The logic underlying the expectation of a positive relationship between the two is that during times of trouble, voters will be more likely to express their frustration with the current situation by supporting new parties. While the NDSV entry into Bulgarian politics 2001 certainly illustrates this argument, other examples show that during periods of great economic distress voters might be willing to support an existing party that is in strong opposition to the incumbent rather than support a new entrant in the system. In fact, the situation in Bulgaria in 1997 and Russian political developments after 1998 provide good illustrations of such a development.

Ethnic Heterogeneity and the Number of Parties
The results of this analysis clearly support H4. The variable is significant and the coefficient is in the hypothesized direction, which point to a positive relationship between the level of ethnic fragmentation/heterogeneity and the number of parties contesting elections. A difference of .20 in the level of ethnic fractionalization—similar to the difference in the level of fractionalization of Poland and the Slovak Republic, for example—would be associated with one more party in the system, everything else being equal.[11]

This finding as well as the experience of the ethnic party discussed in detail in chapters 3 and 4—the DPS in Bulgaria—hold up the argument that the support of ethnic parties is more stable over time. Ethnic party leaders are thus more likely to consider the achievement of their electoral targets to be within reach and choose to form and run alone in elections, which contributes to a higher number of parties in the system overall. This seems to support the findings of other studies that a higher level of ethnic heterogeneity, at least in the post-communist world, can be expected to contribute to a larger number of parties in the system.

Electoral Threshold and the Number of Parties
H5 is also supported by the results of the statistical analysis. The effect of the electoral threshold is significant at the 0.01 level, and the coefficient has a negative sign. This indicates that, as H5 suggested, a higher threshold will discourage parties from forming and running alone, which contributes to a lower number of parties overall. The coefficient of -1.91 indicates that for every 1 percent difference in the level of the threshold, we can expect the number of parties competing in elections to be lowered by almost two, everything else being equal.

This result confirms the earlier discussion of the tendencies in party behavior in the two quite distinct electoral systems of Bulgaria and Hungary, which argued that the electoral regulations seem to provide a powerful constraint on the behavior of political parties. It also concurs with a large body of literature on the effect of the permissiveness of the electoral system on the number of parties in the system. But this analysis differs in that it estimates the absolute number of parties running in elections as its dependent variable instead of using the "effective" number of parties in the system. In other words, it confirms not only that more permissive systems result in higher proportionality of results and thus allow for a higher number of parties *to do better* in the system, but it also suggests that parties also seem to anticipate and/or react to such systems and choose to ally/merge, which leads to less competitors in the system.

Party Funding and the Number of Parties
The hypothesized effect of the nature of party funding on the number of parties seems to be supported by the results of the statistical analysis. Although the significance level is .08, the one directional hypothesis makes this result even more robust. The coefficient indicates that, everything else being equal, we can associate a difference between funding no parties and funding parliamentary parties, or between funding parliamentary parties and funding parties that have previously achieved a certain level of electoral support, with an increase of .6 in the number of parties.

This finding supports the relatively underresearched hypothesis proposed by this study and Roper (2002 and 2003) that the type of party financing might influence the number of parties in the system. In the present context, this supports the proposition that parties will be more likely to seek office in the long run and see themselves as able to carry out effective electoral campaigns, which leads to a choice of a "running alone strategy," and thus to a larger number of contestants in elections. It also supports the proposition that it will be *the type* of funding as opposed to the mere presence of funding in the system that would influence the behavior of political parties. Operationalizing party funding as a dichotomous variable, Roper found no significant difference between the number of parties in the Baltic States (2003). However, it appears that a more precise statistical analysis can support the evidence from case studies provided here and elsewhere (2001) that also confirms the impact of funding on party electoral strategies.[12]

Election Period and the Number of Parties
Finally, the model also supports the idea that parties learn from their experience and adapt to the constraints of the institutional environment and the realities of party competitions. Everything else being equal, we see a uniform decrease in the number of parties of more than one with each election. H1 is thus supported and H9 indirectly so. H9 suggested that the effect of party organization on the electoral strategies of individual parties, otherwise unobservable at the system level, might be corroborated by a general decrease in the number of parties over time. With the passage of time, parties become more established in societies through their organization, and thus dissuade new entries to "run alone" at elections. However, the underlying

assumption for this hypothesis is that parties do develop an organization, which, given the discussion in earlier sections, might or might not be the case. Thus, the implications of the model for H9 are quite limited.

In general, however, the significance of the *election* variable provides support for the proposition that parties in post-communist party systems do learn from their experience, and following an initial boom in party activity that troubled many, we can expect a gradual stabilization in terms of the number of parties in the system.[13] Although this hypothesis was supported by the experience of Hungarian parties examined in chapter 4, it was not fully supported by the discussion of the patterns of party development in Bulgaria. However, it appears that the experience of political parties in this system might be more different rather than similar to that of a typical post-communist system.

CONCLUSION

This chapter has presented a test of the model of party formation and electoral competition presented in chapter 2 by testing the system-level implications of hypotheses 1, 3, 4, 6, 7, and 8. It presented an examination of the nature of the electoral system and party funding provisions in Bulgaria and Hungary that was prompted by the analysis in chapter 4. It found substantial party-level evidence that these system-level factors play an important role in the decisions of parties to form and in their choice of electoral strategies.

It then proceeded to test the model at the system level by engaging in statistical analysis of panel data from 12 post-communist political systems. Using the number of electoral competitors (here called parties) at each election in each system as the unit of analysis and the Prais-Winsten linear regression, the study estimated the impact of five independent variables on the number of parties. The model performed relatively well with all but one coefficient estimated in the hypothesized direction. The analysis thus provided support for the impact of the level of electoral threshold (H4), ethnic heterogeneity (H6), and the length of experience with democratic elections (H1 and H9) on the number of parties competing in elections. Most importantly, however, it provided evidence that the nature of party financing influences the electoral strategies of political parties (H7 and H8), a proposition that has been relatively underresearched in the current literature. Finally, the model found no evidence to support H3 using the current operationalization of expected electoral volatility, a conclusion that supports findings of other studies as well.

Overall, the statistical analysis provides support for the theoretical model of party formation and electoral competition presented in chapter 2. Parties react to electoral success and failure and choose electoral strategies that best promise to deliver their electoral targets within the constraints imposed on them by the institutional context of the political system. Although aberrations clearly exist, the theoretical model appears to provide a good fit, at least at the system level, to the behavior of political parties in the post-communist world.

NOTES

1. Full texts of the electoral and party laws in Hungary are available through *Political Transformation and the Electoral Process in Post-Communist Europe* project http://www2.essex.ac.uk/elect/database/indexCountry.asp?country=HUNGARY&opt=leg.
2. For the full text of the old and new Bulgarian electoral law, see *Political Transformation and the Electoral Process in Post-Communist Europe* http://www2.essex.ac.uk/elect/database/indexCountry.asp?country=BULGARIA&opt=leg.
3. The splits of the MIEP from the MDF and the fragmentation of the FKGP during that period (1991–1994) are discussed in chapter 4 (section, "Observed Behavior: Electoral Performance and the Choice of Strategies").
4. This is done to both keep within the tradition of similar studies, which rarely distinguish between parties running alone and electoral alliances, *and* to reflect the research problem in this work. We are interested in what strategies parties have chosen: an alliance of three parties will here be counted as one "party" or electoral competitor, indicating that these parties have found it necessary to give up part of their autonomy and run together. Thus, we will observe a decrease in the number of competitors, which is likely to eventually lead to a decrease in the number of parties (in the general definition) as well.
5. Although, Reich has recently argued, the parties that *win* the founding elections tend to disappear as an independent entity over the next few elections (2004).
6. The measure of volatility represents the percent of the vote that has switched parties between two elections. Volatility $(V_t) = 1/2 \, \Sigma |\Delta p_{i,t}|$ Where, $\Delta p_{i,t} = p_{i,t} - p_{i,t-1}$, and, p is the percentage of the vote received by party i at time t.
7. However, the hypothesized direction of the relationship is debatable. As other studies have argued, the direction will depend on whether voters blame all established parties for their economic troubles or just

the government incumbent (Reich 2001). However, presently, and in the absence of better measure of expected electoral volatility, the proposition stands.

8. In fact, the effective threshold is the average of the threshold of inclusions (the share of the vote a party needs to gain a seat under the most favorable circumstances) and the threshold of exclusion (the share of the vote a party need to gain a seat under the most unfavorable circumstances) (Lijphart and Gibberd 1977).

9. This is the most straightforward operationalization of the variable, although it ignores several important additional features of each electoral system that relate directly to how much support a party needs to gain representation: the presence of an SMD part; the presence of higher thresholds for alliances; and the presence of second and third tiers. However, the incorporation of these features would require the inclusion of too many dichotomous variables, which makes the model difficult to estimate.

10. Estimated rho values are between $-.97$ to $+1$. However, this could be expected as the choice of electoral strategies of political parties, and hence their number at election, is proposed to reflect their strategies at the immediately preceding election, which thus anticipates a high first-order serial correlation between observations.

11. The parties included in the measure of the dependent variable in the most heterogeneous countries in the sample indeed include ethnic parties: in Latvia, Estonia, and Ukraine, there are parties of the Russian minority; Lithuania has a Polish minority party; in contrast, there are no ethnic parties included in the measure of the dependent variable in the most homogenous countries in the sample (Poland, Hungary, and the Czech Republic) (Rose and Munro 2003). It has to be noted that parties that might have got representation through special minority arrangements have not been included in the count of parties *unless* they have gathered more than 1 percent of the vote at national elections.

12. It has to be noted, however, that the statistically significant effect of this variable is contingent on specifying panel-specific autocorrelation, in other words, controlling for error terms being related from one election to the next. However, this is one of the underlying propositions of this model, which makes the incorporation of first order serial correlation in the model justifiable.

13. The variable is a significant but weak predictor of the number of parties by itself (correlation coefficient of $-.3$).

Chapter 6

Conclusion

This book has been an attempt to describe and explain the process of formation of political parties in the post-communist world and their choice of electoral strategies. Starting from the assumption that this process can be understood within the framework of existing theories of party development, the book has suggested a theoretical model of how and why parties form, and how and why they decide to run alone, seek alliances, merge, disband, or hibernate. As figure 6.1 explains, party evolution is seen as a repeated process in which politicians define goals, translate them into electoral targets, and choose electoral strategies that best promise to deliver these targets.

After each election, and in light of the party's electoral performance, the process starts again with a reevaluation of the goals, and so on. As a result of this electoral process, parties form and then either persist in the system or change by merging or disbanding. As a consequence, party systems acquire a certain set of characteristics in terms of the number and stability of the political parties within them.

Of most importance to this study has been the process that leads to the choice of a certain electoral strategy. Chapter 2 explained this process in detail, paying specific attention to the factors that influence a party's evaluation of its expected electoral support, the adequacy of this support, and the likelihood that it will remain stable. It then developed nine specific hypotheses that reflect the proposed relationships between the choice of electoral strategies and electoral performance, electoral threshold, expected electoral volatility, ideological crowdedness, ethnic heterogeneity, resources availability, and party organizational development. Chapters 3 and 4 provided detailed description and analysis of these relationships based on data from the

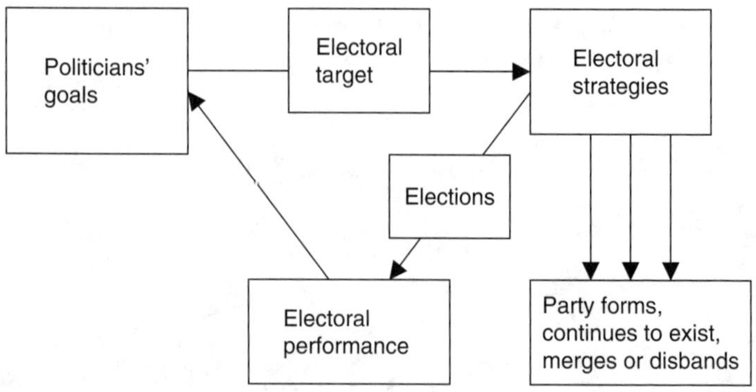

Figure 6.1   Process of party formation and electoral competition: Review.

party systems of Bulgaria and Hungary. Chapter 5 tested the system-level implications of the model, using a statistical analysis of data from 12 post-communist states and qualitative analysis of aggregate trends in Bulgaria and Hungary.

This final chapter offers some more general observations about party behavior in the post-communist world, drawing on the analysis presented here. It could be argued that most observations are based on the experience of parties in two countries only, and thus do not present enough variation to describe and analyze the general tendencies in post-communist party development. However, several factors allow one to claim that one can draw on this analysis to understand the behavior of post-communist parties.

First of all, this analysis has used the party, rather than the party system, as a unit of analysis; the six parties whose evolution has been described in most detail are of quite divergent ideology, organizational experience, and ideological orientation. Each of them has played a different role in the party politics of its respective country, and thus they represent the three different types of party the model differentiated in chapter 2. The BEL, the DPS, and the SZDSZ are executive parties, as their goal has been participation in the executive; Munkaspart is a legislative party, as its ambition has been limited to representation in parliament; and FIDESZ and the BSP are typical prime-ministerial parties, as they have repeatedly attempted to dominate the executive. The success of the six parties in achieving their respective goals has also been quite different.

Ideologically, Munkaspart is reformed Marxist, the BSP is socialist, BEL is social democratic, FIDESZ is conservative, and the SZDSZ and the DPS are liberal (although the DPS is more of an ethnic party that proclaims itself to be liberal). Organizationally, the BSP, the DPS, and Munkaspart can be considered mass-based parties, while the other three are elite-based and run by professionals.

This variation in the nature and experiences of the six parties is further complemented by the variation provided by a comparative analysis of the trends in the two party systems. Bulgaria and Hungary provide very distinctive experiences of post-communism. Hungary is often considered the best performer in both political and economic terms in the group of post-communist countries as its effortless entry into the EU demonstrates. It has also achieved substantial party-system stability. Bulgaria, in contrast, has had major problems along the way of reforming its political and economic system; its party-system has experienced major reshuffles at almost every election. Finding common trends in party behavior in the two systems will thus reflect realities in two quite dissimilar post-communist systems and should thus allow us to use them as indications of general patterns of post-communist party development.

Finally, the conclusions that emerged from the detailed analysis of the Bulgarian and Hungarian parties' experience were further corroborated by the comparative examination of party trends in the post-communist world as revealed through aggregate-level analysis of data from 12 post-communist states. The results of the present work can thus be considered generalizable to the experience of the post-communist world, which allows an elaboration on some general trends of post-communist party development in this chapter.

RATIONAL PARTIES?

This book has proposed to view the behavior of politicians in the post-communist world as rational—in the sense that they are expected to define their political goals, translate them into electoral targets, consider a variety of institutional constraints, and, then, based on all these factors, choose among several strategies the one that is likely to deliver their goals. Within the tradition of studying parties as endogenous institutions, the formation of parties and their persistence in the system are seen as ways of achieving these goals.

Investigation of Bulgarian and Hungarian parties' behavior revealed that politicians do indeed follow a process very similar to the one suggested here in taking the decision to form and in their choice of electoral strategies. They do define goals in electoral terms, evaluate their prospective support, and choose strategies that they believe promise to deliver their electoral targets in the best way. Electoral success does drive their behavior. Analysis of the implications of the theoretical model in the larger setting of 12 post-communist states provided further support for the applicability of this claim to party behavior in the region. In all of the studied party systems, the number of office-seeking parties declines over time. Thus, it seems that parties react to electoral considerations, successful ones persist in the party system while unsuccessful ones gradually disappear.

What does this signify for the general condition of party politics in the region? The evidence presented here is sufficient to give some credibility to an argument that party politics in the post-communist world is no longer as unique as some scholars described it to be in the early 1990s. The fact that a model mostly built on mainstream party theory would describe and explain the behavior of post-communist parties supports this claim. In the first decade of post-communist party development, scholars described a reality of disorganized, weakly grounded, and fluid parties that were assumed to be necessarily different from the Western European ones. By the early 2000s, however, the majority of parties seemed to have achieved a certain level of stability and predictability that would bring post-communist party behavior closer to the nature of party behavior in the established democracies.

There are exceptions to this general rule, and they indicate that electoral considerations do not always explain the behavior of post-communist parties. Based on the Bulgarian and Hungarian parties' experience, we can make several observations that qualify the arguments made earlier in this chapter.

Some parties appear to value their autonomy to a higher degree than the analytical framework presented here allows for. H2 did suggest a certain concern with party autonomy and proposed that parties will be unwilling to forgo it if there is even a small chance of achieving their electoral targets through electoral strategies that do not require them to give up their autonomy. However, it appears that some parties in both Hungary and Bulgaria have chosen to remain autonomous or refused electorally beneficial alliances despite a *clear* indication of their inability to achieve electoral success. The degree to which parties stress this concern varies from observation to observation, but the behavior of the ZP and, in some ways, BEL in Bulgaria and of the Hungarian MDF and Munkaspart do provide examples of this trend.

Munkaspart is probably the most clear-cut example of this concern with autonomy. Despite repeated failure to achieve representation in the Hungarian Parliament, it has refused any cooperation with other parties on the left, remained independent, and contested elections on its own. Similarly, the MDF was in fact faced with the possibility of a merger with FIDESZ after the 2002 elections, but consciously chose to remain an independent entity despite indications that its electoral support could not promise future parliamentary representation in its own right. The clear choice between doing well in the short term by achieving parliamentary representation and persisting as an independent political party was debated within the party, and the decision to choose the latter proved to have been the right one in 2006, but only barely.[1]

The ZP and VMRO in Bulgaria have also taken decisions that speak of a concern with party autonomy. They both left their electoral alliances (ONS and ODS, respectively) in expectation of the 2001 elections; the leaders of both parties referred to their concern with party autonomy as the major reason for the decision to leave the alliances. Both parties joined in new alliances; however, in both cases, they were negotiated specifically with the concern of autonomy in mind (Dzudzev 2003; Murdzov 2003). Neither the VMRO nor the ZP managed to gain parliamentary representation in the 2001 elections.

This pattern of behavior is certainly not a dominant one in either Bulgaria or Hungary. Although it is clearly present in both party systems, it can only be found through a detailed study of individual party behavior. If we were to look at only aggregate data, such as the number of parties contesting elections, these instances of parties persisting in the party system when electoral fortunes would predict their transformation through mergers or alliances would remain unnoticed.

IDEOLOGICAL PARTIES?

Research has often argued that politicians in the post-communist world are not concerned with ideological stances (as illustrated by the high occurrence of splinters and defections), and some studies have assumed parties to be policy neutral (Shabad and Slomczynski 2004; Zielinski et al. 2003; Grofman et al. 2000; Kreuzer and Pettai 2002). This study, however, has demonstrated that ideology matters. Parties do think of their ideological position and consider the dynamics of their respective ideological space when taking the decision to form or not, and then run alone, ally, or merge. All Hungarian and Bulgarian parties examined in detail displayed tendencies to judge their chances of success by considering their own ideological appeal in relation to the existing ideological space. They also tended to be more willing to form alliances with parties that are ideologically closer to them. Some of the clearest examples of attempts to "consolidate the ideological space" are FIDESZ's behavior since the mid-1990s, and the BSP's attempt to bring together all social-democratic parties in Bulgaria since 2000. In both these cases, the driving force behind decisions was the realization that the electorate could only support a limited number of parties of a similar ideological position.

However, this conclusion is not without qualifications. While ideology and ideological positioning matter, other factors sometimes overshadow them in their impact on the choice of electoral strategy. For example, the FKGP in Hungary kept on fragmenting into more and more factions even as elections proved the infeasibility of the small holders' appeal. Similarly, the SDS in Bulgaria experienced a period of splinters in the early 1990s, then seemed to realize that splitting the party was not a viable strategy. But after its defeat in 2001, the party started fragmenting again to produce the SSD, the DSB, and the BSD. The stories of the BZNS and the BSDP in Bulgaria and the KDNP in Hungary are much too similar to go over in detail here. In most of these cases, personal rivalries and past party histories emerge as more important determinants of behavior and eclipse considerations of ideological positioning and electoral success.

ORGANIZED PARTIES?

Party studies have also argued that political parties in the post-communist world are professional and elite based and are generally not concerned with building their organizations. This is generally seen as a natural trend: most of the post-communist political parties developed during a time of a general decline in the importance of party organization and in a specific context of strong antiparty feelings. However, based on data reported in Spirova (2005) as well as in chapter 4 here, this book has argued a slightly different position.

First of all, there is a variation among individual parties regarding the extent to which they find organization building important and invest in it. This variation seems to be at least partially linked to party ideology. The successor parties in both Bulgaria and Hungary exhibit much larger and more extensive organization networks than any other parties in the two systems. Although smaller in absolute terms, the organizations of the Hungarian Munkaspart and the CPoB are similarly impressive. Left-of-center ideology, however, is not a guarantee of a strong organization: BEL, for example, did not see organization to be as important as one would expect a social-democratic party to do;

it did make extensive use of the media and new technology to replace some of the traditional functions of a party organization. Alternatively, parties other than those on the left-of-center can also value organization strongly and build extensive organization networks: the DPS and VMRO in Bulgaria are particularly good examples.

Even the parties that do not have strong organizations and have previously demonstrated distaste for organization building, such as FIDESZ in Hungary, currently appear to be concerned with it. As chapter 3 elaborated, FIDESZ was known as the "voice-mail" party in the 1998 and 2002 elections and was making no concerted attempt to build an organization but instead used expensive and professionally run campaigns to get its message across. However, by 2003, they seemed to have realized that they had exhausted that option of attracting voters and had to turn back to registering new members as an alternative strategy of enlarging their vote. The Bulgarian SDS went through a similar process in the mid-1990s when it decided to end its existence as a loose network of disparate organizations and instead build a single party with a dues-paying membership that could be easily mobilized. Overall, very few of the Bulgarian and Hungarian parties examined here expressed a clear rejection of the idea that organization is important: the CP in Hungary and BEL in Bulgarian were the only two to do so.

In addition, trends in organizational development seem to vary by system. As chapter 4 argued, Bulgarian parties seem to show, in general, a stronger concern for organization building, and to have generally higher member-to-voter ratios than their counterparts in Central Europe. Explanations for this trend do not concern us here; but it is important to realize that general arguments can often obscure the variation that exists among parties, just as arguments about post-communist party development built on the experience of the Central European States might simply not present the whole picture.

The extent to which organizational characteristics influence the behavior of political parties in Bulgaria and Hungary is a separate issue. Ironically, of all parties surveyed in detail, it is the successor parties that display the highest levels of internal party democracy. Partly as a way to distance itself from its nondemocratic past, the BSP allows "ideological platforms," or official factions, to exist within it and has very strictly mandated local participation in the candidate selection process. None of the other parties surveyed in detail display such characteristics. In contrast to the BSP, the other party with a strong organization, the DPS, exhibits the opposite trend. The DPS is strictly hierarchical and allows little room for local initiative and ideological subtlety. In it, as in most of the Hungarian and Bulgarian parties studied, dissenters are encouraged to leave the party.

The little variation in the level of internal party democracy does not allow any sweeping generalizations, but some tentative patterns emerge. It does seem that it is the role attributed to the membership, rather than the actual size of the membership or the extensiveness of the organizational network, that influences the behavior of the party, or least their choice of electoral strategies. Of the parties examined in detail here, it was only the BSP that seemed to be constrained by its membership in any meaningful way. There is not enough evidence to argue that the BSP chose certain electoral strategies because of the demands of its members, but it did seem to react to their discontent with the 2001 choice of a strategy and to alter it at the 2005 elections.

As a consequence, when viewed from the perspective of the aggregate data, the general strength of organizational development does not seem to have a strong impact on the electoral behavior of political parties. We do not notice a more stable dynamic of party interactions in Bulgaria than in Hungary despite a higher concern with developing organization structures there.

PARTIES AND THE RULES OF THE ELECTORAL GAME

The analysis of party behavior at the party level suggested a clear divergence of general patterns of behavior in Bulgaria and Hungary, which indicates that factors at the system level similarly constrain political parties in their decision to form and their choice of electoral strategies. The present work complements a solid body of literature that has found a substantial relationship between electoral systems and the number of parties in both established and new democracies. The examination of individual party behavior in Bulgaria and Hungary showed that, in general, parties do think about the realities imposed by the electoral thresholds when they choose how to run in elections. Alliances and mergers have often been the result of a realization that current electoral support would not surpass the electoral threshold.

The effect of the electoral system on party behavior is particularly prominent in Hungary where small parties are discouraged from running by a mixed PR-SMD system. Not only are they faced with having to surpass a 5 percent national PR threshold, but they are also required to satisfy conditions in the two other tiers of the system, including running candidates in a certain number of SMD districts. The complex and interlocking nature of the electoral rules thus makes it extremely difficult for parties to achieve parliamentary representation unless they have a solid and organized presence throughout the country. In Bulgaria, in contrast, the much more permissive nature of the system allows smaller parties to consider it possible to do well on their own. The 4 percent national threshold is all they need to satisfy in order to achieve parliamentary representation. The willingness of a party such as GOR/BEL/BSD (described in chapter 3), among others, to continue its search for a successful electoral strategy is a clear indication of the more limited constraint of the purely proportional electoral system in Bulgaria.

An analysis of the trends in party behavior at the system level within Bulgaria and Hungary illustrated this argument. Although at the beginning of the examined period both systems had quite a large number of electoral contestants, after four or five cycles of electoral competition, the number of parties running in elections in Hungary is now substantially smaller than in Bulgaria. That the nature of the electoral system impacts the behavior of political parties and, in particular, their choice of electoral strategies was further substantiated by the analysis of party development in 12 post-communist party systems. The statistical model established a significant relationship between the level of the threshold and the number of electoral contestants, which indicates that lower thresholds are associated with a higher number of parties even when the other realities of post-communist party development are accounted for.

This trend is not without exceptions: some parties do refuse to abide by the rules and form and/or persist in the system despite a clear indication that they cannot surpass the electoral threshold. This happens even in Hungary, as the experience of Munkaspart and the CP demonstrates. Here again, system-level patterns clearly obscure some party-level peculiarities. The overall effect of the electoral system can hardly be disputed.

PARTIES AND PUBLIC FINANCING

If the link between electoral rules and parties' choice of electoral strategies only complements previously established relationships, the analysis of the impact of public party financing and party behavior presented here is quite innovative. The detailed examination of the party financing regulations in Bulgaria and Hungary and their impact on party behavior revealed that parties do take into account resource availability when choosing an electoral strategy. Parties will be encouraged to remain outside parliament *but* independent if party financing allows for their maintenance. Alternatively, electoral alliances might result from a concern to secure public financing by achieving representation in parliament.

The system-level analysis established a significant relationship between the type of party financing available in the post-communist systems and the number of parties in each system. Although this proposition has recently been made in the literature (Roper 2003), its limited empirical tests had not shown the presence of a link between the two. In statistical terms, however, financing has been seen as a dichotomous variable—it is either present or absent. Here, the analysis used a different and arguably better operationalization of the provisions of party financing. Financing is seen as one of four possible types ranging from least permissive to most permissive in terms of its hypothesized support for the existence of independent political parties. The statistical analysis carried out here supported the proposition. Thus, it appears that it is the type of financing rather than its mere presence that needs to be accounted for if we are to understand its significance for the process of party competition. This qualification is particularly important as public financing of political parties is a common occurrence in the post-communist world, but its precise shape and form often eludes political scientists and policy makers alike.

PARTIES AND INTERNATIONAL ACTORS

While research on party behavior usually incorporates factors at party and system levels as constraints of this behavior, it rarely goes beyond the domestic party system to look for explanations. However, the discussion in chapters 2 and 3 has shed light on the role played by party groups and party federations at the EU level (Europarties), such as the PES and the EPP.

That Europarties and other international political organizations (such as the Socialist International or the Liberal International) have been involved with parties in the EU-candidate states of post-communist Europe is not news. While we see relatively little, and mostly indirect, impact of these organizations on domestic parties in the member states (Poguntke et al.), they have been actively involved in politics in the candidate states. Europarties have given membership status to parties from the candidate states before EU accession has taken place and even before accession papers have been signed; they have also provided direct financial and personnel assistance to member parties. However, as this research showed, they have gone further;

they have intervened quite directly to influence the electoral behavior of *kin* (not necessarily member) political parties in candidate states. And, political parties in candidate states have accepted, welcomed, and in many cases sought out this interest in them.

While methodological problems prevent the establishment of a systematic relationship, a detailed study of how and why parties choose certain strategies in Bulgaria provided evidence that supports this claim. There, the PES and the EPP have been actively involved in several important events. The PES instigated BEL's formation in 1997; later on it encouraged the creation of the BSP-led alliances, and in many ways gave grounds to BEL to resist joining them. Thus, ironically, in a way it contributed to the fragmentation of the Bulgarian social democracy. The EPP encouraged the creation of the ODS alliance in 1996–97 and its maintenance in 2001, and made repeated, but unsuccessful, efforts to bring the center-right together in 2005.

Parties choose electoral strategies and decide to split, form, run alone, merge, and ally based on an evaluation of their electoral chances within the opportunity structures present in the party system; but they also take into consideration the opinion of their European partners, the Europarties. Legitimacy from the EU level has been so important that parties have chosen strategies that might not have been entirely to their benefit in terms of office-seeking ambition, but have satisfied the will of the Europarties.[2] This clearly points to the need to incorporate international factors in accounts of how parties choose to run in elections, and as a consequence, of explanations about the nature of the party systems in the post-communist world.

UNANSWERED QUESTIONS

There are several reasons that the current analysis has remained limited. The evidence presented and analyzed in this work did not find conclusive evidence to support the proposition of the theoretical model that an expectation of high electoral volatility would be linked to a larger number of new entries into the party system. The analysis of party development in Bulgaria and Hungary presented some evidence that this is indeed the case, but the statistical analysis did not establish a significant relationship between expected volatility operationalized as change in inflation and the number of parties in the system. Arguably, as chapter 5 discussed, this might be an artifact of the operationalization of the variable in the empirical analysis, but it might also point to a different pattern of voters' behavior in times of national crisis. Rather than looking for the new face in politics, they might be more inclined to rally behind the nonincumbent but established parties in the system. For certain, only a deeper investigation into the interaction between expectations of volatility and parties' behavior will shed more light on the particulars of this relationship.

Because of a lack of enough observations, the study also provided only limited insights into the willingness of a party to merge with another during the election immediately following its formation. This problem is common to most attempts to study the phenomenon of party mergers; there are simply not enough of them. It was only the individual party analysis that shed some light on this issue. The proposition that parties will not be willing to forfeit their autonomy by merging without trying an alternative electoral strategy is confirmed by BEL's experiences in Bulgaria; the sheer lack of mergers, especially in the Bulgarian context that should encourage them, also lends support to it. It even appears that parties are more likely to disband or hibernate rather than merge with others. However, no generalizable conclusions on the likelihood of mergers could be reached due to the limited data and some further methodological issues.

THE STUDY OF PARTY POLITICS IN THE POST-COMMUNIST WORLD

The analysis presented here points to several general points related to the study of party politics in the post-communist world. The first one is related to the findings of the cross-national analysis. The statistical analysis showed a significant correlation between consequent observations within party systems, but at the same time, despite its presence, the model estimates are highly significant and point to a common process of party development across states. Although not a groundbreaking finding, this reminds us that we need to account for the specific nature of each system when making comparisons across systems. Comparing post-communist systems cross-sectionally at a certain point in time and arguing that one party system is consolidating faster than another or that the processes of party development in the systems are markedly different might not be warranted.

As this analysis has shown, specific country characteristics such as ethnic heterogeneity do have an impact on the number of parties in the system. Party-level and system-level analysis provided evidence that ethnic parties have more stable support than nonethnic ones. Both the DPS's development in Bulgaria through five electoral cycles, as well as the significant relationship between ethic heterogeneity and the number of parties established by the statistical analysis confirmed this proposition. This could potentially lead to a higher number of parties in ethnically diverse societies, everything else being equal. Ethnic heterogeneity thus might partly explain, for example, the higher number of parties in Latvia compared with those in Hungary, while party behavior might be otherwise driven by similar underlying motivations and decision-making processes.

Further, the analysis provided clear system-level evidence but more mixed party-level evidence on the applicability of the model to party development in the post-communist world. In some cases, the conclusions reached were even contradictory. This leads to a final observation. Understanding party development requires study at both party and party-system level. System-level patterns often obscure the peculiarities of individual parties and limit our understanding of the factors that impact their development. Ignoring the system-level patterns, in turn, prevents us from seeing the trends of party development in absolute terms.

In the present context, individual parties might not all follow the proposed model of party behavior, but enough of them do, allowing us to adduce evidence to support the system-level implications of the model. Because the theoretical model developed here has borrowed heavily from long-standing theories of party behavior in established democracies, we can conclude with some degree of confidence that for all practical purposes, parties and party-system development in the post-communist world are not as unique as party theorists have often argued. Despite being organizationally weaker and heavily dominated by the party elites, in terms of their electoral behavior parties react to basically the same constraints as their Western counterparts.

However, there are exceptions, which only emerge after a careful investigation of the behavior of individual parties. In sharp contradiction to the expectations of the analytical framework here, some parties choose to be "different" and continue to ignore the realities of the electoral process. And although these parties are usually smaller, often marginal, and sometimes short-lived, their presence leaves an impact on the pattern of party behavior in the system.

NOTES

1. In the 2006 elections, the MDF won 11 seats by contesting the elections on its own after it had run in an alliance with FIDESZ in 2002. The party came very close to failing in its effort to secure parliamentary representation however: it got exactly 5 percent of the PR vote (CSPP 2006).

2. The intervention of the Europarties in domestic party politics in candidate countries might actually be counterproductive. In at least two cases, the push for consolidation seems to have created problems within the ideological families by creating further divisions among the parties.

REFERENCES

Agh, Attila. 1994. "The Hungarian Party Systems and Party Theory in the Transition of Central Europe." *Journal of Theoretical Politics* 6(2): 217–238.

———. 1996. "Emergence of New Political Elites." In *Stabilizing Fragile Democracies,* ed. Geoffrey Pridham and Paul G. Lewis. London and New York: Routledge.

———. 1997. "Defeat and Success as Promoters of Party Change." *Party Politics* 3(3): 407–427.

———. 2000. "Party Formation Process and the 1998 Elections in Hungary: Defeat as Promoter of Change for the HSP." *East European Politics and Societies* 14(2): 288–315.

Aldrich, John. 1995. *Why Parties? The Origin and Transformation of Political Parties in America.* Chicago and London: University of Chicago Press.

Alionescu, Ciprian-Calin. 2003. "Parliamentary Representation of Minorities in Romania." Paper presented at the 2003 Annual conference of the Political Studies Association, Leicester, U.K., April 15–17. http://www. psa.ac.uk/cps/2003/Ciprian%20Alionescu.pdf.

Andrews, Josephine, and Jeannette Money. 2002. "Champions and Challengers: Ideology and the Success of Non-Established Parties in Established Party Systems." Paper presented at the 2001 Public Choice Conference, San Diego, CA.

Avramov, Kiril. 2002. Personal interview with author. Sofia.

Bacon, Edwin. 1998. "Russia: Party Formation and the Legacy of the One Party State." In *Political Parties and the Collapse of the Old Orders,* ed. John Kenneth White and Philip John Davies. Albany: State University of New York Press.

Barany, Zoltan. 2001. "Romani Electoral Politics and Behavior." *Journal on Ethnopolitics and Minority Issues in Europe* (Autumn). http://www. ecmi.de/jemie/download/Focus11-2001Barany.pdf. http://www.ecmi. de/jemie/download/Focus11-2001Barany.pdf.

Bartolini, Stefano, and Peter Mair. 2001. "Challenges to Contemporary Political Parties." In *Political Parties and Democracy,* ed. Larry Diamond and Richard Gunther. Baltimore: Johns Hopkins University Press.

BAS (Bulgarian Academy of Sciences). 2001. *Bulgarian Election Results.* http://www.math.bas.bg/izbori/.

BCEC (Bulgarian Central Electoral Commission). 2005. *Elections 2005: Official Results.* http://2005izbori.org/results/index.html.

Beck, Nathaniel, and Jonathan N. Katz. 1995. "What to do (and not to do) with Time-Series Cross-Section Data." *The American Political Science Review* 89(3): 634–647.

Benoit, Kenneth. 1999. "Votes and Seats; the Hungarian Electoral Law and the 1994 Parliamentary Election." In *Founding Elections in Eastern Europe: Elections to the 1994 Hungarian National Assembly,* ed. Gábor Tóka and Zsolt Enyedi. Berlin: Sigma.

———. 2001. "Evaluating Hungary's Mixed-Member Electoral System." In *Mixed-Member Electoral Systems: The Best of Both Worlds?* ed. Matthew Shugart and Martin Wattenberg. Oxford: Oxford University Press.

Bielasiak, Jack. 1997. "Substance and Process in the Development of Party Systems in East Central Europe." *Communist and Post-Communist Studies* 30(1): 23–44.

———. 2003. "Party Competition in Emerging Democracies: Representation and Effectiveness." University of Strathclyde Working Papers, No. 382. Glasgow: University of Strathclyde.

Biezen, Ingrid van. 2003. *Political Parties in New Democracies: Party Organization in Southern and East-Central Europe.* Basingstoke, U.K.: Palgrave.

———. 2004. "Political Parties as Public Utilities." *Party Politics* 10(6): 701–722.

Birch, Sarah, Frances Millard, Kieran Williams, and Marina Popescu. 2002. *Embodying Democracy: Electoral System Design in Post-Communist Europe.* Basingstoke, U.K.: Palgrave-Macmillan.

Birnir, Johanna. 2001 "Party System Stabilization in New Democracies: The Effect of Ethnic Heterogeneity on Volatility of Electoral Preferences." PhD diss., University of California, Los Angeles.

BNS (Bulgarian People's Union). 2005. *Coalition Agreement.* http://www.bns-izbori.info/koalicia.htm.

Bozoki, Andras. 2002. "The Hungarian Socialists." In *The Communist Successor Parties of Central and Eastern Europe,* ed. Andras Bozoki and John Ishiyama. Armonk, NY: M. E. Sharpe.

Bozoki, Andras, and John Ishiyama. 2002. *The Communist Successor Parties of Central and Eastern Europe.* Armonk, NY: M. E. Sharpe.

Browne, Eric, and Dennis Patterson. 1999. "An Empirical Theory of Rational Nominating Behavior Applied to Japanese District Elections." *British Journal of Political Science* 29(2): 259–289.

Browne, Eric C., John P. Frendreis, and Dennis W. Gleiber. 1984. "An Events Approach to the Problem of Cabinet Stability." *Comparative Political Studies* 17(1): 167–197.

———. 1986. "The Process of Cabinet Dissolution: An Exponential Model of Duration and Stability in Western Democracies," *American Journal of Political Science* 30(3): 628–650.

BSD (Bulgarian Social Democracy). 2003. *Political Program of the Bulgarian Social Democracy until 2007.* Sofia.

BSP (Bulgarian Socialist Party). 1995. *Political Report.* Sofia: High Council of BSP.

———. 1997. *Political Report*. Sofia: High Council of BSP.

———. 2000. *Political Report*. Sofia: High Council of BSP.

———. 2002. *Political Report*. Sofia: High Council of BSP.

BSP. 2002. *Report of the High Council of BSP at the 45th Congress*. http://www.bsp.bg/44kongres/otchetVS.html.

Capital. 1997a. February 24–March 2, 1997.

———. 1997b. March 3–9, 1997.

———. 1997c. March 10–16, 1997.

———. 2001a. March 18–24, 2001.

———. 2001b. March 25–31, 2001.

CIA. 2004. *CIA World Factbook*. http://www.cia.gov/cia/publications/factbook/index.html.

Clark, Terry. 1995. "The Lithuanian Political Party System: A Case Study of Democratic Consolidation." *East European Politics and Societies* 9(1): 41–62.

Coalition for Bulgaria. 2001. *Dogovor za Uchredjavane na Koalicija za Bulgaria* [Contract for the Establishment of the Coalition for Bulgaria]. Sofia.

Cox, Gary. 1997. *Making Votes Count*. New York and London: Cambridge University Press.

Crawford, Keith. 1996. *East Central European Politics Today: From Chaos to Stability?* Manchester: Manchester University Press.

Crawford, Sue, and Elinor Ostrom. 1995. "A Grammar of Institutions." *American Political Science Review* 89: 582–600.

Daalder, Hans, and Peter Mair, eds. 1983. *Western European Party Systems: Continuity and Change*. Beverly Hills, CA: Sage Publications.

Dainov, Evgenii. 1999. *Prehodut 1989/1999: Vmesto Istorija* [The Transition: 1989/1999: Instead of a History]. Sofia: Planeta.

Dakowska, Dorota. 2002. "Beyond Conditionality: EU Enlargement, European Party Federations, and the Transnational Activity of German Political Foundations." *Perspectives on European Politics and Society* 3(2): 271–296.

Dal, Kasim. 2003. Personal interview with author. Sofia.

Delsodato, Giorgia. 2002. "Eastward Enlargement by the European Union and Transnational Parties." *International Political Science Review* 22(3): 269–289.

Derleth, James. 2000. *The Politics of Transition in Central and Eastern Europe*. New York: Prentice Hall.

Dexter, Lewis Anthony. 1970. *Elite and Specialized Interviewing*. Evanston, IL: Northwestern University Press.

Diamond, Larry, and Juan Linz. 1988. "Politics, Society and Democracy in Latin America." In *Democracy in Developing Countries: Latin America 1988*, ed. Larry Diamond, Juan Linz, and Seymour Martin Lipset. Boulder: CO: Lynne Rienner.

Diamond, Larry, and Richard Gunther, eds. 2001. *Political Parties and Democracy*. Baltimore: Johns Hopkins University Press.

Diermeier, Daniel, and Randolph Stevenson. 2000. "Cabinet Terminations and Critical Events." *American Political Science Review* 94(3): 627–640.

Dorget, Christelle. 2000. *La légitimation des partis nationaux par le biais des fédérations internationales* (The legitimation of parties through the international federations). *Transitions* 41(1): 135–152.

Duch, Raymond M., and Harvey D. Palmer. 2002. "Strategic Voting in Post-Communist Democracy?" *British Journal of Political Science* 32: 63–91.

Duverger, Maurice. 1969. *Political Parties: Their Organization and Activity in the Modern State*. London: Meuthen.

Dzudzev, Petar. 2003. Personal interview with author. Sofia.

Economist Intelligence Unit. 2003. *Political Forces in Hungary*. October 29. http://www.economist.co.uk/countries/Hungary/profile.cfm?folder= Profile-Political%20Forces.

Engelbrekt, Kjell. 1991. "Bulgarian Socialist Party Prepares for Elections." *RFE/RL Research Report*, September 6, 12–16.

Epstein, Leon. 1967. *Political Parties in Western Democracies*. New York: Frederick A. Praeger.

Feno, Richard, Jr. 1978. *House Members in Their Districts*. Boston: Little, Brown.

FIDESZ (Federation of Young Democrats). 1989. "Federation of Young Democrats Declaration of Political Program and Chronology." *World Affairs* 151(4).

Fodor, Gabor, 2003. Personal interview with author. Budapest.

Fowler, Barbara. 2003. "The Parliamentary Elections in Hungary, April 2002." *Electoral Studies* 22(4): 799–807.

Frendreis, John P., Dennis W. Gleiber, and Eric C. Browne. 1986. "The Study of Cabinet Dissolutions in Parliamentary Democracies." *Legislative Studies Quarterly* 11(4): 619–628.

Friedman, Eben. 2002. "Political Integration of the Romany Minority in Macedonia." *Southeast European Politics Online* 3(2–30).

Giovanni Sartori, "The Influence of Electoral Systems: Faulty Laws or Faulty Methods?," in Grofman and Lijphart, op.cit

Goetz, Klaus. 2000. "Europeanizing the National Executive? Western and Eastern Style," paper prepared for the University Association for Contemporary European Studies' 30th Annual Conference, Budapest, April 6–8.

———. 2001. "Making Sense of Post-Communist Central Administration: Modernization, Europeanization or Latinization?" *Journal of European Public Policy* 8(6): 1032–1051.

Golder, Matt. 2003. "Explaining Variation in the Success of Extreme Right Parties in Western Europe." *Comparative Political Studies* 36(4): 432–466.

Golosov, Grigorii. 1998. "Who Survives? Who Doesn't?" *Political Studies* 4(3): 511–536.

GOR (Citizens Union for the Republic). 1993. "Founding Document." *Trud*, May 31, 1993.

Gospodinova, Velina. 2003. Politicheskta tzena and DPS raste [The Political Price of DPS is Rising]. *Capital*, February 15–21, 2003.

Grabbe, Heather. 2000. "The Sharp Edges of Europe: Extending Schengen Eastwards." *International Affairs* 76 (3): 519–536.

———. 2001. "How Does Europeanization Affect CEE Governance? Conditionality, Diffusion and Diversity." *Journal of European Public Policy* 8(6): 1013–1031.

Grofman, Bernard, and Arend Lijphart, ed. 1986. *Electoral Laws and Their Political Consequence.* New York: Agathon.

Grzymala-Buse, Anna. 2002. *Redeeming the Communist Part: The Regeneration of Communist Parties in East Central Europe.* Cambridge: Cambridge University Press.

Gunther, Richard. 1989. "Electoral Laws, Party Systems, and Elites: The Case of Spain." *American Political Science Review* 83(3): 835–858.

Gunther, Richard, and Larry Diamond. 2001. "Types and Functions of Parties." In *Political Parties and Democracy,* ed. Larry Diamond and Richard Gunther. Baltimore: Johns Hopkins University Press.

Hack, Peter. 2003. Personal interview with author. Budapest.

Harper, M. A. G. 2003. "The 2001 Parliamentary and Presidential Elections in Bulgaria." *Electoral Studies* 22: 325–395.

Hauss, Charles, and David Rayside. 1978. "The Development of New Political Parties." In *Political Parties: Development and Decay,* ed. Louis Miasel and Joseph Cooper. Beverly Hills, CA: Sage.

Hazan, Reuven. 1998. "Party System Change in Israel, 1948–98: A Conceptual and Typological Border-Stretching of Europe?" In *Comparing Party System Change,* ed. Paul Pennings and Jan-Erik Lane. London and New York: Routledge.

Heywood, Paul. 1996. "The Emergence of New Party Systems and Transitions to Democracy: Spain in Comparative Perspective." In *Stabilizing Fragile Democracies,* ed. Pridham, Geoffrey, and Paul G. Lewis. London and New York: Routledge.

Hollis, Wendy. 1999. *Democratic Consolidation in Eastern Europe: The Influence of the Communist Legacy in Hungary, the Czech Republic and Romania.* New York: Columbia University Press.

Horowitz, Donald. 2000. *Ethnic Groups in Conflict.* Berkeley: University of California Press.

Hug, Simon. 2001. *Altering Party Systems. Strategic Behavior and the Emergence of New Political Parties in Western Democracies.* Ann Arbor: University of Michigan Press.

Huntington, Samuel P. 1968. *Political Order in Changing Societies.* New Haven, CT: Yale University Press.

IDEA (International Institute for Democracy and Electoral Assistance). *Handbook on Funding of Political Parties and Election Campaign.* Stockholm. http://www.idea.int/publications/funding_parties/index.cfm.

Ikstens, Janis et al. 2002. "Political Finance in Central Eastern Europe: An Interim Report." *Austrian Journal of Political Science* 31(1).

Ilonszki, Gabriella. 2005. "Systemic and Regulatory Problems in the Background of Party and Campaign Finance in Hungary." Paper presented at the "Workshop on the Effect of Party and Campaign Finance on Post-Communist Party Development," Riga, Latvia, October 20–23.

Ilonszki, Gabriella, and Sandor Kurtan. 2002. "The Year in Review: Hungary." *European Journal of Political Research* 41: 968–974.

Ishiyama, John. 1997. "The Sickle or the Rose," *Comparative Political Studies* 30(3): 299–330.

———. 1999a. "Sickles in to Roses: The Communist Successor Parties and Democratic Consolidation in Comparative Perspective." Paper presented at the Midwest Political Science Association meeting, Chicago, IL, April 15–17.

———. 1999b. "The Communist Successor Parties and Party Organizational Development in Post-Communist Parties." *Political Research Quarterly* 52(1): 87–112.

———, ed. 1995. *Communist Successor Parties in Post-Communist Politics.* Commack, NY: Nova Science.

Ishiyama, John, and Andras Bozoki. 2001. "Adaptation and Change: Characterizing the Survival Strategies of the Communist Successor Parties." *The Journal of Communist Studies and Transition Politics* 17(3): 32–51.

Jackman, Robert, and Kevin Volpert. 1996. "Conditions Favoring Parties in the Extreme Right in Western Europe." *British Journal of Political Science* 26(2): 501–521.

Kalinova, Evgenija, and Iskra Baeva. 2000. *Bulgarskite prehodi: 1944–1999* [The Bulgarian Transitions: 1944–1999]. Sofia: Tilia.

Kamov, Nikolaj. 1998. Interview. *Capital,* 1998 (8): 10.

Karasimeonov, Georgi. 1996. "Bulgaria's New Party System." In *Stabilizing Fragile Democracies,* ed. Geoffrey Pridham and Paul G. Lewis. London and New York: Routledge.

Karasimeonov, Georgi. 2003. *Novata Partiina Sistema v Bulgaria* [The New Party System in Bulgaria]. Sofia: GorexPress.

Katz, Richard, and Peter Mair. 1995. "Changing Models of Party Organization and Party Democracy: The Emergence of the Cartel Party." *Party Politics* 1(1): 5–28.

Keri, Laszlo, and Ádam Levendel. 1995. "The First Three Years of a Multi-Party System in Hungary." In *Party Formation in East-Central Europe,* ed. Gordon Wightman. Brookfield, VT: Edward Elgar.

King, Gary, James E. Alt, Nancy Elizabeth Burns, and Michael Laver. 1990. "A Unified Model of Cabinet Dissolution in Parliamentary Democracies." *American Journal of Political Science* 34(3): 846–871.

Kiss, Csilla. 2002. "From Liberalism to Conservatism: The Federation of Young Democrats in Post-Communist Hungary." *East European Politics and Societies* 16(3): 739–763.

———. 1995a. "The Formation of Party Cleavages in Post-Communist Democracies." *Party Politics* 1(4): 447–472.

———. 1995b. *Party System in East Central Europe: Consolidation or Fluidity?* Studies in Public Policy, No. 241. Center for the Study of Public Policy, University of Strathclyde, Glasgow.

Kitschelt, Herbert, Zdenka Mansfeldova, Radoslaw Markoviski, and Gabor Toka. 1999. *Post-Communist Party Systems.* Cambridge: Cambridge University Press.

Klima, Michael. 1998. "Consolidation and Stabilization of the Party System in the Czech Republic." *Political Studies* 46(3): 492–510.

Konstantinov, Mihail. 2000. "Electoral Law and the Electoral Systems in the Balkans; Possibilities for Changes in the Bulgarian Electoral Law." Stenographic notes. Center for the Study of Democracy. Sofia. http://www.csd.bg/fileSrc.php?id=164.

———. 2001. "*What Is New in the New Election Law?*" Comments on the new Law on Election of Members of Parliament. Center for the Study of Democracy. Sofia. http://www.csd.bg/artShow.php?id= 11913.

Koole, Ruud. 1996. "Cadre, Catch-All or Cartel? A Comment on the Notion of the Cartel Party." *Party Politics* 2(?): 507–523.

Kopa, Mihaly. 2003. Personal interview with author. Budapest.

Kopecky, Petr. 1995. "Developing party organization in East-Central Europe." *Party Politics* 1(4): 515–534.

Kopecky, Petr, and Cas Mudde. 2000. "Explaining Different Paths of Democratization: The Czech and Slovak Republics." *Journal of Communist Studies and Transition Politics* 16(3): 63–84.

———. 2002. "The Two Sides of Euroscepticism: Party Positions on European Integration in East Central Europe." *European Union Politics* 3(3): 297–326.

Kostadinova, Tatiana. 2005. "Party Campaign Finance in Bulgaria." Paper presented at the "Workshop on the Effect of Party and Campaign Finance on Post-Communist Party Development," Riga, Latvia, October 20–23.

Kreuzer, Marcus, and Vello Pettai. 2001. "Institutions and Party Development in the Baltic States." In *Party Development and Democratization*, ed. Paul Lewis. London: Frank Cass: 107–126.

———. 2002 "The Calculus of Party Affiliation in Post-Communist Democracies: Party Switching, Fusions, Fissions and the Institutionalization of the Party Systems." Paper presented at the 2002 APSA annual meeting, Boston, MA, August 29–September 2.

Kripavicius, Algis. 1998. "The Post-Communist Transition and Institutionalization of Lithuania's Parties." *Political Studies* 46(3): 465–491.

Krusteva, Penka. 2003. Personal interview with author. Sofia.

Kumanov, Milen, and Tanya Nikolova. 1999. *Political Parties, Organizations and Movements in Bulgaria and Their Leaders, 1879–1999.* [In Bulgarian.] Sofia: Ariadna.

Kupa, Mihaly. 2003. Personal interview with author. Budapest.

Kutov, Ivaylo. 2004. Personal interview with author. Sofia.

Lacardie, Paul. 2000. "Prophets, Purifiers, and Prolocutors." *Party Politics* 6(2): 175–187.

Lane, Jan-Erik, and Svante Ersson. 1987. *Politics and Society in Western Europe.* London: Sage Publications.

Law on the Election of Members of the National Assembly. 1991. Promulgated State Gazette No. 69/22.08.1991; amended State Gazette 70, 76 & 98/1991; 66/1995. http://www2.essex.ac.uk/elect/database/legislationAll.asp?country=bulgaria&legislation=bg9195.

Law on Political Parties. 1990. *Durzhaven Vestnik,* April 10.

———. 2001. *Durzhaven Vestnik,* March 28.

Law on the Operation and Financial Functioning of Political Parties in Hungary. 1989. http://www2.essex.ac.uk/elect/database/legislationAll.asp?country=hungary&legislation=hu89.

Lawson, Kay, Andrea Rommele, and Georgi Karasimeonov, eds. 1999. *Cleavages, Parties and Voters: Studies from Bulgaria, the Czech Republic, Hungary, Poland and Romania.* Westport, CT: Praeger.

Lewis, Paul G. 1994a. "Democratization and Party Development in Eastern Europe." *Democratization* 1(3).

———. 1994b. "Political Institutionalization and Party Development in Post-Communist Poland." *Europe-Asia Studies* 46(5): 779–799.

———. 1998. "Party Funding in Post-Communist East Central Europe." In *Funding Democratization,* ed. Peter Burnell and Alan Ware. Manchester and New York: Manchester University Press.

———. 2000. *Political Parties in Post-Communist Eastern Europe.* London and New York: Routledge.

———. 2001a. "The 'Third Wave' of Democracy in Eastern Europe." *Party Politics* 7(5): 543–565.

———, ed. 1996. *Party Structure and Organization in East-Central Europe.* Cheltenham, U.K.: Edgar Elgar.

———. 2001b. *Party Development and Democratic Change in Post-Communist Europe: The First Decade.* London: Frank Cass.

Lieber, Robert J. 1975. "European Elite Attitudes Revisited: The Future of the European Community and European-American Relations." *British Journal of Political Science* 5(3): 323–340.

Lijphart, Arend. 1975. "The Comparable-Cases Strategy in Comparative Research." *Comparative Political Studies* 8(2): 158–173.

———. 1990. "The Political Consequences of Electroal Laws, 1945–1985." *American Political Science Review* 84: 481–96.

———. 1994. *Electoral Systems and Party Systems: A Study of Twenty-Seven Democracies, 1945–1990.* New York: Oxford University Press.

Linz, Juan, and Alfred Stepan. 1996. *Problems of Democratic Transition and Consolidation.* Baltimore: Johns Hopkins University Press.

Lipset, Seymor M., and Stein Rokkan, eds. 1967. *Party Systems and Voter Alignments,* New York: Free Press.

Lomax, Bill. 1995. "Factions and Factionalism in Hungary's New Party System." *Democratization* (Spring): 125–137.

Long, Scot. 1997. *Regression Models for Categorical and Limited Dependent Variables.* Thousand Oaks, CA: Sage Publications.

Mainwaring, Scott P. 1992. "Transitions to Democracy and Democratic Consolidation: Theoretical and Comparative issues." In *Issues in Democratic Consolidation: New South American Democracies in Comparative*

Perspective, ed. Scott P. Mainwaring, Guillermo O'Donnell, and J. Samuel Valenzuela. Notre Dame, IN: University of Notre Dame Press.

———. 1999. *Rethinking Party Systems in the Third Wave of Democratization.* Stanford: Stanford University Press.

Mair, Peter. 1990. "The Electoral Payoffs of Fission and Fusion." *British Journal of Political Science* 20(1): 131–142.

———. 1997. *Party System Change: Approaches and Interpretations.* Oxford: Clarendon Press.

———, ed. 1990. *The West European Party System.* New York: Oxford University Press.

Mandzukov, Mitko. 2000a. *I evrolevicata kacna v klientelistko gnezdo* [BEL Joins the Clientelistic Parties]. *Capital*, no. 17.

———. 2000b. *Predizboren Haos v Levicata* [Pre-Election Chaos in the Left]. *Capital*, no. 36.

Mandzukov, Mitko, and Velina Gospodinova. 2001. *Sudruzhnici po Nevolja* [Partners with No Other Choice]. *Capital*, no. 18 (May 1–6, 2003).

Markowski, Radoslaw. 1995. "Ideological Dimension in Eastern European Context: Popular Identification and Party Format." Paper presented at Workshop on Public Opinion and Party Formation in Post-Communist and Authoritarian Democracies," Duke University, Durham, North Carolina, March 24–25.

McFaul, Michael. 2001. "Explaining Party Formation and Non-Formation in Russia." *Comparative Political Studies* 34(10).

Michael Pinto-Duschinsky (2002) "Financing Politics: A Global View" in Journal of Democracy, Volume 13, Number 4, October 2002.

Milanov, Milan. 2002. Personal interview with author. Sofia.

Miller, Arthur, Gwyn Erb, William Reisinger, and Vicki Hesli. 2000. "Emerging Party Systems in Post-Soviet Societies: Fact or Fiction?" *Journal of Politics* 62(2): 491–510.

Minkenberg, Michael. 2000. "The Radical Right in Post-Socialist Central and Eastern Europe: Comparative Observations and Interpretations." *East European Politics and Societies* 16(2).

Mladenov, Nikolaj. 2003. Personal interview with author. Sofia.

Moraski, Bryon, and Gerhard Lowenberg. 1999. "The Effect of Legal Thresholds on the Revival of Former Communist Parties in East-Central Europe." *Journal of Politics* 61: 151–170 .

Muller, Wolfgang C., and Kaare Strom, ed. 1999. *Policy, Office or Votes? How Political Parties in Western Europe Make Hard Decisions.* New York: Cambridge University Press.

Muller-Rommel, Ferdinand. 1989. *New Politics in Western Europe.* Boulder, CO: Westview Press.

Murdzhov, Miroslav. 2003. Personal interview with author. Sofia.

Murer, Jeffrey. 1995. "Challenging Expectations: A Comparative Study of the Communist Successor Parties of Hungary, Bulgaria and Romania." In *Communist Successor Parties in Post-Communist Politics,* ed. John Ishiyama. Commack, NY: Nova Science.

———. 2002. "Mainstreaming Extremism: The Romanian PDSR and the Bulgarian Socialists in Comparative Perspective." In *The Communist Successor Parties of Central and Eastern Europe*, ed. Andras Bozoki and John Ishiyama. Armonk, NY: M. E. Sharpe.

Nassmacher, Karl-Heinz. 2004. "Monitoring, Control and Enforcement of Political Finance Regulation." *IDEA Handbook on Funding of Political Parties and Election Campaign.* Stockholm: IDEA. http://www.idea.int/publications/funding_parties/index.cfm.

Navracsics, Tibor. 2003. Personal interview with author. Budapest.

NCIOM (National Center for the Study of Public Opinion). 2001. *Obshtestveno Mnenie Fevruary-Mart I Mart–April 2001* [Opinion Polls, February, March, April 2001]. http://www.parliament.bg/nciom/ (accessed May 2004).

Nedelchev, Mihail. 2000. *Radicaldemocratism: Opit za Liberarlno povedie v Bulgaria* [Radical Democratism: An Attempt for Liberal Political Behavior in Bulgaria]. Sofia: Grazhdanian.

Nie, Norman, Sidney Verba and Jae-On Kim. 1978. *Participation and Political Equality: A Cross-National Comparison.* Cambridge: Cambridge University Press.

Niedermeter, Oscar. 1998. "German Unification and Party System Change." In *Comparing Party System Change,* ed. Paul Pennings and Jan-Erik Lane. 1998. London and New York: Routledge.

Norris, Pippa. 2004. *Electoral Engineering: Voting Rules and Political Behavior.* Cambridge: Cambridge University Press.

O'Donnel, Guillermo. 1988. *Bureaucratic Authoritarianism: Argentina 1966–1973 in Comparative Perspective.* Berkeley: University of California Press.

Okolicsanyi, Karoly. 1991. "The Finances of the New Political Parties." *RFE/RL Report on Eastern Europe.* June 28, 1991.

Olson, David. 1998. "Party Formation and Party System Consolidation in the New Democracies of Central Europe." *Political Studies,* 46(3): 432–464.

Ordeshook, Peter, and Olga Shvetsova. 1994. "Ethic Heterogeneity, District Magnitude, and the Number of Parties." *American Journal of Political Science* 38(1): 100–123.

Palfrey, Thomas, 1984. "Spatial Equilibrium with Entry." *Review of Economic Studies* 51(1): 139–156.

Panebianco, Angelo. 1988. *Political Parties: Organization and Power.* Cambridge: Cambridge University Press.

Panev, Bajcho. 2000. "Electoral Law and the Electoral Systems in the Balkans; Possibilities for Changes in the Bulgarian Electoral Law." Stenographic notes. Center for the Study of Democracy. http://www.csd.bg/fileSrc.php?id=164.

Pataki, Judith. 1991. "Main Opposition Party Divided." *RFE/RL Research Report,* November 22, 13–17.

———. 1992. "Hungary's Free Democrats Elect New Leadership." *RFE/RL Research Report,* December 18, 41–44.

Peabody, Robert L., Susan Webb Hammond, Jean Torcom, Lynne P. Brown, Carolyn Thompson, and Robin Kolodny. 1990. "Interviewing Political Elites (in The Profession)." *Political Science and Politics* 23(3): 451–455.

Pederson, Morgens. 1979. "The Dynamics of European Party Systems: Changing Patterns of Electoral Volatility." *European Journal of Political Research* 7(1): 1–26.

Pennings, Paul, and Jan-Erik Lane, eds. 1998. *Comparing Party System Change*. London and New York: Routledge.

Perea, E. A., 2002. "Individual Characteristics, Institutional Incentives and Electoral Abstention in Western Europe." *European Journal of Political Research* 41(5): 643–672, 31.

Perkins, Doug. 1996. "Structure and Choice: The Role of Organizations, Patronage and the Media in Party Formation." *Party Politics* 2(3).

Petrov, Zahari. 2004. Personal interview with author. Sofia.

Pettai, Vello, and Marcus Kreuzer. 2001. "Institutions and Party Development in the Baltic States." In *Party Development and Democratic Change in Post-Communist Europe,* ed. Paul G. Lewis. London: Frank Cass.

Pinchev, Georgi. 2002. Personal interview with author. Sofia.

Pinto-Duschinsky, Michael. 2002. "Financing Politics: A Global View." *Journal of Democracy* 13(4): 69–86.

Pirgova, Maria. 2002. *Bulgarskijat parlamentarism v uslovijata na globalen prehod* [Bulgarian Parliamentarism in a Global Transition]. Sofia: Paradigma.

Poguntke, Thomas, Nicholas Aylott, Robert Ladrech, and Kurt Richard Luther. Forthcoming. "The Europeanization of National Party Organizations: A Conceptual Analysis." *European Journal of Political Research*.

Political Transformation and the Electoral Process in Post-Communist Europe project. Database. University of Essex, http://www.essex.ac.uk/elections/.

Powell, G. Bingham. 1982. *Contemporary Democracies: Participation, Stability and Violence*. Cambridge, MA: Harvard University Press.

Powell, G. Bingham, and Georg Vanberg. 2000. "Election Laws, Disproportionality and Median Correspondence: Implications for Two Visions of Democracy." *British Journal of Political Science* 30: 383–411.

Pridham, Geoffrey. 1995. "Political Parties and Their Strategies in the Transition from Authoritarian Rule: The Comparative Perspective." In *Party Formation in East Central Europe,* ed. Gordon Wightman. Brookfield, VT: Edward Elgar.

Pridham, Geoffrey, and Paul G. Lewis. 1996. *Stabilizing Fragile Democracies*. London and New York: Routledge.

Protsyk, Oleh. 2002. *Campaign and Party Finance in Ukraine: Dilemmas of Regulation in the Context of Weakly Institutionalized Political and Legal Systems. IFES Report.* Washington, D.C.: International Foundation for Election Systems, May. www.policy.hu/protsyk/recentpubl.html.

Przeworski, Adam. 1975. "Institutionalization of Voting Patterns, or is Mobilization the Source of Decay?" *American Political Science Review* 69(1): 49–67.

Przeworski, Adam, and Henry Teune. 1982. *The Logic of Comparative Social Inquiry.* Malabar, FL: R. E. Krieger.

Putnam, Robert. 1973. *The Beliefs of Politicians. Ideology, Conflict and Democracy in Britain and Italy.* New Haven, CT: Yale University Press.

Rabushka, Alvin, and Kenneth A. Shepsle. 1972. *Politics in Plural Societies; a Theory of Democratic Instability.* Columbus, OH: Merrill.

Racz, Barnabas. 2000. "The Hungarian Socialists in Opposition: Stagnation or Renaissance." *Europe-Asia Studies* 52 (2): 319–47.

Racz, Barnabas, and Istvan Kukorelli. 1995. "The Second Generation Post-Communist Elections in Hungary in 1994." *Europe-Asia Studies* 47(2): 251–279.

Rae, Douglas. 1971. *The Political Consequences of Electoral Laws.* New Haven, CT: Yale University Press.

Randall Calvert. 1995b. "Rational Actors, Equilibrium and Social Institutions." In *Explaining Social Institutions,* ed. Jack Knight and Itai Sened. Ann Arbor: University of Michigan Press.

Randall, Vicky, and Lars Svasand. 2002. "Party Institutionalization in New Democracies." *Party Politics* 8(1): 5–31.

Reich, Gary M. 2001. "Coordinating Party Choice in Founding Elections: Why Timing Matters." *Comparative Political Studies* 34(10): 1237–1263.

———. 2004. "The Evolution of New Party Systems: Are Early Elections Exceptional?" *Electoral Studies* 23(2): 185–362.

Reilly, Benjamin. 2003. "Political Engineering of Parties and Party Systems." Paper presented at the 2003 APSA annual meeting, Philadelphia, August 28–31.

Reti, Tamas. 1998. "Hungary's Upcoming Elections; Political Prospects & The Economic Dimension". *WWICS Eastern European Series.* http://wwics.si.edu/index.cfm?topic_id=1422&fuseaction=topics.publications&doc_id=18905&group_id=7427.

Rochon, Thomas. 1985. "Mobilizes and Challengers: Towards a Theory of New Party Success." *International Journal of Political Science* 6(4): 419–439.

Rohrschneider, Robert. 1993. "New Party and Old Left Realignments." *Journal of Politics* 55(3): 682–701.

Roper, Steven. 2002. "The Influence of Romanian Campaign Finance Laws on Party System Development and Corruption." *Party Politics* 8(2): 175–192.

———. 2003. "Explaining Party System Development: A Cross-National Comparison of Post-Communist Party Finance." Paper presented at the 2003 APSA annual meeting, Philadelphia, Pennsylvania, August 28–31.

Rose, Richard. 1974. *The Problem of Party Government.* London: Macmillan.

———. 1995. "Mobilizing Demobilized Voters in Post-Communist Societies." *Party Politics* 1(4): 549–563.

Rose, Richard, and Neil Munro. 2003. *Elections and Parties in New European Democracies.* Washington: CQ.

Rueschemeyer, Dietrich, Evelyne Stephens, and John D. Stephens. 1992. *Capitalist Development and Democracy.* Chicago: University of Chicago Press.

Sartori, Giovanni. 1976. *Parties and Party Systems.* Cambridge: Cambridge University Press.

Scarrow, Susan. 1994. "The Paradox of Enrollment: Assessing the Costs and Benefits of Party Memberships." *European Journal of Political Research* 25(1): 41–60.

———. 1996. *Parties and Their Members: Organizing for Victory in Britain and Germany.* Oxford: Oxford University Press.

Schimmelfennig, Frank. 2001. "The Community Trap: Liberal Norms, Rhetorical Action, and the Eastern Enlargement of the European Union." *International Organization* 55(1): 47–80.

Schlesinger, Joseph A. 1994. *Political Parties and the Winning of Office.* Ann Arbor: University of Michigan Press.

Schmitter, Philippe. 2001. "Parties are Not What They Once Were." In *Political Parties and Democracy,* ed. Larry Diamond and Richard Gunther. Baltimore: Johns Hopkins University Press.

Schopflin, George. 2002. "New Old Hungary: A Contested Transformation." *RFE/RL East European Perspectives* 4(10). http://www.rferl.org/reports/eepreport/2002/05/10-150502.asp.

Schuessler, Alexander. 2000. *A Logic of Expressive Choice.* Princeton, NJ: Princeton University Press.

Shabad, Goldie, and Kazimierz M. Slomczynski. 2004. "Inter-Party Mobility among Parliamentary Candidates in Post-Communist East Central Europe," *Party Politics* 10(1): 151–176.

Shafir, Michael. 2000. "The Hungarian Democratic Federation of Romania" in The Politics of National Minority Participation in Post-Communist Europe, ed. Jonathan P. Stein. Armonk, NY: M. E. Sharpe.

Shepsle, Kenneth, and Ronald Cohen. 1990. "Multiparty Competition, Entry and Entry Deterrence in Spatial Models of Elections." In *Readings in the Spatial Theory of Voting,* ed. James Enelow and Melvin Hinich. New York: Cambridge University Press, 12–45.

Sjoblom, Gunner. 1983. "Political Change and Political Accountability." In *Western European Party Systems: Continuity and Change,* ed. Hans Daalder and Peter Mair. Beverly Hills, CA: Sage.

Smelser, Neil J. 1975. "The Methodology of Comparative Analysis." In *Comparative Research Methods,* ed. Donald P. Warwick and Samuel Osherson. Englewood Cliffs, NJ: Prentice-Hall.

Smilov, Daniel. 1999. "Structural Corruption of Party Funding Models: Governmental Favoritism in Bulgaria and Russia." Paper presented at the Princeton University/Central European University joint conference on Corruption, Budapest, October 30–November 6.

Smilov, Daniel. 2001. *Party Financing: Preliminary Findings*. International Policy Fellowship research paper. http://www.policy.hu/smilov/osi-international-policy-fellows/preliminary-findings/odyframe.htm.

Spirova, Maria. 2005. "Political Parties in Bulgaria: Organizational Trends in Comparative Perspectives." *Party Politics* 11(5): 601–622.

Standart. 1995. *Rezultatite* [Results from the Local Elections]. October 31.

Staridolska, Elena, and Velina Gospodinova. 2005. *Putevoditel za Politecheski Nomadi* [A Guide for Political Nomads]. *Capital,* May 14–20.

Stein, Jonathan P., ed. 2000. *The Politics of National Minority Participation in Post-Communist Europe.* Armonk, NY: M. E. Sharpe.

Stimpson, James A. 1985. "Regression in Space and Time: A Statistical Essay." *American Journal of Political Science* 29(4): 914–947.

Stockton, Hans. 2001. "Political Parties, Party Systems, and Democracy in East Asia." *Comparative Political Studies* 34(1): 94–119.

Stoianova, Julia. 2003. Personal interview with author. Sofia.

Strom, Kaare. 1990. "A Behavioral Theory of Competitive Political Parties." *American Journal of Political Science* 34: 565–598.

Strom, Kaare, and Jorn Y. Leipart. 1993. "Policy, Institutions, and Coalition Avoidance: Norwegian Governments, 1945–1990." *The American Political Science Review* 87 (December): 870–887.

Swain, Nigel. 1991. *Extremist Parties in Hungary.* Working Paper No. 7 of the Center for Central and East European Studies, University of Liverpool, U.K.

Szczerbiak, Aleks. 1999. "The Impact of the 1998 Local Elections on the Emerging Polish Party System." *Journal of Communist Studies and Transition Politics* 15(3): 80–100.

———. 2001. "Party Structure in Post-Communist Poland." *Journal of Communist Studies and Transition Politics* 17(2): 94–130.

Szoke, Mihaly. 2003. Personal interview with author. Budapest.

Taagepera, Rein, and Matthew Soberg Shugart. 1989. *Seats and Votes: The Effects and Determinants of Electoral Systems.* New Haven, CT: Yale University Press.

Tamás, Bernard. 1999. "Parties on Stage: Evaluating the Performance of Hungarian Parties." In *Elections to the Hungarian National Assembly 1994,* ed. Gábor Tóka and Zsolt Enyedi. Berlin: Sigma, 13–51.

Tatarli, Ibrahim. 2003. *Dvizehnie za Prava I Svobodi: Studii* [Movement for Rights and Freedoms: Essays]. Sofia.

Terziev, Svetoslav. 2001. *Zashto SDS atakuva carskite hora na mezhdnaroden teren* [Why the SDS is Attacking the King's Men on International Ground?]. *Sega,* October 2.

Toka, Gabor. 1995a. "Parties and their Voters in 1990 and 1994." In *Lawful revolution in Hungary, 1989–1994,* ed. Bela Kiraly and Andras Bozoki. New York: Columbia University Press.

———, ed. 1995b. *The 1990 Elections to the Hungarian National Assembly.* Berlin: Edition Sigma.

Tomov, Alexander. 1993. Interview. *Trud.* May 3.

Toole, James. 2000. "From Above or Below? Elite Competition, Social Interests, and the Development of East Central European Party Systems." Dissertation presented to the faculty of the Graduate School of Arts and Science, Brandeis University, Waltham, MA.

———. 2003. "Straddling the East-West Divide: Party Organization and Communist Legacies in East Central Europe." *Europe-Asia Studies* 55(1): 101–118.

Tzachevski, Venelin. 2003. *DPS kaza sbogom na ethnicheskoto si lice* [DPS Bids Farewell to its Ethnic Image]. *Standart*, March 7.

Tzenova, Radka. 2004. *Izbiratelnata Sistema I ravnishteto na Partijna Fragmentacia v Bulgaria* (1991–2001) [The Electoral System and the Fragmentation of the Party System in Bulgaria 1991–2001]. *University of National and World Economy Research Papers.* Sofia: UNSS. http://www.unwe.acad.bg/research/?id=505.

Vajda, Janos. 2003. Personal interview with author. Budapest.

Vanev, Georgi. 2003. Personal interview with author. Sofia.

Vassilev, Rosen. 2001. "Post-Communist Bulgaria's Ethnopolitics." *Global Review of Ethnopolitics* 1(2).

Vencislavova, Jana. 2005. BSP trugna na izbori [BSP towards Elections]. *Mediapool,* May 3. http://www.mediapool.bg/show/?storyid=104495.

Vermeersch, Peter. 2002. "Ethnic Mobilization and the Political Conditionality of the European Union Accession; the Case of the Roma in Slovakia." *Journal of Ethnic and Migration Studies* 28(1): 83–101.

———. 2003. "EU Enlargement and Minority Rights Policies in Central Europe: Explaining Policy Shifts in the Czech Republic, Hungary and Poland." Paper presented at the eighth annual world convention of the Association for the Study of Nationalities, Columbia University, New York, April 3–5.

Videnov, Zhan. 1994. Interview. *Standart,* December 12.

Waller, Michael, and Georgi Karasimeonov. 1996. "Party Organization in Post-Communist Bulgaria." In *Party Structure and Organization in East-Central Europe,* ed. Paul Lewis. Cheltenham, UK: Edgar Elgar.

Warwick, Paul V. 1992. "Rising Hazards: An Underlying Dynamic of Parliamentary Government." *American Journal of Political Science* 36(4): 857–876.

Wellhofer, E. Spencer. 2001. "Party Realignment and Voter Transition in Italy, 1987–1996." *Comparative Political Studies* 34(2): 156–187.

Whitefield, Stephen. 2002. "Political Cleavages and Post-Communist Politics." Annual Review of Political Science 5: 181–200.

Wightman, Gordon, ed. 1995. *Party Formation in East Central Europe.* Brookfield, VT: Edward Elgar.

Willey, Joseph. 1998. "Institutional Arrangements and the Success of New Parties in Old Democracies." *Political Studies* 46(2): 651–668.

William Riker, "Duverger's Law Revisited," in Bernard Grofman and Arend Lijphart, *Electoral Laws and Their Political Consequences,* (New York: Agathon Press, 1986), p 30.

Wyman, Matthew, Stephen White, Bill Miller, and Paul Heywood. 1995. "The Place of 'Party' in Post-Communist Europe." *Party Politics* 1(4): 535–548.

Yanai, Nathan. 1999. "Why Do Political Parties Survive?" *Party Politics* 5(1): 5–19.

Yanova, Miroslava. 2000. "Electoral Law and the Electoral Systems in the Balkans; Possibilities for Changes in the Bulgarian Electoral Law." Stenographic notes. Center for the Study of Democracy. http://www.csd.bg/fileSrc.php?id=164.

Zankov, Roumen. 2003a. Personal interview with author.

———. 2003b. Follow-up interview.

Zielinski, Jakub, Kazimierz M. Slomczynski, and Goldie Shabad. 2003. "Electoral Control in New Democracies: Fluid Party Systems as Perverse Incentives." Paper presented at the 2003 APSA annual meeting, Philadelphia, August 28–31.

Further Reading

Anckar, Carsten. 2000. "Size and Party System Fragmentation." *Party Politics* 6(3): 305–329.

Anckar, Dag, and Carsten Anckar. 2000. "Democracies without Parties." *Comparative Political Studies* 33(2): 225–247.

Bernhard, Michael. 2000. "Institutional Choice After Communism: A Critique of Theory Building in an Empirical Wasteland." *East European Politics and Societies* 14(2): 316–347.

Biezen, Ingrid van. 2000. "On the Internal Balance of Party Power." *Party Politics* 6(4): 395–419.

CECLE (Central Electoral Commission for Local Elections). 2003. "Low Voter Turnout in the Big Cities." *Mediapool.* http://www.mediapool.bg/site/mizbori_03/2003/10/26/01_261003mi.shtml.

Chhibber, Pradeep, and Mariano Torcal. 1997. "Elite Strategy, Social Cleavages, and Party Systems in a New Democracy." *Comparative Political Studies* 30(1): 76–107.

CSPP. 2006. *Center for the Study of Public Policy Election Database.* http://www.abdn.ac.uk/cspp/catalog7_0.shtml.

Dix, Robert. 1992. "Democratization and the Institutionalization of Latin American Political Parties." *Comparative Political Studies* 24(4): 488–511.

Downs, Anthony. 1957. *An Economic Theory of Democracy.* New York: Harper & Row.

EC (European Commission). 2003. *Copenhagen European Council, Membership Criteria.* http://europa.eu.int/comm/enlargement/intro/criteria.htm.

EPP (European People's Party). 2003. *European People's Party Resolution on Local Elections in Bulgaria.* http://www.eppe.org/default.asp?CAT2=0&CAT1=173&CAT0=105&shortcut=299.

Fedderesen, Timothy et al. 1990. "Rational Voting and Candidate Entry under Plurality Vote." *American Journal of Political Science* 34(4): 1005–1016.

Gebethner, Stanislaw. 1996. "Parliamentary and Electoral Parties in Poland." In *Party Structure and Organization in East-Central Europe*, ed. Paul Lewis. Cheltenham, U.K.: Edgar Elgar.

Gelman, Vladimir, and Inesa Tarussia. 2000. "Studies of Political Elites in Russia: Issues and Alternatives." *Communist and Post-Communist Studies* 33(3): 311–329.

Grofman, Bernard, Evald Mikkel, and Rein Taagepera. 2000. "Fission and Fusion of Parties in Estonia, 1987–1999." *Journal of Baltic Studies* 31(4): 329–357.

Harmel, Robert, and John D. Robertson. 1985. "Formation and Success of New Parties." *International Political Science Review* 6(4): 501–523.

Huntington, Samuel P. 1965. "Political Development and Political Decay." *World Politics* 17(3): 386–430.

Huntington, Samuel P. 1993. *The Third Wave: Democratization in the Late Twentieth Century.* Norman: University of Oklahoma Press.

IFES (International Foundation for Election Systems). 2003. *Central and Eastern European Electoral Law Compendium.* Washington. CD-ROM.

Janda, Kenneth, and Tyler Coleman. 1998. "Effects of Party Organization on Performance during the 'Golden Age' of Parties." *Political Studies* 66: 611–632.

Janova, Mira. 2002. *Report at the National Conference of BEL.* Author's personal notes.

Kanev, Dobrin. 2001. "The Legislative Aspects of Party Finance and Political Corruption in Bulgaria." *South-East Europe Review* 2001(2): 133–142.

Karasimeonov, Georgi. 2002. "The New Party System in Bulgaria: Current Situation and its Future" [in Bulgarian]. *Razum* 1: 2.

Kitschelt, Herbert. 1988. "Left-Libertarian Parties: Explaining Innovation in Competitive Party Systems." *World Politics* 40(2): 194–234.

———. 2001. "Divergent Paths of Post-Communist Democracies." In *Political Parties and Democracy,* ed. Larry Diamond and Richard Gunther. Baltimore: Johns Hopkins University Press.

Korasteleva, Elena. 2000. "Electoral Volatility in Post-Communist Belarus." *Party Politics* 6(3): 343–359.

Lawson, Kay, and Peter H. Merkl. 1988. *When Parties Fail: Emerging Alternative Organizations.* Princeton, NJ: Princeton University Press.

Leiserson, Avery. 1958. *Parties and Politics.* New York: Alfred A. Knopp.

Lijphart, Arend. 1999. *Patterns of Democracy.* New Haven, CT: Yale University Press.

Lijphart, Arend, and Robert Gibberd. 1977. "Thresholds and Payoffs in List Systems of Proportional Representation." *European Journal of Political Research* 5: 219–244.

Lipset, Seymour M. 1959. "Some Social Requisites of Democracy: Economic Development and Political Legitimacy." *American Political Science Review* 53(1): 69–105.

———. 2000. "The Indispensability of Political Parties." *Journal of Democracy* 11(1): 48–56.

Mainwaring, Scott P. 1998. "Party Systems in the Third Wave." *Journal of Democracy* 9(3): 67–81.

Mair, Peter. 1996. *What is Different about Post-Communist Party Systems?* Glasgow: University of Strathclyde.

Maisel, Charles, and David Rayside. 1978. *Political Parties: Development and Decay.* Beverly Hills, CA: Sage Publications.

Mandzukov, Mitko. 2000. *Levicata pak shte se obedinjava* [The Left Will Unite Again]. *Capital*, no. 23.

Mansfeldova, Zdenka. 1994. "The Emerging New Czech Political Elite." Paper presented for the twenty-second annual joint session of the European Consortium for Political Research, Madrid, April 17–22.

Maor, Moshe. 1997. *Political Parties and Party Systems: Comparative Approaches and the British Experience*. New York: Routledge.

Moser, Robert. 1999. "Electoral Systems and the Number of Parties in Post-Communist States." *World Politics* 51(3): 359–384.

NCIOM (National Center for the Study of Public Opinion). 2003. *Major Political Trends in Society*. http://www.parliament.bg/nciom/ Nciom2002.htm (accessed January 2003).

———. 2004. *Major Political Trends in Society*. http://www.parliament. bg/nciom (accessed May 2004).

O'Donnell, Guillero, and Philippe Schmitter. 1986. *Transition from Authoritarian Rule: Prospects for Democracy*. Baltimore: Johns Hopkins University Press.

OMDA. 2000. *Information about the Agrarian Parties in Bulgaria*. http://www.omda.bg/bulg/news/archcoment/bzns0120.htm (accessed November 2002).

Petkova, Lilia. 2002. "The Ethnic Turks in Bulgaria: Social Integration and Impact on Bulgarian-Turkish Relations, 1947–2000." *Global Review of Ethnopolitics* 1(4).

Ragin, Charles C. 1987. The Comparative Methods: Moving Beyond Qualitative and Quantitative Strategies. Berkeley: University of California Press.

Ribareva, Iren, and Vjara Nikolova. 2000. *Protestut na 39-te: Dolumentalen Razkaz*. [The Protest of the 39: A Story in Documents]. Sofia.

Rose, Richard, and Thomas Mackie. 1988. "Do Parties Persist or Fail?" In *When Parties Fail*, ed. Kay Lawson and Peter Markl. Princeton, NJ: Princeton University Press.

Rose, Richard, Neil Munro, and Tom Mackie. 1998. *Elections in Central and Eastern Europe*. http://www.cspp.strath.ac.uk/abs300.html.

Spourdalakis, Michalis. 1996. "Securing Democracy in Post-Authoritarian Greece." In *Stabilizing Fragile Democracies*, ed. Geoffrey Pridham and Paul G. Lewis. London and New York: Routledge.

Strom, Kaare. 1985. "Party Goals and Government Performance in Parliamentary Democracies." *The American Political Science Review* 79(3): 738–753.

Stroschein, Sherrill. 2001. "Measuring Ethnic Party Success in Romania, Slovakia and Ukraine." *Problems of Post-Communism* 48(4): 59–69.

Szczerbiak, Aleks. 1999. "Testing Party Models in East-Central Europe." *Party Politics* 5(4): 523–539.

Taggart, Paul, and Aleks Szczerbiak. 2004. "Contemporary Euroscepticism in the Party Systems of the European Union Candidate States of Central and Eastern Europe." *European Journal of Political Research* 43(1): 1–27.

Tazs, Barnabas. 2000. "The Hungarian Socialists in Opposition: Stagnation or Renaissance." *Europe Asia Studies* 52(2): 319–347.

Toka, Gabor, and Zsolt Enyedi, ed. 1999. *The 1994 Election to the Hungarian National Assembly.* Berlin: Sigma.

Toole, James. 2000. "Government Formation and Party System Stabilization in East Central Europe." *Party Politics* 6(4): 441–463.

Tzekov, Petjo. 2002. "Jane from Sandanski." *SEGA.* http://www.segabg.com/ 29072002/p0050003.asp.

Waller, Michael. 1995. "The Adaptation of the Former Communist Parties of East-Central Europe: A Case of Social Democratization?" *Party Politics* (1): 473–490.

Warwick, Paul V. 1994. *Governmental Survival in Contemporary Democracies.* Cambridge: Cambridge University Press. Wittman, Donald. 1973. "Parties as Utility Maximizes." *American Political Science Review* 67: 490–498.

Woolbridge, Jeffrey. 2001. *Econometric Analysis of Cross Section and Panel Data. Econometric Analysis of Cross Section and Panel Data.* Boston: MIT Press.

Yanova, Elena. 2005. *Dogan dade 15 dni* [Dogan Gave 15 Days]. *Standart,* April 9. http://www.standartnews.com/archive/2005/04/09/theday/ s4403_12.htm.

Appendix A

Sample Interview Questions
Questions for the MSZP in Hungary

1. Introductions.
2. Can you tell me what has been the most important accomplishment of the MSZP over the years?
3. What has been the main goal of the party?
4. How have you tried to achieve it?
5. Why did the MSZP decide to ask its members to join anew in 1989? Was that seen as a political risk?
6. Have you ever considered forming an electoral alliance with another party? Why?
7. How does the MSZP decide how to appear in local elections and in national elections? Who takes this decision? Do any external factors influence it?
8. How important is the party organization for the development of the party?
   a. How many members do you have?
   b. How many local organizations do you have?
   c. How many employees does the MSZP have?
   d. Has there been any change in the attitude toward party organization over the 1990s?
9. What is the MSZP's relationship with Munkaspart? Is there any cooperation at any level?
10. Has there ever been any consideration for closer cooperation with other parties?

APPENDIX B

COMPLETE ELECTION RESULTS FOR BULGARIA, 1990–2005

Table 1 Bulgarian election results, 1990 (Grand National Assembly)

Party/Coalition	PR vote %	PR seats	SMD seats	Total seats
BSP (Bulgarian Socialist Party)	47.15	97	114	211
SDS (Union of Democratic Forces)	36.21	75	69	144
DPS (Movement for Rights and Freedoms)	8.03	12	11	23
BZNS (Bulgarian Agrarian National Union)	6.02	16	0	16
Fatherland Front	0	0	2	2
Fatherland Party of Labor	0.6	0	1	1
Social Democratic Party	0.72	0	1	1
Alternative Socialist Party	0.36	0	0	0
Alternative Socialist Association	0.26	0	0	0
Liberal Party–Pernik	0.25	0	0	0
Union of Disabled	0.17	0	0	0
Union of Nonparty Members	0.16	0	0	0
Independents	0	0	2	2
Other 29 parties and associations	1.12	0	0	0
Total[1]	100	200	200	400

[1] Percentages are rounded off and may not add up to 100.

Table 2 Bulgarian election results, 1991 elections (36th National Assembly)

Party/Coalition	Vote %	Number of seats	Seats %
SDS (Union of Democratic Forces)	34.36	110	45.8
BSP (Preelectoral Union of the BSP, BLP, OPT, PKhZhD, KhRP, NLP "St. Stambolov," SMS, FBSM, SDPD, and "ERA-3")	33.14	106	44.2
DPS (Movement for Rights and Freedoms)	7.55	24	10
BZNS(e) (Bulgarian Agrarian National Union–United)	3.86		
BZNS-NP (Bulgarian Agrarian National Union–"Nikola Petkov")	3.44		
SDS-C (Union of Democratic Forces–Centre)	3.2		
SDS-L (Union of Democratic Forces–Liberal)	2.81		
KTsB (Kingdom of Bulgaria Federation)	1.82		
BBB (Bulgarian Business Block)	1.32		
BNRP (Bulgarian National Radical Party)	1.13		
BBP (Bulgarian Business Party)	0.93		
KTKS ("Freedom" Coalition for the Turnovo Constitution)	0.72		
BKP (Bulgarian Communist Party)	0.71		
PFP (Political Transformation Forum)	0.55		
DBD (Movement of Nonpartisans for Democracy)	0.41		
LP (Liberal Party–Pernik)	0.34		
BNS (Coalition of the Bulgarian National Union—Bulgarian Fatherland Party and New Democracy Bulgarian National Union)	0.31		
BNDP (Bulgarian National Democratic Party)	0.28		
PLK (Liberal Congress Party)	0.26		
NPS (National Patriotic Union Party)	0.26		
BDP (Bulgarian Democratic Party)	0.25		
NDP (Independent Democratic Party)	0.23		
SKP (Free Cooperative Party)	0.22		
SBG (Union of Nonpartisan Guarantors)	0.18		
BRMP (Bulgarian Revolutionary Party of Youth–Varna)	0.15		
BKP(m) (Bulgarian Communist Party–Marxist)	0.14		
KhP (Radical Christian Party)	0.12		
BPSDP (Bulgarian Workers' Social-Democratic Party)	0.11		
PBO (Bulgarian Eagle Party)	0.09		
BRSP (Bulgarian Worker-Rural Party–Varna)	0.07		
SBSSGB (Organization of Invalids and Underprivileged Citizens of Bulgaria)	0.06		
SDP (Free Democratic Party)	0.03		
BDPESS (Bulgarian Democratic Party for European and World States)	0.02		
PSD-ts (Party for Free Democracy–Centre)	0.02		
ODSPS (United Democratic Union "Party for Justice")	0		
PSB (Party of Proprietors of Bulgaria)	0		

(Continued)

Table 2 (*Continued*)

Party/Coalition	Vote %	Number of seats	Seats %
KhRDP (Christian Radical Democratic Party)	0		
PKKF (Constitutional Forum Political Club)	0		
Independents (19)	0.95		
Total[1]	100	240	100

[1] Percentages are rounded off and may not add up to 100.

Table 3 Bulgarian election results, 1994 elections (37th National Assembly)

Party/Coalition	Vote %	Number of seats	Seats %
BSPASEK (Coalition of the Bulgarian Socialist Party, the Bulgarian National Agrarian Union "Alexander Stamboliiski," and Ecoglasnost Political Club)	43.5	125	52.08
SDS (Union of Democratic Forces)	24.23	69	28.75
BZNS, DP (People's Union of the Bulgarian Agrarian National Union and the Democratic Party)	6.51	18	7.5
DPS (Movement for Rights and Freedoms)	5.44	15	6.25
BBB (Bulgarian Business Block)	4.73	13	5.42
DAR ("Democratic Alternative for the Republic" Political Union)	3.79		
BKP (Bulgarian Communist Party)	1.51		
SNI (New Choice Union)	1.49		
PS (Patriotic Union)	1.43		
FTsB (Kingdom of Bulgaria Federation)	1.41		
NDKDTsB (Kingdom of Bulgaria National Movement for Crowned Democracy)	0.78		
SMSTsB (Kingdom of Bulgaria Union of Monarchist Forces)	0.61		
BNRP (Bulgarian National–Radical Party)	0.54		
DPSpr. (Democratic Party of Justice)	0.46		
DZPBSSG (Movement for the Protection of Pensioners, the Unemployed, and Underprivileged Citizens)	0.36		
PDP (Party of Democratic Change)	0.27		
BZNS-TK (Bulgarian Agrarian National Union Confederation–"Turnovo Constitution" National Block)	0.25		
OSBSSGB (Organisation of Invalids and Underprivileged Citizens of Bulgaria)	0.25		
DNB (Forward Bulgaria Movement)	0.19		

Table 3 (*Continued*)

Party/Coalition	Vote %	Number of seats	Seats %
Era-3 (Era-3 Union of Democratic Parties and Movements)	0.17		
KhDS (Christian-Democratic Union)	0.16		
SDP (Free Democratic Party)	0.14		
Preobrazhenie. (Transfiguration Forum)	0.14		
DPB (Democratic Party of Bulgaria)	0.12		
OS (Alliance for Socialism)	0.12		
BLZPChG (Bulgarian League for the Protection of the Rights of People and Citizens)	0.11		
SS (Union of Justice)	0.1		
BRMP (Bulgarian Revolutionary Party of Youth)	0.09		
SKP (Free Cooperative Party)	0.08		
SSD (Union of Free)	0.08		
BRSDP (Bulgarian Workers' Social-Democratic Party)	0.07		
BRSP (Bulgarian Worker-Rural Party)	0.07		
BOPNS –(Bulgarian Fatherland Party–"National Union")	0.07		
BNS (Bulgarian National Union)	0.07		
PSB (Party of Proprietors of Bulgaria)	0.07		
FPSB (Front of Progressive Forces of Bulgaria)	0.07		
NLPSS (Stefan Stambolov Popular-Liberal Party)	0.06		
DPT (Democratic Party of Labour)	0.05		
RPB (Republican Party of Bulgaria)	0.04		
BDPESShch (Bulgarian Democratic Party for European and World States)	0.04		
PBO (Bulgarian Eagle Party)	0.03		
SBG (Union of Nonpartisan Guarantors)	0.03		
SBO (Union of Bulgarian Communities)	0.02		
DGI-SDS (Civic Initiative DGI-SDS Movement)	0.01		
Edinstvo. (Unity Party)	0		
ONDO (Alliance of the Nation–Movement of the Downtrodden)	0		
KhRP (Christian Republican Party)	0		
NKhS (National-Christian Union)	0		
Eight independents	0.24		
Total[1]	100	240	100

[1] Percentages are rounded off and may not add up to 100.

Table 4 Bulgarian election results, 1997 elections (38th National Assembly)

Party/Coalition	Vote %	Number of seats	Seats %
ODS (Alliance of Democratic Forces—SDS, DP, BZNS, BSDP)	49.15	137	57.55
DemLev (Democratic Left—Bulgarian Socialist Party, Ecoglasnost Political Club)	22.44	58	25.03
ONS (Alliance of National Salvation—Bulgarian Agrarian National Union–Nikola Petkov, Movement for Rights and Freedoms, Green Party, Party of the Democratic Centre, New Choice, Federation of the Bulgarian Kingdom)	9.44	19	9
EvroLev (Euroleft)	5.57	14	4.4
BBB (Bulgarian Business Block)	5.27	12	4.02
BKP (Bulgarian Communist Party)	1.3	0	0
OT (Alliance for the King)	1.12	0	0
BKhristK (Bulgarian Christian Coalition)	0.66	0	0
DPSpravedlivost (Democratic Party of Justice in the Republic of Bulgaria)	0.56	0	0
PBZheni (Party of Bulgarian Women)	0.41	0	0
LForum (Liberal Forum)	0.33	0	0
KorDem (Crowned Democracy)	0.29	0	0
BRSotsP (Bulgarian Workers' Socialist Party)	0.23	0	0
BZNS-ts (Bulgarian Agrarian National Union–Centre)	0.25	0	0
DAR (Democratic Alternative for the Republic)	0.24	0	0
BPLiber (Bulgarian Party of Liberals)	0.19	0	0
BNRP (Bulgarian National-Radical Party)	0.18	0	0
BNDP (Bulgarian National Democratic Party)	0.17	0	0
NPLF (Popular Patriotic Left Front)	0.17	0	0
BRSelP (Bulgarian Workers'-Agrarian Party)	0.17	0	0
SDR (Union for Democratic Development)	0.15	0	0
KhDS (Christian-Democratic Union)	0.15	0	0
NapredB (Forward Bulgaria Coalition)	0.16	0	0
SKoopP (Free Cooperative Party)	0.14	0	0
DemLiga (Democratic League)	0.11	0	0
NovaDem (New Democracy)	0.08	0	0
Preobrazhenie (Transfiguration Forum)	0.09	0	0
BDPESShch (Bulgarian Democratic Party for European and World States)	0.09	0	0
BNEP-VT (Bulgarian National Ecological Party–Veliko Turnovo)	0.08	0	0
BZelFed (Bulgarian Green Federation)	0.08	0	0
BRMP (Bulgarian Revolutionary Youth Party)	0.05	0	0
BNDVPut (Bulgarian National Movement for the Eternal Path)	0.05	0	0
BOPNS (Bulgarian Fatherland Party–National Union)	0.05	0	0

Table 4 (*Continued*)

Party/Coalition	Vote %	Number of seats	Seats %
FPSB (Front of Progressive Forces of Bulgaria)	0.03	0	0
ON-DO (Alliance of the Nation—Movement of the Downtrodden, "ON-DO" Political Party)	0.01	0	0
NarPart (Popular Party)			
NPvSDS (Bulgarian Agrarian National Union—Nikola Petkov in SDS)			
PDP (Party of Democratic Change)			
SBO (Union of Bulgarian Communities)			
Independents	0.53	0	0
Total	100	240	100

Table 5 Bulgarian election results, 2001 elections (39th National Assembly)

Party/Coalition	Vote %	Number of seats	Seats %
NDSV (National Movement Simeon the Second)	42.74	120	50
ODS (United Democratic Forces—SDS, People's Union: BZNS-NS and DP, BSDP, National MRF)	18.18	51	21.25
"Coalition for Bulgaria" (BSP, OPT, CPoB, BSDP-2+)	17.15	48	20
DPS (DPS, Liberal Union, EuroRoma)	7.45	21	8.75
Gergiovden-VMRO	3.63		
Alliance "Simeon II"	3.44		
National Union for Tzar Simeon II	1.7		
Bulgarian Euroleft, BESDP—United Social-Democrats, BZNS	0.98		
Union Bulgaria	0.74		
Alliance "National Union Tzar Kiro"	0.6		
NU Fatherland and Left	0.48		
George Ganchev's Block	0.38		
United Agrarian Forces (UAF) (National League—BZNS and BZNS "Nikola Petkov")	0.34		
Bulgarian Workers' Party (communists)	0.28		
Democratic Party of Justice in RB	0.24		
Bulgarian Workers' Socialist Party	0.24		
Bulgarian Communist Party "Fatherland"	0.21		
Patriotism 2000	0.13		
Union of Patriotic Forces and Reserve Soldiers "Defense"	0.11		
Bulgarian Democratic Party for United States of Europe and the World	0.11		

(*Continued*)

Table 5 (*Continued*)

Party/Coalition	Vote %	Number of seats	Seats %
Movement for Defense of Retired, Unemployed, and Socially Weak Citizens–Front of the Progressive Forces in Bulgaria	0.1		
Bulgarian National Party "Social Union"	0.1		
Alternative Social-Liberal Party	0.09		
Free Cooperation Party	0.09		
Bulgarian National-Radical Party	0.07		
Social Liberal Movement "Justice"	0.06		
National Movement for New Era	0.05		
Fatherland Party of Labor	0.04		
Alliance for Preservation of the Wealth of Bulgaria	0.03		
Party of the Workers and Social-Democratic Intelligentsia	0.02		
Bulgarian Fatherland Party "National Union"	0.01		
NPLPOPC (National Party of Labor, Private Owners, Producers and Creators)	0.01		
BNF (Bulgarian National Front)	0		
Bulgarian Business Block	0		
Party of the Middle Class	0		
Union of the Nation–Movement of the Deprived	0		
Party of the Greens	0		
Bulgarian National Movement of the Eternal Road (BNMOER)	0		
Democratic Alliance	0		
Christian-Social Union	0		
Movement for National Revival "Uplift"	0		
Movement People's Power	0		
Free People's Party	0		
Restored Macedonian Patriotic Organization (RMPO)–Bulgarian Democratic Movement (BDM)	0		
BZNS "Pladne"	0		
BZNS-United	0		
Alternative Socialist Alliance–Independents	0		
Alliance for the People	0		
All-Bulgarian National Movement Fatherland	0		
Workers' Youth Union	0		
Union of the Persecuted in Bulgaria after September 9, 1944	0		
Bulgarian Middle Class	0		
Movement for New Political Morality	0		
Bulgarian Party "Liberals"	0		
Independents	0.21	0	0
Total	100	240	100

Table 6 Bulgarian election results, 2005 elections (40th National Assembly)

Party/Coalition	Vote %	Number of seats	Seats %
"Coalition for Bulgaria" (BSP, PBS, PD Social-Democrats, DSH, Party "Roma," KPB, BZNS-Al., Stamboliski, ZP)	30.95	82	33.98
NDSV	19.88	53	21.80
DPS	12.81	34	14.07
Coalition "Ataka"	8.14	21	8.93
ODS (SDS, DP, Gergiovden, BZNS-NS–BZNS, DROM)	7.68	20	8.44
DSB	6.44	17	7.07
Coalition BNS (SSD, BZNS, VMRO)	5.19	13	5.70
NV (New Time)	2.95		
Coalition of the Rose (BSD, NDPS, OBT)	1.30		
EuroRoma	1.25		
BHK (Bulgarian Christian Coalition)	0.58		
FAGO	0.50		
Independents	0.35		
OPPB (United Party of the Pensioners)	0.35		
NK "Long Live Bulgaria"	0.35		
DSB-UB	0.33		
Dvizhenie "Napred Bulgaria"	0.28		
Coalition "Dostojna Bulgaria"	0.23		
SDN "Granite"	0.16		
"Chamber of Experts"	0.10		
PSD	0.06		
"Poden Kraj"	0.06		
NZP "Nikola Petkov"	0.05		

APPENDIX C

COMPLETE ELECTION RESULTS FOR HUNGARY, 1990–2002

Table 1 Hungarian election results, 1990 elections

Party/Coalition	PR vote %	SMD seats	Total seats	Seats %
MDF (Hungarian Democratic Forum)	24.73	114	164	42.49
SZDSZ (Alliance of Free Democrats)	21.39	35	92	23.83
FKGP (Independent Smallholders Party)	11.73	11	44	11.4
MSZP (Hungarian Socialist Party)	10.89	1	33	8.55
FIDESZ (Federation of Young Democrats)	8.95	1	21	5.44
KDNP (Christian Democratic People's Party)	6.46	3	21	5.44
MSZMP (Hungarian Socialist Workers' Party)	3.68	0	0	0
MSZDP (Social Democratic Party of Hungary)	3.55	0	0	0
ASZ (Agrarian Alliance)	3.13	1	1	0.26
VP (Entrepreneurs' Party)	1.89	0	0	0
HVK (Patriotic Elections Coalition)	1.87	0	0	0
MNP (Hungarian People's Party)	0.75	0	0	0
MZP (Green Party of Hungary)	0.36	0	0	0
NKgP (National Smallholders Party)	0.2	0	0	0
SKK (Somogy County Christian Coalition)	0.12	0	0	0
MSZAP (Hungarian Cooperative and Agrarian Party)	0.1	0	0	0
SZP (Freedom Party)	0.06	0	0	0
FMDP (Independent Hungarian Democratic Party)	0.06	0	0	0
MFP (Hungarian Independence Party)	0.04	0	0	0
Total[1]	100	166	376	100

[1] Percentages are rounded off and may not add up to 100.

Table 2 Hungarian election results, 1991 elections

Party/Coalition	PR vote %	SMD seats	Total seats	Seats %
MSZP (Hungarian Socialist Party)	32.99	149	209	54.15
SZDSZ (Alliance of Free Democrats)	19.74	16	69	17.88
MDF (Hungarian Democratic Forum)	11.74	5	38	9.84
FKGP (Independent Smallholders Party)	8.82	1	26	6.74
KDNP (Christian Democratic People's Party)	7.03	3	22	5.7
FIDESZ (Federation of Young Democrats)	7.02	0	20	5.18
Munkaspart [ex-MSZMP]	3.19	0	0	0
KP (Republican Party)	2.55	0	0	0
ASZ (Agrarian Alliance)	2.1	1	1	0.26
MIEP (Party of Hungarian Justice and Life)	1.59	0	0	0
MSZDP (Social Democratic Party of Hungary)	0.95	0	0	0
EkgP (United Smallholders Party)	0.82	0	0	0
VP (Party of Entrepreneurs)	0.62	0	0	0
NDSZ (National Alliance of Democrats)	0.52	0	0	0
MZP (Green Party of Hungary)	0.16	0	0	0
KFKGP (Compromise Independent Smallholders Party)	0.11	0	0	0
Total[1]		175	384	

[1] Percentages are rounded off and may not add up to 100.

Table 3 Hungarian election results, 1998 elections

Party/Coalition	PR vote %	SMD seats	Total seats	Seats %
MSZP (Hungarian Socialist Party)	32.92	54	134	34.72
FIDESZ-MPP (FIDESZ–Hungarian Civic Party)	29.48	55	113	29.27
FIDESZ-MPP–MDF joint candidates	–	35	50	12.95
FKGP (Independent Smallholders Party)	13.15	12	48	12.44
SZDSZ (Alliance of Free Democrats)	7.57	2	24	6.22
MIEP (Party of Hungarian Justice and Life)	5.47	0	14	3.63
Munkaspart (Workers' Party)	3.95	0	0	0
MDF-FIDESZ-MPP joint candidates	–	15	15	3.89
MDF (Hungarian Democratic Forum)	2.8	2	2	0.52
KDNP (Christian Democratic People's Party)	2.31	0	0	0
MDNP (Hungarian Democratic People's Party)	1.34	0	0	0
USZM (New Alliance for Hungary)	0.49	0	0	0
EMU (Together for Hungary Union)	0.19	0	0	0
NF (Forum of National Minorities)	0.13	0	0	0
MSZDP (Social Democratic Party of Hungary)	0.08	0	0	0
MSzZP (Social Green Party of Hungary)	0.07	0	0	0
VP (Party of Entrepreneurs)	0.05	0	0	0
Total[1]	100	175	398	100

[1] Percentages are rounded off and may not add up to 100.

Table 4 Hungarian election results, 2002 elections

Party/Coalition	PR vote %	SMD seats	Total seats	Seats %
MSZP (Hungarian Socialist Party)	42.05	78	178	46
FIDESZ MDF joint list	41.07	95	188	48
SZDSZ (Alliance of Free Democrats)	5.57	2	19	5
MSZP-SZDSZ joint candidates	0	1	0	0.03
MIEP (Hungarian Truth and Life Party)		0	0	0
OMC (Alliance for Hungary–Center Party)	3.9	0	0	0
Munkaspart	2.16	0	0	0
FKGP (Independent Smallholders Party)	0.75	0	0	0
UBP (New Left Party)	0.06	0	0	0
RKGP (Reform Party of Smallholders)	0.02	0	0	0
SDP (Social Democratic Party)	0.02	0	0	0
MRP (Hungarian Roma Party)	0.01	0	0	0
KGPKGSP (Smallholders Party)	0.01	0	0	0
MAVEP (United Party of Hungarian Entrepreneurs)	0.01	0	0	0
Total[1]		176	385	

[1]Percentages are rounded off and may not add up to 100.

Appendix D

Bulgarian and Hungarian governments

Table 1 Governments in Bulgaria, 1990–2005

Government	Years	Type	Parliamentary support by
Lukanov Government	June 1990–January 1991	Majority	BSP
Popov Government	February 1991–November 1991	Expert	BSP, SDS, BZNS
Dimitrov Government	November 1991–October 1992	Majority	SDS, DPS
Berov Government	November 1992–September 1994	Minority	DPS, BSP
Indzova Government	September 1994–January 1995	Caretaker	—
Videnov Government	January 1995–January 1997	Majority	BSP
Sofijanski Government	February–April 1997	Caretaker	—
Kostov Government	May 1997–June 2001	Majority	ODS
Sax-Coburg-Gotha Government	July 2001–June 2005	Coalition	NDSV, DPS
Stanishev Government	August 2005–Present	Coalition	BSP, NDSV, DPS

Table 2 Governments in Hungary, 1990–2003

Government	Years	Type	Parliamentary support by
Antall Government	1990–1994	Coalition	MDF, FKGP, KDNP
Horn Government	1994–1998	Coalition	MSZP-SZDSZ
Orban Government	1998–2002	Coalition	FIDESZ-MPP, MDF, FKGP, MIEP
Medgyessy Government	2002–(2004)	Coalition	MSZP, SZDSZ
Gyurcsany I Government	2004–2006	Coalition	MSZP, SZDSZ
Gyurcsany II Government	2004–present	Coalition	MSZP, SZDSZ

APPENDIX E

VALUES OF THE DEPENDENT AND INDEPENDENT VARIABLES OF INTEREST, PANEL DATA SET

Country	Election	Number of parties	Electoral threshold	Party funding provisions	Index of ethnic heterogeneity	Inflation, change %
Bulgaria	1	4	4	1	0.285187	272.52
	2	10	4	1	0.285187	1322
	3	10	4	1	0.285187	31.8
	4	7	4	1	0.285187	770.32
	5	8	4	2	0.285187	−28.65
Czech	2	15			0.107254	
Republic	3	10	5	2	0.107254	−4.04
	4	9	5	2	0.107254	24.32
	5	6	5	2	0.107254	−62.07
Estonia	1	12	5	0	0.493675	
	2	11	5	2	0.493675	−19.9
	3	10	5	2	0.493675	−59.84
Hungary	1	11	4	2	0.18901	70.92
	2	10	5	2	0.18901	−15.97
	3	9	5	2	0.18901	−22.18
	4	6	5	2	0.18901	−42.9
Latvia	1	11	4	0	0.576305	−55.29
	2	14	5	0	0.576305	−29.5
	3	10	5	0	0.576305	−44.79
	4	11	5	0	0.576305	−21.62
Lithuania	1	11	5	0	0.337198	
	2	17	4	0	0.337198	−37.92
	3	17	5	2	0.337198	34.02

(*Continued*)

(*Continued*)

Country	Election	Number of parties	Electoral threshold	Party funding provisions	Index of ethnic heterogeneity	Inflation, change %
Poland	1	16	0	0	0.064164	127.1
	2	15	5	1	0.064164	−18.67
	3	10	5	1	0.064164	−23.9
	4	8	5	1	0.064164	−45.64
Romania	1	9	5	1	0.193976	
	2	7	5	1	0.193976	−8.42
	3	11	5	1	0.193976	20.43
	4	9	5	1	0.193976	−0.3
Russia	1	11	5	3	0.333078	
	2	18	5	3	0.333078	−35.81
	3	10	5	3	0.333078	209.65
	5	11	5	3	0.333078	−26.52
Slovakia	1	12	5	2	0.253922	
	2	7	5	2	0.253922	9.64
	3	13	5	2	0.253922	−54.66
Ukraine	1	25	3	0	0.364701	−81.18
	2	14	3	0	0.364701	−33.65
	3	20	3	0	0.364701	−93.67
Slovenia	1	16	3	2	0.15345	
	2	12	3	2	0.15345	−26.28
	3	9	4	2	0.15345	24.33